Matsuri

Matsuri

FESTIVALS OF A
JAPANESE TOWN

MICHAEL ASHKENAZI

 UNIVERSITY OF HAWAII PRESS
HONOLULU

98 97 96   5 4 3 2

Library of Congress Cataloging-in-Publication Data

Ashkenazi, Michael.
    Matsuri : festivals of a Japanese town / Michael Ashkenazi.
        p.   cm.
    Includes index.
    ISBN 0-8248-1385-5. —ISBN 0-8248-1421-5 (pbk.)
    1. Fasts and feasts—Shinto. 2. Yuzawa-shi (Japan)—Religious
life and customs. 3. Festivals—Japan—Yuzawa-shi. I. Title.
BL2224.7.A84   1993
394.2'68299561'0952113—dc20   92-31751
                                                          CIP

Designed by Kenneth Miyamoto

To Jeanne, with love

Contents

Acknowledgments

THE RESEARCH on which this work is based was generously funded by the Japan Foundation. The assistance of the foundation and its staff, particularly of the Exchange of Persons Department and Library, is gratefully acknowledged. The final draft of the book was written while I was a fellow of the Canada-Israel Foundation for Academic Exchange at the University of Calgary. I am grateful to both the foundation and my colleagues in the Department of Anthropology of the university for granting me the time to complete the work.

A great many people both in and out of Yuzawa assisted me in this project. I can mention only a few by name, but the people of Yuzawa as a whole deserve my utmost thanks for unfailing and unstinting kindness during and after the period of research and for taking me into their homes and confidence. Thanks are due the five *kannushi* of Yuzawa, without whose cooperation the research would not have been possible. Otomo Hiromitsu, Kumagai Masao, Takashina Sayoshi, Yoshida Katsuyori, and Miura Taiichi devoted much time to explaining their points of view and the rationale of many of the rituals I observed. They not only permitted my attendance at many rituals, but actually encouraged it. I am grateful to Okuyama Heitaro, deputy mayor of Yuzawa, and his family both for smoothing my way and for their hospitality. The *wakamono-kai* of Maemori-chō were the focus of much of my attention during their preparations for the Daimyō Gyōretsu. I cannot thank them enough for their patience with my many questions and with the problems posed by having a foreign researcher in their midst. Special thanks go to Hirayama Zaiichiro, the *wakamono-kaichō* of Maemori-chō. He displayed unflagging good humor, patience, and leadership during his tenure and, notwithstanding the considerable burdens of office, took a great deal of trouble to make me feel welcome. I would also like to thank Fukuda Magoichi and Ito Yutaro for their hospitality and explanations of the Daimyō Gyōretsu, the history of Yuzawa, and the functions of the *sōdan-kai* of the *wakamono-kai* of Maemori-chō. The members of the Yanagi-machi *wakamono-kai* encouraged me to join them in their activities and submitted to endless questions. Messrs. Nagano and Nagai of the Omachi *wakamono-kai* supplied a great deal of information about the town and their group. Tomiya Matsunosuke of Omachi, a scholar of Yuzawa, explained the recent history of Yuzawa to me and encouraged me in my work. Mr. Saito of Uchidate-machi became a personal friend and spent many hours with me discussing traditional religion in Yuzawa. Tamura Hajime, besides being my teacher, introduced me to Ura-machi and explained the relationship of its temples and shrines to its *chōnai-kai*. The members of the 1980 *tōban* of Ura-machi were extremely kind, allowing me not only to participate in all their festivals but also to interview them at their places of business. In addition, many of them introduced me to others who they thought might further my research. Mr. Shimohashi of the Shuzo Kaikan elaborated on the economic problems of the town. Mr. Hayakawa explained the history of Kanaike-jinja, introduced me to people in the neighborhood, and also served as a mine of information about local arts and crafts.

I am particularly grateful to Messrs. Ishikawa, Kadono, Ito, Haga, and other members of the Yuzawa Iaido club, all of whom taught me much about Yuzawa. Because of their kindness I was afforded entrance to many places I would have had no access to on my own. Not the least of the advantages such access provided was the companionship I enjoyed and the skills I was taught at the club. Particular thanks go to Aso Jiro *sensei*, who encouraged me to practice what he taught and also introduced me to his extensive family in the countryside.

The members of the Yuzawa Rotary Club and of the South Yuzawa Rotary Club were always helpful, and I relied on them for many introductions. Mr. Miyoshi, a retired schoolteacher and a nature enthusiast, discussed Yuzawa's history and its festivals with me. Mr. Otomo Shigeo of the Yuzawa municipality ferreted out the details of Yuzawa's *bunka-zai*, as well as other material and statistical data about the town.

Mr. Okamatsu Koyo deserves special thanks for having first introduced me to Yuzawa. He and his family provided a much-needed base for our first month in Yuzawa.

In Tokyo I am grateful to Professor Sonoda Minoru of the Nihon Bunka

Kenkyu-sho of Kokugakuin University for his encouragement and the use of his institute's facilities. The staff of the Oriens Institute Library in Meidaimae and of the Anthropology Library at Tokyo University were extremely kind and allowed me the run of their respective premises.

Professors William Kelly and John Middleton, both of Yale University, and Professor Yoneyama Toshinao of Kyoto University read several early drafts of this book and were unsparing in their advice. I am also grateful to Professor M. G. Smith, who impressed upon me the rigor of his methodology and theoretical approach and contributed immeasurably to the spirit of the book. I owe thanks to the anonymous reviewers of the manuscript; their comments, even where I disagreed with them, stimulated my thinking and contributed materially to the book. Patricia Crosby, my editor at the University of Hawaii Press, offered advice and support in the best tradition of the *nakōdo*.

Three people deserve special mention. My son Oren, aged two at the time of the research, assisted by being his charming self and interrupting my work whenever necessary. He also deserves credit for having been instrumental in gaining my family and me acceptance as residents of Yuzawa; his presence served quite often as a bridge with people who might not otherwise have talked to me.

Okuyama Shunzo served as our mentor, friend, and resident philosopher. Besides furnishing numerous introductions, he smoothed our way as much as possible and coached me in the proper etiquette for every occasion. He and his family made our stay in Yuzawa both pleasant and productive, and our close relationship persists to this day. I am forever in his debt.

My wife, Jeanne, was involved in this research from the beginning. She shared the pleasures and difficulties of fieldwork, encouraged me during its analysis, and was a necessary critic, editor, logician, and calligrapher throughout the preparation of the manuscript. Her knowledge of Yuzawa and her own keen professional insight into things Japanese and the editing and writing of books have been invaluable.

While I have received welcome aid from many persons, the responsibility for what is written here is my own. Wherever possible, I have disguised the identities of those mentioned. I have purposely obscured some personal details, feeling that individuals who assisted me with their comments are entitled to their privacy. I have tried to the best of my ability to present a true picture of Yuzawa. As I am, after all, an outsider, that picture is a personal one that might not be subscribed to by Yuzawa's residents. I hope that this book will repay in some small measure all that I owe these people.

Elements of Chapters 3, 4, and 7 have appeared in *Cultural Dynamics, Asian Folklore Journal,* and *Ethnology.* I am grateful to the editors and anonymous referees of those journals. Japanese names are given in Japanese order, that is, surname first followed by given name.

Matsuri in Context

MINAMISHIN-MACHI, a neighborhood founded in the seventeenth century, lines both sides of the main road leading from the train station through the business district of Yuzawa. A large concrete arch marks the approach to the neighborhood shrine, Shimizu-jinja. Spanning the shrine entrance above a row of shops is the neighborhood hall. Passing under the hall, one comes to a courtyard with two buildings and a children's playground. Straight ahead at the end of a concrete path is the *jinja* (shrine), a plain wooden structure with a pitched roof. A small concrete building, the repository, houses the *shintai,* an object that represents the deity. Several stone stelae clutter the yard. In the yard also is a curative well, no longer in use, from which the *jinja* draws its name: *shimizu* means pure water. The *jinja* was originally dedicated to Kannon, the Buddhist deity of mercy, and a painting dating from the sixth year of the Meiji reign that hangs in the neighborhood hall depicts the well being uncovered under the supervision of a Buddhist priest. Today the shrine is wholly Shinto.

At 6 A.M. on the day of the *matsuri* (festival) several members of the *wakamono-kai* (young men's association) assemble at the neighborhood hall. They sweep the shrine grounds and clean the shrine, airing its interior and polishing the shrine utensils. A group of four struggles to hang the long festival banners. The *torii,* to which the banners attach, poses a problem; it is too close to the road, and the flags might constitute a traffic hazard. Eventually the banners are safely secured, and at 8 A.M. the men, satisfied that preparations have been completed, disperse; all of them have jobs or business to attend to during the day.

The men reassemble in the late afternoon to finish the morning's work. A nearby parking lot is furnished with a "stage" (the bed of a large truck) for the evening's entertainment. The men string and test lanterns. Large paired lanterns are hung flanking the shrine entrance. Fruit and vegeta-

ble offerings are arrayed on raised trays at the altar. Some men bring twin
bottles of sake wrapped in special paper, with the donor's name inscribed
in ink. These too go on the altar.

Outside in the street the neighborhood shops that would normally be
closing remain open. Several itinerant peddlers *(tekiya)* and carnival
operators put the finishing touches on their booths. There are goldfish to
be caught with a wafer cup, quoit games, popgun shoots, and faro
wheels. Candied apples, plastic masks of TV characters, toys, and balloons tempt the young. The peddlers, who travel from *matsuri* to *matsuri,* are inured to the excitement and converse about their own affairs.

As evening falls the neighborhood's residents drop by the *jinja* with
sake or cash offerings; 1,000- to 5,000-yen offerings are common, the
money placed in a special decorated envelope inscribed with the donor's
name. The stream of visitors quickens after dinnertime. Many carry a tray
or purse with a candle and a small twist of white paper containing a handful of rice and a coin. They throw the paper and its contents or sometimes
just a coin into the offertory box that stands at the entrance to the shrine.
Candles are lit and placed on the multispiked candelabrum behind the
offertory box. Each visitor rings the bell suspended from the roof of the
jinja, claps twice, bows over joined hands, claps, and bows deeply once
more. One of the men on duty offers visitors a sip of sake, a morsel of rice
cooked with red beans, a piece of dried squid, and an amulet consisting
of a slip of paper printed with the name of the shrine and the deity.

At 6 P.M. the *kannushi* (priest) who performs the shrine's festival ritual
every year arrives with a small suitcase of equipment and vestments.
Using a cutting board and knife, he folds and cuts strips of white paper
and attaches them to evergreen sprigs to make altar offerings for use in
the ritual. During his preparations in the neighborhood hall, he talks
with the men present about his recent trip abroad. Later he dons his vestments: a tall, brimless black gauze hat, long culottes, and a brocade silk
surplice or coat with long semidetached sleeves. The priest proceeds to
the shrine, accompanied by some of the young men. He takes a brocade-
covered box containing the *shintai* from the repository. Using both
hands, the priest carries the small box to the shrine and places it on the
altar.

The organizers gather in the shrine, and the priest performs a ritual
during which the men lay on the altar the evergreen offerings prepared
earlier. At the end of the ritual the priest thanks the participants, and
they all accept a sip of sake from a container that had been on the altar

during the ritual. While a few men stay at the shrine to offer sake and amulets to visitors, the rest proceed to the neighborhood hall, where a local restaurant has catered a meal that includes large amounts of beer and sake. During the lively dinner some of the men excuse themselves to relieve those who have stayed at the shrine and to start the evening's entertainment.

While the feast for the festival managers is going on upstairs in the hall, more visitors flock to the shrine. Outside the precincts the street is packed. Children crowd before the booths. Some hold small fireworks and sparklers that cast a red or green glare over the crowds when they are set off. On the truck bed in the parking lot one of the *wakamono-kai* members acts as master of ceremonies and introduces hopeful singers, who are accompanied by canned music played at earsplitting volume. The crowd laughs good-naturedly at the performers' blunders. Business is brisk at the booths and in the neighborhood's shops, which are all specially decorated for the event. Some shops put on small shows of their own or offer goods at loudly advertised reduced prices. Coffee shops and booths selling cold beer, sake, grilled foods, and sweets are heavily patronized; occasionally one sees a face flushed from overindulgence, which during the festival is tolerated and even encouraged.

Meanwhile, in the hall the young men of the *wakamono-kai* chat or play cards on the mat floor, drink more beer, munch snacks. Occasionally a few venture outside to watch the festivities or replace one of their number on duty. Finally, the head of the association thanks the priest and gives him an envelope containing "car fare": an honorarium. At about midnight the police clear the blocked street and the festival-goers wend their way home, some in bright summer kimono, some clutching balloons or prizes from the game booths, many less than sober.

The following morning, formally the main festival day, is anticlimactic. Because this festival is small and is held on a work day, little occurs. The peddlers have already left for a festival in another town. The truck stage is disassembled and the area cleared of litter. The priest arrives and performs an early ritual, but he does not linger at the shrine. He is a salaried employee in a large firm and has to get to work at his office. The vessels used in the ritual are sorted and stored away in boxes. The offerings of rice wrapped in twists of paper are collected, to be distributed later to the young men who helped manage the festival. The coins thrown into the offertory box and enclosed with the rice are carefully counted and the sum recorded in the shrine's logbook. The book also documents who donated sake and money and the amounts given. The sake will be used in the association's parties or gatherings; the money goes into the shrine's treasury toward future repairs or the purchase of altar necessities. The offerings of vegetables and fruits are distributed to whoever among the managers wants them. The last act of the festival is the distribution of paper amulets and cakes of pounded glutinous rice to all the financial contributors: those households that are part of the deity's demesne and thus privileged to share the deity's food.

The main festival of Shimizu-jinja is over for another year. The same men will not run it next year; their term of office expires with the festival. Their successors will receive the shrine's books, bank account, and seal. For most of the neighborhood's three hundred residents this has been a satisfactory festival. The visitors from surrounding neighborhoods in Yuzawa have enjoyed themselves. The *kannushi* is pleased to have discharged his duty and can now turn his attention to upcoming ritual duties. Although individuals and even small groups will visit the shrine throughout the year to conduct rituals, on the whole Shimizu-jinja, like most small shrines in Japan, will have the shuttered appearance of an abandoned building. The children playing on the small jungle gym and swings are the sole sign of life on the shrine grounds.

Matsuri in Yuzawa and Japan

In modern Japan *matsuri* (the word means both "festival" and "fête" in the religious sense) has come to mean a public festival, and most rural and urban communities in Japan have a *matsuri* during the year. A number of famous ones have nationwide, even international, renown. The large *matsuri* full of color and spectacle are particularly attractive to tourists, but the smaller festivals, those that occur annually in almost any Japanese community, perhaps better reveal the anthropological significance of the *matsuri*. Such festivals, which usually occur in and around a Shinto *jinja,* are commonly part of the annual round of rituals of a particular shrine. It is the main ritual of a shrine that is usually the occasion of a public festival. The festival of Minamishin-machi in the town of Yuzawa, a rural town in Akita prefecture, is typical.

Minamishin-machi is one of the thirty-nine officially recognized neighborhoods of Yuzawa, the town that is the administrative seat and commercial center of the municipality of Yuzawa-shi. The neighborhood is composed largely of the families of its shopkeepers. Neighborhood businesses include clothing shops, bakeries and other food shops, a book-shop, several bars, and coffee shops. Recently, a large department store chain announced plans to open a branch on the empty lot near the shrine. Aside from having a relatively large number of shops, Minamishin-machi is typical of the other neighborhoods that form Yuzawa's commercial and municipal core, especially in terms of size and socioeconomic composition.

Of Yuzawa-shi's 39,000 residents, 18,000 live in the town, the rest in outlying villages and hamlets. The town lies on Highway 13, which links Akita City (the capital of Akita prefecture) to the north and Yamagata City to the south, a one-and-a-half kilometer strip of densely packed houses and buildings between the highway and the wooded eastern slopes of the mountains that border the Omono River valley. Yuzawa is noted for its sake brewing; at the industry's peak there were twenty-one breweries in and around town. To its residents the town exemplifies the culture of southern Akita. Also, it is considered an affluent town in a region known historically for its poverty and isolation.

Yuzawa is divided, as are all Japanese towns, into *chō* (neighborhoods). Most *chō* have some form of community organization that runs their affairs, some of which are quite complex. Many *chō* are associated with a Shinto shrine, either inside the neighborhood's designated boundaries or nearby. In larger, better-established, and wealthier *chō*, neighborhood business is often conducted in a hall built on the shrine grounds; in others the shrine doubles as community center. The grounds of shrines often serve as community meeting places, and some are furnished with childrens' play equipment, such as swings and jungle gyms. In addition to *chō*-maintained shrines (the major ones are listed on the map), small shrine structures—some the size of a single room, others hardly larger than a hatbox—pepper the town.

Rituals are performed in or before each shrine at least once a year. At neighborhood shrines, the main ritual is usually accompanied by a public festival. The largest and most elaborate such festival in Yuzawa, the Daimyō Gyōretsu, accompanies the main ritual of Atago-jinja, the town's largest shrine and shrine of several of its neighborhoods.

Of Yuzawa's thirty-nine official neighborhoods, twenty-three have shrines, each with its own festival. The remaining neighborhoods are either new, associated with a neighborhood that has a festival, or in the process of starting one themselves. Other shrines, such as that of the sweet-makers' association and those of descent groups, also have yearly

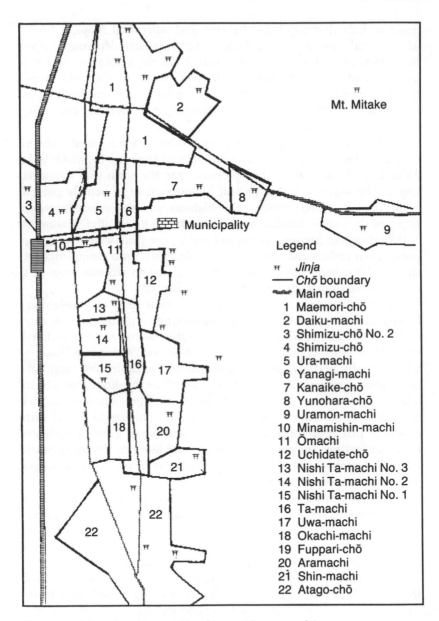

Yuzawa neighborhoods mentioned in text (not to scale)

rituals, though the accompanying public festivals, if there are any, are generally simple. Particularly the larger festivals often have some organized entertainment, including such public activities as games, and possibly a parade.

The main concerns of this book derive from features of the festivals apparent to even the casual observer. Most *matsuri* involve a considerable investment of time and money. Streets and houses are decorated and people mobilized. A great deal of planning goes into orchestrating the variety of activities that take place within a *matsuri*'s limited time. The festivals draw large crowds, who dress up, eat, drink, participate in and observe the activities, and generally seem to have an unreservedly good time. Another readily apparent characteristic of *matsuri* is that they take place in or near a Shinto shrine.

In other words, *matsuri* manifest several social phenomena. First, if only to judge from the name, they have a religious basis; moreover, those that take place around a shrine include one or more ritual elements. *Matsuri* are also festivals in the usual sense and shed light, therefore, on the question of what constitutes public entertainment. Third, the larger and more complex *matsuri* require considerable organization and management. Finally, they take place in a modern society that has undergone and is still undergoing radical change. A detailed exploration of *matsuri* in terms of these four contexts—contexts I shall define further in the following paragraphs—forms the subject of this book.

Ritual in *Matsuri*

In Japan a *matsuri* ritual is usually performed by a trained *kannushi* (Shinto priest) or bonze (Buddhist priest) in a shrine or in a place designated a shrine for the purpose. There may be more than one ritual and one shrine involved in a single *matsuri*. Moreover, there are many rituals performed in Japan that are not associated with shrines or festivals.

To the casual observer, even the major ritual of a shrine hardly appears to be an important part of a festival; casual observation thus seems to reinforce the academic view that traditional Shinto—a major component of Japanese faith—has little relevance as religion. Few people attend these rituals, and, as the foregoing description of the Shimizu-jinja *matsuri* shows, most festival-goers are neither present when the ritual is performed nor aware of its time and venue. Yet rituals are not the perfunctory affairs such lack of attendance might lead one to assume. Evidence to the contrary can be seen in the rising number of nonfestival rituals performed annually throughout Yuzawa and in the many festivals that have lost most of their festive quality but retain their rituals.

Japan's religion is, like many faiths, mainly evident in sets of religiously oriented overt actions. Most people are not as familiar with the specific doctrinal teachings of their religion as they are with its rituals. This is as true for religions having an involved and elaborate dogma, such as Christianity (see, for example, Christian 1972), as it is for those, like Shinto that are based on little, if any, doctrine. What Japanese religion offers the average individual is a large and comprehensive set of modes, or rituals, for approaching, addressing, and interacting with the powerful nonhuman entities called *kami*.

Festivals and the rituals involved in them are also important social affairs. In addition to its purported religious benefits, a ritual is an opportunity to demonstrate wealth, power, status, good fellowship, and cooperation. Indeed, the requirements of ritual often inhibit conflict, whether it be differences of opinion or personality. Even when lay practitioners profess not to share the religious beliefs that clergy would say underlie the ritual, they will often maintain and even embellish a ritual. They may do so because they have a social stake in the ritual or possibly because they believe the ritual is integral to the festival they are performing. We find, therefore, as Roof (1974, 297) has noted, that laypersons emphasize the social functions of rituals and ritual-related activities (and by so doing muffle expressions of conflict), whereas clergy emphasize ritual's religious content, though not to the point of antagonizing their "clientele."

Festivity and Entertainment

The variety of events and activities in addition to ritual that occur at festivals constitute the festive element, the aspect least amenable to analytical definition and explanation. "Festivity" combines two elements: leisure and entertainment. "Leisure" implies chosen activities—particularly entertainment. As I shall subsequently show, *matsuri* have been and still are a source of entertainment. Thus, participation in them is a matter of choice. However, the context in which that choice is made has changed. Modern life, in the economically successful Japan since the 1970s, as elsewhere, has given people unprecedented opportunities for leisure. Moreover, compared with premodern Japan, where few entertainment opportunities presumably existed, today, television, films, computer games, and toys of various kinds compete for the public's attention. Festivities must therefore be seen within the framework of leisure activities and entertainment available to the average Japanese.

Two other issues that complicate an analysis of the festive element concern the nature of festivity. First, festivity involves several types of activity often undertaken simultaneously by many people. These activities are not all discrete nor are they necessarily unique to festivals. People engage in most, if not all, of them outside of festivals as well. One such activity, for example, is social interaction. While public social intercourse between acquaintances in Yuzawa is normally relatively formal, the modalities of interaction in festivals range from the highly formalized ritual to quite informal interactions. Such nonformal activities as strolling, eating while standing, and wearing leisure clothes are more frequent and indulged in by a greater number of people during festivals than at other times. During the festival, daily life and conduct intermingle with unusual behaviors of various types.

The second issue is that the number and categories of individuals who participate in a festival are generally not limited or restricted. In other words, "festivity" has neither clearly marked limits nor analytical boundaries to separate it from nonfestive life.

To summarize, festivity in *matsuri* in Yuzawa has three qualities. First, it is entertaining. Festival-goers are, on the whole, intent on entertaining themselves and others, and they see the *matsuri* as a form of recreation. What defines festivity in contrast to daily life is its unusual, entertaining, and social "image." (I use the term in the sense used by Richardson [1982] for other unbounded situations, such as markets.) The festivity creates and is maintained by this image. It is felt and shared in, experienced rather than just seen. The participation in and acceptance of the image by large numbers of people generates and strengthens it. Its acceptance, however, is conditional upon a significant number of participants acting in a way that shows their enjoyment.

Second, in the space—territory and time—of festivity, economic and other transactions take place. The unusual atmosphere created by festivity transcends that of a commercial market, political rally, or spectator event by simultaneously involving festival-goers in a variety of events and by offering events in various fields of interest rather than just one.

Third, festivity involves a mass of people. "Festival participants" do not constitute a single group, caste, or other social category. The numbers and composition of this mass are in constant flux as new individuals arrive and others depart and as those present attend to nonfestival matters. Analytically, the mass of individuals in a festival differs little from a group in any other arbitrarily selected situation or arbitrarily selected and defined area in daily life.

Festival Organization

Festivals require an organized group to run them. Rituals, whether or not part of a festival, must be run by a social unit. Other festival events, too, require some managing and organizing body to supply food, drink, and entertainment, to control traffic, to create the setting for the festival by decorating the area, announcing events, and preparing or performing those events.

The presence of these organizations gives rise to two questions. First, how do these organizations affect the continuity, change, or decline of festivals? Second, how does the organization of one facet of a festival, the festivity, merge with the organization of its other facet, ritual? Such organizations can presumably vary in many ways. In general it can be safely assumed that the organizational forms used are those familiar to the members of the culture from other circumstances.

The Changing Society

Any group's organization is subject to change over time as the society it is part of changes and as the group's composition and objectives change. These changes affect festival-related organizations, festivity, and rituals. One must be wary, however, of assuming that change affects them all equally and similarly. The change I am concerned with is both internal— the way particular festivals are performed—and external—the disappearance or continuation of festivals in a culture. I am not concerned with general "sociocultural change" as Kushner et al. (1962) have called it, but, rather, with changes in a specific institution as a result of a given, well-documented series of changes in Japan.

Three hypotheses offered by anthropologists regarding changes in aspects of *matsuri* are relevant here. Morioka (1975) has proposed a demographic cause for what he sees as a decline in the performance of *matsuri:* as population movement increases, the social structures that support and maintain shrines and festivals disintegrate. As a consequence, large numbers of rural and urban festivals are going into decline. Morioka's data are drawn largely from a Tokyo bedroom community that has developed in the postwar years from a traditional farming community. Robertson (1987), in contrast, shows how the urbanizing rural communities studied decades earlier by Morioka try to use the traditional idiom of a *matsuri* to reinforce, and even create, a communal spirit. This phenomenon reflects changes in Japan in the past thirty years (Davis 1976, 1977a; and Kelly 1990).

Davis draws from historical data to show changes in festival organization and participation in two fishing villages along the Inland Sea. The economic and political decline of a propertied class led to changes in the frequency and elaboration of the villages' festivals. Davis sees the change as a decline resulting from the economic and social restructuring of village communities and from encroachment of historically unpropertied families into the ritual privileges of propertied groups. Kelly discusses the recreation of "traditional" festival activities as an indirect consequence of the enrichment of Japan and as a direct result of leisure-time pursuits and the search for "authentic" experience.

While I generally agree that population mobility in the modern era has done much to change traditional religious institutions and consequently the maintenance of *matsuri*, I hesitate to support Morioka's contention that "Shinto is decaying" (1975, 164). Changes in *matsuri* cannot be seen as a simple decline, either of Shinto or of the *matsuri* institution. Different causes affect change in different elements of *matsuri*, and no single cause underlies all of them. To generally understand the process of ongoing change in *matsuri* it is necessary first to analyze changes separately from the direction of changes in each element. *Matsuri* are not a strictly religious institution, and changes in *matsuri* practice cannot be declared the death knell of a particular religious institution.

The Festival System

The three foci of this study constitute an artifical division of a set of *matsuri* in a community into those matters relating to rituals, those relating to festivity, and those relating to the organization and management of *matsuri* as events. Activities rather easily dealt with formally under the label of one or another of these divisions in reality occur more or less simultaneously; separating them requires doing some violence to the seamless continuity between, say, ritual activity and organizational process.

The sources of change and its implications must also be traced within a coherent framework, because many events co-occur, and all are interrelated in complex ways. The festivals in a given geographical area, all of which engage the same populace, are related by similar rituals and familiar cultural idioms; they also differ as a whole from festivals outside the area. The concept of a festival system, while not providing geographical determination for these similarities or differences, is useful as an analytical construct for discussing and explaining changes in individual festivals. Festivals in Yuzawa, as we shall see, are interrelated on several levels. The same idioms are used, many of the same people participate, and certain organizational and group ties percolate through the various *matsuri*. It is this localized similarity among festivals that I call a festival system: a set of festivals that share idioms, personnel, and a local timeframe. In practical terms, the often fuzzy boundaries of any particular festival system correspond to demographic and residential divisions. The festival system of Yuzawa corresponds to a great degree to a community centered in the town of Yuzawa. At a greater remove, the Yuzawa festival system is an element in a larger festival system encompassing the whole of Japan in the same, though more diffuse, ways. Changes in a particular festival are likely to diffuse more rapidly within the system than without it, thus reinforcing the image, at least, of uniqueness and difference.

The concept of Yuzawa as a distinct community is bolstered by the distinctiveness of its major festivals. At the same time Yuzawa's festival repertoire is not exhausted by its three great festivals. The numerous other festivals of the town are also related in several ways: the same people attend, the same priests officiate. Certain methods of performing general customs are considered very "Yuzawan" by the town's residents. The festivals within Yuzawa may therefore be seen to be more affected by one another than by festivals outside Yuzawa, though that influence too is not lacking.

In addition to its usefulness as a cultural construct, I use the term "festival system" socioanalytically to distinguish one festival population from another. Generally, the network of social ties that binds festival-goers in Yuzawa and the social communication and exchanges individuals have with others because of festivity and ritual activities are more intense and frequent within Yuzawa than they are between Yuzawans and outsiders. Nevertheless, the Yuzawa festival system is part of a larger festival system. The same factors that operate in Yuzawa to form a cultural and social commonality operate on a national level to create a national festival system that is an aspect of Japanese culture. To understand the continuity of Yuzawa's festivals it is necessary to understand how they are related within Yuzawa's festival system and how Yuzawa's festival system interacts with the broader national system socially and culturally.

An Overview

One of my main reasons for choosing Yuzawa as a research site was the absence of tourists during its festivals. It is certain that *matsuri* that attract large numbers of tourists are likely to be heavily influenced by the economics and dynamics of the tourist industry. Such influence inevitably complicates the analysis by introducing a massive and complex variable that can obscure the influence of other factors. In Yuzawa, where tourist influences are minimal, it was possible to concentrate on endogenous factors. The size and relative affluence of the town also contributed to my choice of this particular site. The population of about 18,000 was a sufficiently large organic unit to exhibit a variety of festival forms and patterns, yet it did not exceed the maximum size that I as a single researcher could deal with. Yuzawa's relative affluence meant, a priori, that there would be economic resources for maintaining at least some *matsuri*.

A word is perhaps necessary about the point of view I have adopted in analyzing Yuzawa's *matsuri*. It has become commonplace in anthropology to discuss difficult human issues in terms of the creation and exchange of meanings, communications, and symbols. I have written elsewhere (Ashkenazi 1988a) about the lack of methodological rigor that the ideas of symbolization tend to bring about. Briefly stated, the choice of objects that appear to be symbolic, that is, that represent other concepts, very often depends on the pragmatic concerns of the people involved, not on their need to find highly esoteric methods of communicating their ideas. It is not that I believe that humans do not use or create symbols. It is, rather, that given the poverty of the methodological tools available to anthropologists, the siren call of symbolic analysis is all too seductive. Unhappily perhaps, I was taught to apply Occam's razor rather rigorously to the material at hand. Where other explanations, simpler ones, serve as well or better, it is they that must be accepted in the first instance. Undoubtedly it is possible to examine the symbolic structures that underlie the festivals described here. By doing so, however, I believe that crucial empirical elements will be lost to the reader: festivals are run by people, organized and organizing themselves in some ways, who adopt, change, and reject symbols as the need arises. Perhaps there is an element of prejudice in my decision to restrict the discussion, as far as possible, to the simplest and most direct explanation, adhering as much as I can to the explanations and suggestions made by the participants themselves. At some later date I or someone else using this material might be able to reconstruct the symbolic and intellectual processes that underlie the performance of Yuzawa's *matsuri*. At this point, however, I believe it to be sufficient to document them.

This study is therefore about the maintenance of festivals, specifically, the festivals—*matsuri*—of an urban Japanese environment. Social and cultural conditions have changed in Japan over the centuries. The changes of the twentieth century have been almost revolutionary. Yet *matsuri* persist as a cultural form. It must be assumed, therefore, that in some way *matsuri* are flexible enough to adjust to these changing circumstances. To solve the puzzle three related questions must be answered: To what degree do *matsuri* persist in a modern environment? What mechanisms and behaviors ensure their persistence? And, finally, why are they maintained? In a broader context, the aim of this study is to explain how traditional or traditional-seeming phenomena are maintained in a modern society. While the question of change has been debated ad nauseam among anthropologists and sociologists,[1] few such studies address the major question dealt with here, that of how changes articulate with the retention of traditional practices.

To answer this rather broad set of questions, I discuss the elements that make up *matsuri* as analytically separate concepts. The organization of the book reflects the dilemma of having to deal sequentially with a complex dynamic system. Chapter 2 deals with the relevant background to Yuzawa's festivals. Understanding the background requires understanding national and local contexts. Thus the chapter covers the essential concepts of the analysis that follows and then presents some relevant economic and social data about Japan and Yuzawa.

Chapters 3, 4, and 5 constitute an examination of the details of any given *matsuri* and an attempt to tease out general rules. The discussion moves from the highly structured, very formal events in *matsuri* rituals through less formal parades, gradually reaching the (seemingly) unstructured events that constitute festivity.

Dealing successfully with a large number of people requires, I would argue, some well-practiced and clearly thought out organizational practices. Chapters 6 and 7 concentrate on these organizational practices from two viewpoints. In Chapter 6 the emphasis is on answering one major question: How are festivals managed effectively? As shall be seen, one answer is that management is through an intimate and complex set of ties between the organizational frameworks of all the festivals in Yuzawa. A second answer is found in the practical organizational experience transmitted in time-honored and yet modifiable ways.

Whereas Chapter 6 deals essentially with overarching managerial issues that are the province of the "owners" of *matsuri,* Chapter 7 deals with a different personnel element. The priests, whose primary responsibility is for the proper conduct of rituals, are examined in this chapter as a separate and cardinal component of the festival system. Just as intergroup ties are one component in maintaining a festival system, so, too, priests and their network constitute an important component and factor in both change and continuity of ritual form, which, as we shall have seen in Chapter 3, have direct consequences for *matsuri* as a whole.

The final two chapters are a return to the general concerns of the relationship between change and continuity in *matsuri* performance. Chapter 8 provides an analytical framework that allows the observer of a set of festivals to understand the process and consequences of change. The chapter elaborates on the concept of "festival system": a set of festivals related through territorial proximity, shared personnel, and shared or similar practices. Chapter 9 summarizes the findings and relates them to data from Japan and elsewhere and to some broad theoretical considerations about festivals that have arisen recently in anthropology.

2

The Background

Yuzawa's *matsuri* must be understood in context, against the background of events, behaviors, and institutions that comprise Japanese society in general and Yuzawa in particular. This chapter is intended to summarize briefly only those background elements relevant to the discussion at hand.

Japanese Religion

Festivals in Japan are associated primarily with religious ritual. Viewed from a Western perspective, from which most definitions of religion derive, a discussion of Japan's "religion" is problematic. The problem derives partly, at least, from the biases inherent in most anthropological studies of religion. The "Japanese religious complex" (Sopher 1967) is composed of two main elements, Buddhism and Shinto, which have influenced one another for centuries. However, "Japanese traditions tend to be mutually syncretistic, rather than mutually exclusive" (Earhart 1969, 3).

Several sects of Buddhism compete more or less amiably, many "Buddhists" are also "Shintoists," and a host of common practices derive from both or neither. Buddhism and Shinto have generally divided religious functions between them, Buddhism dealing largely with the dead and the afterworld, Shinto, with everyday matters. Like most generalizations, this too is full of exceptions. There are Shinto mortuary and funeral rituals, and Buddhist rites for good fortune and blessing. Some sects, such as Shugendō, have taken on aspects of both (Norbeck 1970, 45). Others, such as Mahikari (Davis 1980), have introduced elements of Christianity and beliefs in the lost continent of Mu into their canons. In a 1981 statistic, the Agency for Cultural Affairs (1981, 12) estimates adherents of Shinto at 84,000,000 and of Buddhism at 85,000,000 out of a population

16

of 117,000,000. Yet such numbers are both unreliable and of limited significance because, as Anesaki (1970) points out, the great majority of people adhere to both.[1] Shinto emphasizes ritual and has resisted attempts over the past forty years to provide it with a coherent and generally accepted doctrine. Buddhism, by contrast, is doctrine oriented, with doctrinal as well as organizational differences separating various sects. However, at the level of common religious practice, Shinto and Buddhism often blend imperceptibly into one another, generally ignoring doctrine altogether (Davis 1977a, 6).

Japanese religious history has been characterized by the importation and accretion of foreign elements onto existing practice (Anesaki 1963; Kitagawa 1966) and by government interference in religious practice and organization (Lokowandt 1978; Murakami 1980; R. J. Smith 1974, 213) to the point of dictating the forms of rituals. Between 1869 and 1873, the Restoration government decreed the separation—*shinbutsu bunri*—of Buddhist and Shinto institutions and practices, which had generally been mixed. Religious institutions were forced to belong doctrinally to one or the other.

"The meaning of the word 'Shinto' as well as changes over time in customs and beliefs would indicate that Shinto emerged as an independent religion only in modern times, and then only as a result of political policy" (Kuroda 1981, 20). From 1903 to about 1912 the government engaged in a campaign to merge the myriad small country shrines (Fridell 1973). In the late 1920s, acting to "rationalize" shrine practices and to utilize religion in its political control of the country, the government enacted a series of precise guidelines on shrine practices, offerings, and rituals (Akita Shinto-shi 1979, 160–162; Murakami 1980, 66–68). After World War II, the Occupation authorities and later the Japanese government enacted legislation defining and circumscribing, albeit liberally, the nature of religious bodies (Creemers 1968; Agency for Cultural Affairs 1981, 166–168).

Shinto has historically lacked the central organizations that the Buddhist sects' main temples have established. When the government Bureau of Shrines in the Home Ministry was abolished by the Allied Occupation authorities' "Shinto directive" of 1945, leading Shinto scholars and priests founded Jinja Honchō, a federation of Shinto shrines to which, it is claimed, 80 percent of the shrines in the country belong. Through its prefectural branches and through Kokugakuin University in Tokyo, Jinja Honchō tries to influence and control the academic and practical qualifications of *kannushi* by offering special courses and awarding certificates of competence (Sadler 1974). Women *kannushi,* while not unknown, are uncommon, and the role usually open to women is that of *miko* (shrine maiden), a role with a lengthy history in Japan (Okano 1976).

Primarily two sorts of religious structures dot the landscape of Japan. Temples *(tera* or *otera)* are usually affiliated with and function as branches of the Japanese Buddhist sects. Shinto establishments—shrines *(jinja, miya,* or the suffix *-gu)*—are often unrelated, except remotely, to central or large shrines. Often very small and, unlike *otera,* more often than not lacking a resident priest, *jinja* are usually identifiable by the square, gatelike arch called *torii* that marks the approach to the shrine. The Agency for Cultural Affairs (1981, 239) estimates the number of shrines at 80,000, the Jinja Honchō (1964, 2) at about 100,000. These are gross underestimates, since only *jinja* with a resident priest and an affiliation in some national shrine organization are counted. Many more shrines, some larger, some smaller, dot the countryside and the cities. A conservative estimate is that the official numbers are too low by a factor of five.[2] Each shrine has one or more festivals a year, which are celebrated with varying degrees of pomp and ceremony.

A word must be added here regarding Shinto thought, and specifically its theology. The Shinto godhead is polytheistic, with numerous deities serving in tandem in a vague hierarchy. Amaterasu-Ō-Mikami, whose main shrine is at Ise in Mie prefecture, is the titular main deity, but this primacy means little insofar as the hierarchy of shrines and festival rituals is concerned.

Shinto addresses itself primarily to *kami,* powerful nonhuman moot entities. (I call such entities "moot" for the same reason that I avoid the term "supernatural" in discussing religion. As Saliba [1976, 184] has shown, the use of that concept is controversial, and more than likely reflects a European bias rather than a valid scientific criterion.) Perhaps the best definition comes from a Shinto source: *kami* are simply "the objects of worship in Shinto" (Shinto Committee 1958). They have a physical aspect in the form of a *shintai,* some object associated with the *kami,* which may be a statue, a stirrup, a naturally shaped stone, a natural feature, or simply a block of wood with the *kami*'s name written on it. What is important for the following discussion is that *kami,* like their worshipers, are social beings with clear social obligations.

Kami have in common two characteristics. First, they are considered to possess or exhibit purity (both a state and a quality), or *hare* (Namahira 1977). Human beings, animals, and inanimate objects may have *hare* as well. *Hare* can be acquired or increased through proper actions, for example, through refraining from contact with blood and meat, practicing austerities, bathing, scattering salt or other purificatory actions. Second, by virtue of *hare*, the *kami* also possess high *social* status. The degree of status is, given the Japanese penchant for arranging statuses in discrete vertical order, ranked.

The concept of *kami* has been dealt with by a number of writers, including Spae (1972) and Jinja Honchō (1964). These discussions and analyses share what I would call an "ideologized" version of the *kami* concept, which largely represents the point of view of *professionals* interested in the issue for their own ends, whether these ends are academic or ideological. In a detailed study, R. J. Smith (1974) has shown that the average Japanese has a wide range of beliefs about the dead (a form of *kami*). In a later study, Roberts et al. (1986) have shown that a similar range can be found in the popular understanding of the *kami* concept. This confusion, or ambivalence, is also reflected in the degree of divergence between a *kami*'s supposed (or official) rank according to Jinja Honchō and the actual ranking of local shrines created for the *kami*, which depends on other factors entirely. To illustrate, the shrine of Amaterasu-Ō-Mikami, the Shinto pantheon's primary *kami*, is not Yuzawa's main shrine, but one of the town's smaller, less noticeable shrines. Neither is the annual festival of the Ise shrine (the central shrine of Amaterasu-Ō-Mikami) particularly noted in Yuzawa.

The Festive Year

The timing of festivals is determined by the ritual calendar, but this timing, in Japan as a whole, and in Yuzawa in particular, is complicated by the number of calendrical systems in use. The year is divided according to a number of systems of different geneses, ranging from ancient native Japanese seasonal observances through Chinese lunar observations to the Gregorian calendar, according to which national holidays are celebrated. Nationally, there is a distinction between the new calendar (Gregorian), according to which such nationally significant days as Constitution Day, the Emperor's birthday, and Coming-of-Age Day are observed, and the old Chinese lunar calendar, according to which such significant nationally recognized dates (but not holidays) as O-bon and

Setsubun are celebrated. A system of lucky or unlucky days, years, and hours—*yakudoshi*—derived from the Chinese, an annual "flower calendar" that matches blooming periods of flowers to months, and the individual calendars of shrines and temples for celebrating events in their particular ritual cycle add to the complexity of observable occasions.

Certain events listed in each of these calendars are significant only to the particular system the calendar observes. In many cases, nonetheless, such events are of national or at least local importance. In some cases, important events in one calendar coincide with those of some, or many, others. The most significant date, one that serves as a turning point for most calendars, is Shōgatsu (New Year), in which the new years of Buddhist temples, Shinto shrines, and the national calendar coincide.[3] In Yuzawa, the calendars of all Buddhist temples, Atago-jinja (the town's major shrine), and some smaller shrines list the event, and these places of worship are open for visits during most of the night. Other shrines are inactive. Most people visit a shrine or a temple or both during the night of December 31.

Other events occur in some ritual calendars but not in others. In the calendar in which they appear they may be very prominent *for that calendar* and for its public, but not for others. For example, Hina *matsuri* (the doll festival, or as it is known in the West, Girls' Day) is celebrated nationally in most households, but it is neither a recognized official holiday nor celebrated in most temples or shrines. The discussion of the ritual year below concentrates, therefore, on those events that relate to *matsuri*, and specifically to *matsuri* in Yuzawa.

The ritual year of Japan, Yuzawa included, starts with the events of the New Year. Most individuals and families make it a point to visit a shrine at that time. Atago-jinja is, of course, open, and members of the shrine's support organization offer *miki* (consecrated wine) and amulets. The same is true of Yunohara Hitachi Inari-jinja in Maemori-chō, though here the crowd is usually drawn only from Maemori and Daiku-machi residents.

The New Year is mostly celebrated at home, however, among family and friends. Visiting is common. Some Japanese, but by no means all, maintain traditional rituals, such as drawing the first water of the year, lighting the first fire, or serving the traditional *nanakusa* (seven herbs) gruel as a first meal. Some households perform special household rituals during the three-day holiday.

The first major festival of the year is Inukko *matsuri*, the Dog Festival. Yuzawa winters are snowy, and the mid-February festival combines a religious ritual with a popular snow-sculpture festival. Households erect small shrines and build snow sculptures of dogs. Since the construction of roads, few people build snow sculptures in front of their houses, as they used to in the past. Instead, the baseball field near the municipality is turned into an "Inukko concourse," where households, school classes, shops, and clubs are encouraged to construct imaginative sculptures. On the hill beside the concourse volunteers erect a shrine before which a ritual is performed by a priest attended by representatives of the municipality. The same priest performs two other rituals during the evening, one before a shrine erected by the Traffic Safety Commission (a voluntary body that assists the traffic police) and one at a *dondo-yaki*, a bonfire in which New Year decorations are ritually burned.

In a somewhat smaller festival, shrines dedicated to Inari, the *kami* of rice and prosperity, usually celebrate *hatsu uma*, the first Day of the Horse after the ritual end of winter. In most cases this consists of little more than a ritual in the shrine.

Several neighborhood shrines start celebrating their festivals in the spring, and the frequency of ritual activities grows as the summer advances. Festivals are heralded by a series of three, five, or seven sound bombs that resound throughout the Omono valley. One important event is the festival of Kashima-jinja in Maemori-chō. The *wakamono-kai* who run the event use the opportunity of the festival for discussing the Daimyō Gyōretsu, the major ritual of summer. The seventh day of the seventh month (traditional calendar) celebrates Tanabata, the Star Festival. Households and shops erect green bamboo fronds hung with colored slips of paper over the streets. Lanterns painted with pictures on various themes, whose size varies from fifty centimeters to about four meters to a side, are hung from the bamboos and lit at night.

Yuzawa's major festival, the Daimyō Gyōretsu, which is also the annual festival of Atago-jinja, is celebrated on the third weekend of August. The rituals of other, smaller neighborhood shrines cluster usually in late August to October. The valley then resounds with sound bombs, and several festivals sometimes occur in Yuzawa on the same day. October 15 marks the annual festival of Hachiman shrines throughout Japan. Yuzawa's sole Hachiman shrine runs a small festival that includes a traditional archery exhibition. By November the leaves are starting to turn, and, usually after the first snowfall, small children and their parents visit Atago-jinja for the *shichi-go-san* festival, celebrated nationally for children aged seven, five, and three.

Throughout the year there are also a large number of private rituals, some of which are related to the season. Farmers have their fields purified after the snows. Weddings occur throughout the year (except for November, the *kami*-less month), as does the introduction of newborns to the *kami*. Construction picks up during the summer, and there are a variety of rituals relating to house construction, new cars, and new businesses. During fall, the time to prepare for winter, rituals are performed for taxi-cab companies and heavy equipment, which are affected by the heavy snowfall of the region.

As can be seen, the ritual year in Yuzawa is a combination of several elements. Some derive from national calendrical cycles, others from largely local events. It is important to realize that, though the national calendrical cycles are of great importance in many spheres of life, for the religious and ritual lives of individuals, the local cycle predominates. Although people celebrate national holidays and, for example, the events marked on the flower calendar, these are of less importance to the community than are the special local events that reflect on Yuzawa itself. We turn, therefore, to a brief examination of the town.

Introduction to Yuzawa

Yuzawa-shi, the southernmost *shi*[4] of Akita prefecture, is predominantly rural, dotted with farms in small hamlets, several semiurban village centers and townlets, and one town. Some of the town's thirty-nine neighborhoods, called *chō* or *machi,*[5] are further subdivided so that the total number of neighborhood units is seventy-nine. A neighborhood is defined operationally as those houses that share in the circulation of a *kairanban,* a communal message box passed from house to house. Each neighborhood elects a headman, the *chōnai-kaichō,* usually a retired male. The *chōnai-kaichō*'s major function is to transmit messages from the town administration to his neighborhood.[6]

Neighborhoods average 206 residents, although the largest aggregate neighborhood of Maemori-chō numbers close to 1,300.[7] Neighborhoods still reflect the social arrangements of the Edo period. Uwa-machi, Ara-machi, and Naikan-machi were settled by *bushi* families (warrior stratum of Edo period) positioned to defend the *daimyō*'s manor. *Ashigaru* (foot-soldiers who also worked as craftsmen) settled near the irrigation canals and temple grounds that served as fortifications. *Chōnin* (craftsmen and merchants) settled in a strip from Maemori to Fuppari, and servants lived in outlying neighborhoods such as Nishi Tamachi and Minamishin-machi. Yuzawa has been growing since the end of World War II, absorbing the rice paddies that border the town. Several of the newer neighborhoods such as Sengoku-chō have therefore no "history," having been founded only in the past twenty years.

The municipality uses the neighborhoods to pass on messages to the population. Local governments in Japan are generally tightly supervised by higher-echelon governments (Steiner 1965). Yuzawa's municipal government is elected, but, like that of others in Japan, its autonomy is restricted by the prefectural and national governments.[8] Even though in many cases their activities are duplicated elsewhere by municipal activities, neighborhoods are a forum for community and leisure activities and assist the municipality in such areas as public hygiene.[9] To defray costs, each resident household is required to pay a monthly sum (about 750 yen in 1980).

Rice, lumber, and fruit dominate Yuzawa's agriculture-based economy. The residents consider Yuzawa a relatively affluent town by Tohoku[10] standards. Yuzawa's prosperity is due to the large-scale manufacture of sake in the first half of this century. Sake brewing still figures prominently in the local economy; a local sake company is one of the largest employers in the area. Yuzawa's traditional crafts, particularly woodworking and dyeing, are either struggling for survival or (as in the case of silk spinning) no longer practiced. Major regional banks and offices, police headquarters, and the district court operate from Yuzawa. Some Yuzawa companies—a department store, furniture factory, sake company, and confectionery—have opened branches elsewhere in the prefecture and in the metropolis.

The economy today is bolstered by a thriving fruit industry, by branches of several industrial concerns, and to a degree by the town's municipal position and tourism. There is some demographic change, although the population remains more or less constant: the number of newcomers, many of whom are from the surrounding countryside, nearly offsets the number of younger men and women who leave for larger cities. Since the mid-1970s Yuzawa has enjoyed a steady growth in housing. Many rice fields around town have been converted to building lots, and at least three new residential neighborhoods—Sengoku-chō, Ura-mon-machi, and Okada-machi—have come into existence on former farming land. The town mostly consists of single-family dwellings, with a small number of usually small, two-storied apartment houses. The town center, where most commercial establishments—shops, supermarkets, banks—and administrative offices are situated, corresponds to the original seven neighborhoods created by *chōnin* in the Edo period.

Yuzawa is built on the eastern slopes of the mountains that border the Omono River, which flows to the sea near Akita City north of Yuzawa. In recent years much of the rice land between the town and the river has been converted to urban use, and the highway that runs from Yamagata prefecture to Akita City has become lined with office buildings and houses. Nonetheless, the town retains its bucolic atmosphere. There are small vegetable plots within town, and the mountains into which the town climbs are still covered with pine and cryptomeria. Standing on a high point, one can still see the cone of Chōkai-san, a large extinct volcano to the west. People often know one another by name, at least, and there always seems to be time to pass a few minutes talking to an acquaintance on the way to or from some errand.

Residents of the town include both blue- and white-collar families and a few professionals—doctors, engineers, teachers, lawyers (the district court is in Yuzawa). Some older residents still support themselves by wood and bamboo crafting. With the inclusion of formerly farming hamlets and areas in the town and the greater ease of transportation, there are also some farming households, although few individuals that I knew in town subsisted entirely on agriculture. (Many families, however, maintain a small plot for kitchen vegetables.) The town is fortunately situated, with one side against a forested mountain, which residents use for recreation and for agricultural purposes. Pawlonia wood is raised commercially, and there are also scattered truck gardens in forest clearings.

The town has thirty-five public shrines of varying sorts and perhaps twice that number of shrines in people's yards, as well as ten Buddhist temples, one Tenrikyō temple, and two Christian churches. Roughly speaking, shrines may be owned and run by a community or neighborhood association of some sort (public shrines), by a private voluntary association (*kōjū* shrines), or by a kin- or, more properly, ancestor-based association (*ujiko* shrines).

The shrines are distributed throughout the town in various settings. Twenty-eight neighborhoods have shrines within or near their borders, four neighborhoods have a shrine outside the neighborhood, and the rest currently have no shrine. Several neighborhoods (e.g., Yanagi-machi, Maemori) support more than one communal shrine. In addition about ten shrines are maintained by worshiper associations *(kōjū* or *ujiko)*. I was unable to determine the exact number of such shrines since *ujiko* do not advertise and it is difficult to ascertain merely by sight whether a given shrine is abandoned or maintained, and if so how. Moreover, *kōjū* and *ujiko* shrines are often on private property, and not all owners were ready to cooperate with the research.

Most shrines are solitary, but there are several shrine parks where several distinct shrines have been built on the same precincts, usually with one host and several guest shrines (Ashkenazi 1981). This is the case in the Yunohara Hitachi Inari, Shinmeisha, and Atago shrine precincts, as well as on the grounds of two temples, Seiryoji (Soto Zen sect) and Tōsenji (Tendai sect).

Yuzawa's newer neighborhoods have few shrines, although in a number of instances *ujigami* (*kami* of kin associations) shrines, usually smaller than the average size in older neighborhoods, can be found. The modern Japanese architecture of the newer neighborhoods constructed since World War II, and particularly since the early 1970s, does not accommodate *kamidana* (shelves within a house fitted with a small shrine for ancestral and household *kami*). Nor does it provide enough yard space for the erection of major *ujigami* shrine structures, such as can be seen in older neighborhoods where the yards are larger. New neighborhoods often lack religious facilities of any kind.

Yuzawa's major tourist attractions are the winter Inukko *matsuri;* the Tanabata *matsuri* (in July), which celebrates the mythical reunion of the cowherd and the weaver girl in heaven; and the Daimyō Gyōretsu (in August), Yuzawa's major festival. Other shrines have festivals, too, but their celebration is limited to neighborhood boundaries, and they are not major attractions.

Entertainment in Yuzawa includes *pachinko* (pinball) parlors and video arcades, bowling centers, a cinema, a large cultural center with auditoriums and lecture rooms, a civic center that offers various classes and exhibitions, a ski slope, several sports grounds, and numerous coffee shops. There are also two sports-cum-vacation complexes and several spas within easy driving distance. Most of these are open year round. Many families own cars, and fishing, camping, or sightseeing trips for families or groups organized by intra- and interneighborhood associations are common. The growing demand for leisure resources has increased the construction of elaborate facilities such as Ikoi-no-Mura, a resort in the hinterlands of Yuzawa-shi. Among other things, Yuzawa residents are proud of their alcohol consumption. Six sake breweries still operate within the town. I was told there are 350 bars but was unable to verify that number personally notwithstanding strenuous efforts. Most men (and some women) drink at a bar at least once a week.

Entertainment and Leisure in Modern Japan

Japanese national affluence after about 1965, including a rise in the standard of living and general prosperity in the countryside (Dore 1978; Johnson 1976), has been accompanied by an increase in leisure activities and an improvement in living conditions for most of the population. By the late 1980s the Japanese government was concerned that Japanese spent too little time in leisure activities, although, indefatigable as usual in the pursuit of statistics, it was aware of the trend almost two decades earlier (Economic Planning Agency 1972, 84). The steady rise in income has since increased the demand for entertainment, and possibilities ranging from tourism to hobbies to home electronic diversions have kept pace with the demand.[11]

Television, as Fukutake notes (1974, 96), has become a prime source of entertainment. It is also a medium for learning about places away from one's immediate ken. H. D. W. Smith (1973) suggests that because television as well as other forms of mass communication are largely controlled by the metropolis (i.e., Tokyo and Osaka), they tend to reflect metropolitan attitudes and practices. Metropolitan media tend to stereotype the bucolic and backward *inaka* (countryside),[12] and the metropolitan viewpoint is, more often than not, shown on local television.

Growth in leisure and entertainment has been paralleled by a related phenomenon. Many functions of Japanese society take place within the framework of voluntary associations. Some, like the *buraku* (hamlet) associations, have a long history (Johnson 1976; Ushiomi 1964) and perhaps have served as models for the urban neighborhood associations of today. Others are recent affinity groupings that bring together people with a particular interest (e.g., a sport or a hobby). These serve various functions in community life, not the least of which is to bring together those individuals with similar tastes for leisure-time activities. As Plath (1969, 146) has noted, such associations can generally be divided into two types: those whose recruitment is based on residence—neighborhood associations, shrine support organizations, volunteer firemen—and those whose recruitment is based on occupation or interest—flower arranging, tea ceremony, tennis, nature walks. In smaller communities these two types tend to overlap so that membership in one tends to become ipso facto membership in others. In larger communities and in the cities, membership tends to cross-cut, with members of one association members of another, and communal activities are more diffuse.

As we shall see, this desire for entertainment affects, indeed helps determine, the persistence of *matsuri*. While some elements of *matsuri*, such as the rituals, can and do exist apart from their entertainment value, the same is not true of the festivities. The essence of festivity is entertainment, or, at least, entertainment is indistinguishable from it. In fact, as we shall see later, *matsuri* organizers are aware of and utilize their festivals' entertainment potential to the best of their ability.

Historical Note

The history of Japan as a nation is not one of the concerns here. However, it is necessary to provide some historical details that relate to phenomena to be dealt with in the following pages. One of Yuzawa's major festivals, the Daimyō Gyōretsu, will be used extensively for illustration. The genesis of the festival is tied intimately to the history of Yuzawa, which emerged as a town only in the seventeenth century with the arrival of the Satake clan. While there is some awareness of the pre-Satake period, called the Onodera period locally, the arrival of the Satake and their retainers, servants, shrines, and customs is the start of local ethnohistory. Families, establishments, several shrines, and festivals relate themselves in some way to the clan's arrival. Current social and festival arrangements in Yuzawa owe much to the social system that held sway in Japan from the seventeenth century to the end of the nineteenth.

In 1600, an alliance led by the *daimyō* Tokugawa Ieyasu of Edo defeated the supporters of Toyotomi Hideyori at Sekigahara, ushering in the 269-year-long Edo period. The postbattle political arrangements reassigned the Satake clan from their fief at Mito (modern Ibaragi prefecture northeast of Tokyo) to a smaller fief in remote Ugo province (modern Akita prefecture). The southern branch of the Satake was assigned a ten-thousand-*koku*[13] fief in Yuzawa (Yamashita and Hisaei 1963).

To control their reluctant subject clans, the Tokugawa government resorted to various mechanisms, the most prominent being the *sankin kōtai*. Under *sankin kōtai*, *daimyō* had to spend a certain portion of the year in the shogunal capital of Edo, where they were required to maintain a mansion. When leaving Edo to reside in their fiefs, *daimyō* had to leave children and wives behind as hostages. The *sankin kōtai* requirements—

arrival and departure dates, numbers and equipment of followers, gifts, and so forth—were minutely regulated (Tsukahira 1966). By the nineteenth century the tremendous expense of the system had led to heavy *daimyō* indebtedness to local merchants in many places, and the system's formal abolition before the Meiji Restoration in 1868 was greeted with relief (Hall 1971, 261). By then, as Tsukahira notes, the system was no longer effectively operating in any case.

Edo-period Japanese society was organized into four formally defined social strata: warriors, farmers, craftsmen, and merchants. All government functions were performed by the warriors. In reality the distinctions between the warrior and other strata were not so clear-cut (Moore 1968), and many *bushi* worked clandestinely as craftsmen or farmers, some even giving up the *bushi* title entirely. Rich merchants and farmers could often aspire to *bushi* rank, notwithstanding legal strictures against the practice.

The modern town of Yuzawa is a physical expansion of Yuzawa of the Edo period. Neighborhoods that had been empty fields are now crowded with houses, though the geographical names of the places have not been changed. The municipality building is built near the site of the *daimyō*'s mansion, and the arrangements for local neighborhood government derive from practices started in the Edo period. The physical setting, changed as it is by paved roads and telephone wires, can still evoke shadows of the past. Sights seen in photographs taken in 1880 can be identified today.

The Edo period, or, as it is known locally, the Satake period, has some of the features of a mythical time. It is evoked as the cradle of modern Yuzawa and its subdivisions and even as an explanation of some of the tensions that Yuzawa, like any other community, experiences. References to the Satake abound, and explanations of origin for the locations of shrines and their genesis and for local customs and preferences are often that these have ". . . come down to us from the Satake period." This is unquestionably true of the genesis of the three main festivals, each of which originated, in local view, from that period. The repetition of the festivals *in a historical context* becomes one way to point out, to themselves and to outsiders alike, the depth of the local population's concept of Yuzawa as a social and cultural entity.

Yuzawa—The Image of Reality

To explicate Yuzawa's *matsuri,* it is necessary to relate them to the context in which they are performed and continue to exist. Three broad factors are "behind the scenes" players, as it were. As partially religious phenomena, *matsuri* must be seen within the context of Japanese religion. That is not to say that all of Japanese religion is encompassed in *matsuri*, nor that religion is all there is to them. Here I have only given sufficient detail to enable the reader to understand some of the basic religious issues that relate to Yuzawa's *matsuri*.

I emphasize that these are *Yuzawa's* festivals. They are not unique to Yuzawa. To the contrary. Many such festivals are to be found throughout Japan. For Yuzawa residents, however, their *matsuri* are an element in what makes their town stand out *for them*. The image its residents have of Yuzawa will emerge as we trace individual elements in the town's *matsuri*, but it is no less important to give an objective picture of the town and its place in Japan.

Two other elements of the total picture are also important. As we shall see throughout the book, *matsuri* fit into two areas of modern life: religious behaviors and forms of entertainment for the general public. Entertainment and leisure are consequences of modernity and, particularly in Japan, of the leisure created by a newly affluent society. The alternatives available to Yuzawa residents, the ways in which they pass their time, directly influence the success and continuation of the town's *matsuri*, since many elements of festivities play toward a public out to enjoy itself.

In addition, Yuzawa, besides being a community, a place, a collection of buildings, is also a concept in people's minds. As in other societies, this is a composite image. And, as in other societies, part of that image is based on ideas about what amounts to a "mythical time." By this I mean that historical "truths," whatever they are for the historian (and Yuzawa has some excellent historians), are brushed aside in favor of mythical images of the community that define it and give its actions license. Thus, in historical reality, perhaps, Yuzawa is a minor *han* of defeated Kantō barons, but in the eyes of its people it is *Daimyō Gyōretsu no machi,* the city of the Lord's Parade.

All of these factors are implicit in the performance of Yuzawa's *matsuri*, in the behavior of participants and other residents, in the ways in which the town reacts to the events it puts on. There is no need to explicate to one another what being a "ten-thousand-*koku* fief" means; all in Yuzawa know. And neither is it necessary to explain, except to strangers, that work will be suspended early in Atago-chō when the paraders are practicing.

3

Rituals

Rituals are central to most festivals. They exist and are performed, however, for reasons and in circumstances that transcend the confines of festivals. Even identifying the limits of what ought to be called "ritual" constitutes a complicated problem all its own. A close relationship exists between shrine rituals, rituals performed outside of shrines, events such as parades that accompany many festivals, and certain behaviors in daily life. As I have noted, I am far from convinced of the validity of imputing psychological or supernatural motives as a basis for identifying ritual behavior, behavior that is eminently human, observable, and thus analyzable using empirical methods. My theoretical approach emphasizes observable phenomena. To examine Yuzawa's rituals I have therefore extracted common features from several different behaviors in the town. To illustrate these common features I begin this chapter with several skeletal descriptions of rituals that I observed under different circumstances. I then analyze these rituals with reference to daily interaction behaviors and a body of theory, extracting their similarities through careful examination. To slightly simplify a complex discussion, I deal with festival parades in the following chapter.

As previously noted, the core of most festivals in Yuzawa is a formal, religious ritual. Rituals are performed in Yuzawa in various circumstances, including important personal events (e.g., funerals, weddings), and some special public efforts (e.g., opening a new bridge). Although festival rituals are the major concern here, it is necessary to discuss Shinto rituals in Yuzawa in general in order to place these festival rituals in context. Describing a selection of rituals in the order in which they occur in the course of one year in Yuzawa will help to clarify the discussion. The rituals chosen represent a range of ritual behaviors. Such inclusivity shows the breadth of the behavioral rules implicit in performing rituals that are to be discussed.

Rituals in Yuzawa

Shichi-go-san is a rite of passage conducted for children of three, five, and seven years of age. The event, which is for families and individuals, rather than the community, occurs around November 15. In Yuzawa, *shichi-go-san* usually occurs after the first snowfall. The incumbent priest of Atago-jinja conducts *shichi-go-san* rituals upon request. Family groups start arriving in the early morning. Often only the mother accompanies her children, but sometimes a father or grandmother comes too. The cold and snow deter many from wearing kimono, and many people arrive in formal Western dress. The ritual takes place in one of the rooms of the priest's house, which is fitted out as a shrine. The room is bare except for a small three-tiered altar on the far side. The schematic arrangement of shrines can be seen in Figure 1.

On the uppermost tier of the shrine's altar are a metal mirror and some paper streamers attached to upright wands. The middle tier bears five raised trays *(sanbō)* with a variety of foodstuffs as offerings *(osonaemono)* and gift packages for the children. The lowest tier has a pair of lit candles.

The simple ritual is replicated with some variations at any ritual conducted by a Shinto priest. The priest announces the start of the ritual by banging a drum. Seating himself at point A (see Figure 2, p. 46 below), he then faces the altar and chants a short invocation. While chanting he kneels, trunk erect, feet tucked under buttocks in *seiza* (formal sitting on *tatami* mats). After purifying the premises and those present by waving a streamer-tipped wand over them, he reads a prayer from a scroll. The priest gives the child a *tamagushi*, that is, a sprig of *sakaki (Cleyera ochnacea; Cleyera japonica)* tied with flax and paper streamers. Instructed by the priest, who removes himself carefully to a position away from the altar, the child places the *tamagushi* on a low table before the altar. The child and parents clap their hands and bow to the altar. The ritual ends as the priest sounds a drum. The children in their finery are rewarded with a small gift, a decorated paper bag filled with traditional "thousand years" sweets.

Of Yuzawa's six resident *kannushi*, only two make their living solely as ritual experts. One, who inherited his position from his father and was trained in the profession before the war, has a touch of missionary zeal. He proudly told me of introducing several innovations to his ritual practice, including the purification of cars against traffic accidents. A taxi

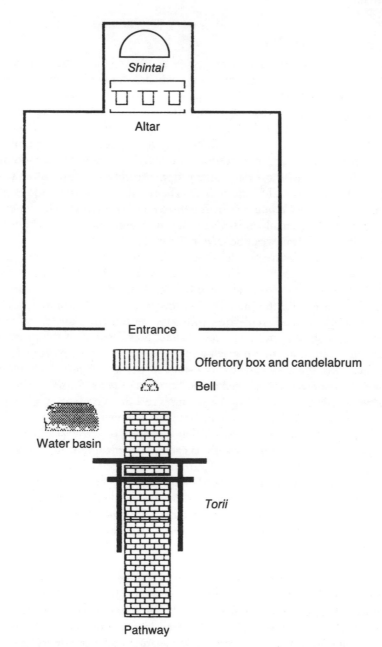

Figure 1. Schematic drawing of a *jinja*

company requests his services whenever it acquires a new car. "Their cars have had fewer accidents ever since I started purifying them," he said. Two new cars were waiting for him the day I watched him work. It was his second ritual that day and several more were in the offing. The cars were parked in the taxi garage, their motors running, their doors, trunks, hoods, and radiator caps open. A small altar was set up with paraphernalia brought by the *kannushi:* salt, candle, sake bottle, and a glass of water. The drivers of these two cars waited in attendance; other drivers ignored the ritual. The manager came out to thank the *kannushi,* then disappeared back into his office. The ritual was similar to the one described for *shichi-go-san* with one difference: the *kannushi* took care to wave the purifying wand over the cars' doors, trunk, and engine, as well as over the drivers. After the *kannushi* left, the drivers emptied the glass of water into the radiators and strewed the remaining salt[1] in the direction of the cars.

One of Yuzawa's smaller neighborhoods, Shin-chō, was originally settled by samurai families. A *kōjū* (ritual association) of these families erected a small shrine on a hill above the neighborhood. Of these families, only two still live in the area. The *bettō* (stewards) of the shrine hold a small ritual on the shrine's yearly festival day. The ritual is performed by a Tendai sect Buddhist priest whose family has officiated at this and several other shrines for several generations. The shrine itself is deserted; the ritual is held in the *bettō's* home. The priest arrives and dons his robes. The *bettō* has had an altar made up in a corner of the guest room. The priest cuts the shapes of two foxes, several Chinese characters, and Sanskrit letters out of sheets of white paper, attaches them to wands, and sets them upright in a rice pile before the *shintai* of the shrine. In this particular shrine the *shintai* is a statue of Inari, the *kami* of prosperity and rice, riding on his messenger, the fox. The ritual differs significantly from one performed by a *kannushi.* The priest chants a text in which Chinese, Japanese, and Indian deities are invoked, rolls a set of beads, and invokes power with finger gestures called *mudra.* At the end of the ritual he tells the *bettō* to place the paper cutouts in the shrine itself. The ritual ends with a feast, from which the bonze excuses himself to attend another ritual.

The New Year is the occasion for families to get together, to visit with relatives and eventually with friends. The Saga family is descended from samurai stock, part of the contingent that was quartered with the Yuzawa *daimyō* by his own overlord, the main house Satake in Akita City. Before the New Year, the Saga place an offering, traditional in their family, of woven rice-straw images, vegetables, pounded rice cakes, and sake on small lacquered trays in their home's *tokonoma* (niche).

On each of the three days of the celebration, the family gathers before the *tokonoma*. Mr. Saga senior (he has two married sons) kneels before the altar. The family members follow suit. He claps his hands, then recites a short invocation, raising each of the trays to the scroll in the *tokonoma*. The scroll bears the name of the Saga house's *kami,* given to a Saga ancestor by the Satake *daimyō.* The elder Saga then offers each of the family members sips of sake from the special sake container used only on this occasion. They all bow and clap again.

In the rather lengthy theoretical discussion that follows, we will examine the theoretical premises of the examples just given.

Aspects of Ritual

Ceremony

All four of the events described above are, at the least, superficially similar. They belong to a class of human behaviors variously called "ritual" or "ceremonial." They are "similar" to the unprejudiced eye because they seem to have a number of features in common. Indeed, some of these features are shared by events outside Japanese society. The problem is in identifying these common features in a definitive manner, a manner that, on the one hand, allows comparisons outside Japanese society, while on the other is not so broad as to encompass events that may not belong in the same class or set of classes (assuming the possibility that there may be subsets of these events). Goody's (1977) stricture "against ritual" is indeed important. Goody cautions against identifying ritual by, for example, its symbolic content because such identification forces the observer to accept almost any event as ritual since most human events have some symbolic content. It is more fruitful to examine rituals in terms of their observable behavioral characteristics, thus avoiding many of the problems associated with purely interpretative analyses. It is possible, therefore, to consider rituals as a special case of a larger set of human behavioral events and to attempt to isolate those features that pertain particularly to rituals.

A convenient way to do so is to examine human behaviors in terms of the "interaction code" (Skorupski 1976, 75–77) that constitutes the metarules defining how communications are passed in any given society (no distinction being made between verbal and other interactive communicative media). The interaction code, which governs the method of passing messages in a culture (though not their content), includes rules on daily communication and interaction as well as rules regarding infrequent occasions, such as ceremonies. A high degree of elaboration and formality in behavior characterizes ceremonial behaviors. These can be more or less elaborate either in the *complexity* of the formula or script of the behavior or in its *scale*—that is, the resources expended in the behavior. Another aspect of the interaction code is *formality*. Formality in social interactions marks and emphasizes a particular event or set of behaviors. This emphasis, as Skorupski notes, puts the marked behaviors "on the record," making them public and setting them off from other behavior. Ceremonial activity consists of sets of behaviors more complex and more formal than others in use in any given culture.

Ceremonial activity may be conceptualized as a behavioral frame, "a form which gives certain meanings to its contents" (Moore and Myerhoff 1977, 8). "Rituals" in this sense are framed ceremonial activities displaying a great deal of formality and complexity for a particular social end. What any ritual "does" or "says" or "means" depends on the confluence of its morphological characteristics as a frame and the specific contents loaded onto that frame. Contents may be social messages (e.g., as suggested by Leach 1968, 1976) or messages about ideologies (e.g., as demonstrated by Lane 1981), states of nature (e.g., see Rappaport 1967), or some other human concern. What is significant in all of these cases is ritual's capacity as a frame emphasizing the content.

To return to the Japanese examples described earlier, each of the ritual examples is an elaboration in terms of expense, effort, and modes of behavior when compared to the actions of daily life. The specific content or message being emphasized and underlined by the ritual is varied and may have different interpretations for different people. The *shichi-go-san* ritual, for instance, has several interpretations. For the priest, the ritual formally introduces children to the *kami*'s presence; for the parents, it ensures their offspring's health, marks his or her growth, or is a gesture to keep up with their neighbors; for the children, the fancy clothes, an unusual gift, and the "thousand years candy" are of greater salience than any supposed message.

Religious ritual differs from other forms of ritual or ceremonial in one major respect. While all ceremonial is social action, religious ritual involves at least one "moot entity," a social persona lacking demonstrable empirical referents. *"Kami,"* "God," "gods," "spirits," and "demons," all of whom are social persona in rituals involving them, fall into this category. They are, therefore, real participants in rituals addressed to them.[2] To maintain a degree of unity in the terms used, I follow Gluckman (1962), Goody (1977), and Skorupski (1976) in reserving the term "ritual" here for the ceremonialization of religious action. In the performance of ritual, one party to the interaction is a moot entity. All actions addressed to the moot entities, deferring to their wishes and desires or recapitulating their actions, are religious actions.

The conceptualization of ceremonial action and ritual as one end of a continuum of social behaviors is not without problems. We must be able to distinguish clearly between ritual actions and others. This is particularly important in the case of Japanese festivals. On the one hand, many of the events and actions that take place during *matsuri* include religious and symbolic elements. On the other, Japanese behavior toward the *kami* can often be offhanded, indistinguishable from behaviors directed at human beings. Elements that are shared to differing degrees by ceremonial and customary social actions are useful for disentangling these apparent complexities.

Formality

Formality is a key concept for understanding ritual. The concept reappears in a number of definitions. Ritual is "formal behavior" (Benedict 1937), "saying something in a formal way" (Firth 1963, 176). The term "refers to formalized, institutionalized, and usually group activity" (Middleton 1970, 502). Rituals are "sequences of formal acts and utterances" (Rappaport 1979, 175). Most users of the term "formality" tend to assume that it has some self-evident referent. As Irvine (1979, 778, 779) shows, the label "formality" actually disguises several characteristics, only some of which may be applicable in any particular usage. Irvine formulates the four possible aspects of formality as paraphrased below:

1. Increased communicative code structuring: the addition of extra rules or conventions to the communicative code that organizes behavior in social settings. I take Irvine's "communicative code" to be equivalent to the interaction code in Skorupski's sense.
2. Code consistency: the attempt to keep all aspects of a situation—speech, dress, gestures, activities—as consistent as possible. By maintaining consis-

tency in his presentation or performance, an actor demonstrates that he takes his actions and his role seriously and that the action is "for real" and on the record, what Skorupski has called "overt."

3. Invoking positional identity: by invoking social identities, actors make the acting in the situation, the "presentation of self" appear more formal. "The wider, or more public, the scope of the social identities involved . . . the more formal the occasion is."

4. The emergence of a central situational focus: "The ways in which a main focus of attention . . . is differentiated from side involvements" indicate a formal event.

Two examples of formality in nonreligious situations will illustrate what I mean by formality and will also show how ritual is similar to other forms of ceremonial behavior in Yuzawa.

Once a year, the Yuzawa Historical Association sponsors a walk to the site of Yuzawa Castle in the town's central park. Those who join the walk assemble near the municipality building in the early morning. Before the climb, association members distribute a pamphlet entitled "The History of Yuzawa Castle," register participants, and assign themselves to various positions in the line of march. People stand around, greet friends, and read the literature. Then the deputy mayor arrives; he is dressed in white shirt and tie in contrast to the hikers in casual clothes. Conversation stops and heads quickly turn toward the official, who stands waiting. He bows, and all present respond before he gives a short speech. During the speech attention is fully focused on him. All private conversations end, and association members cease their movements and activities. After the speech, normal activity resumes. Later, at a lookout site on the castle heights, a senior member of the association gives an orientation talk. Like the other hikers, he is dressed in casual clothes. While he is talking, some hikers listen attentively; others chat, search for mushrooms or wild vegetables, or point out their houses below. There is a noticeable difference in the attention paid to the two speeches.

In the midwinter Inukko *matsuri,* one of Yuzawa's three main festivals, old New Year's decorations and other ritual paraphernalia are burned at a night ritual called *dondo-yaki.* In the evening, people bring items for burning, and as the hour for the ritual approaches, they begin crowding around the site. Most are bundled up because a blizzard is blowing. A *kannushi* performs the rituals and the deputy mayor is among those who make an offering at the altar. Before approaching the altar, the deputy mayor takes off his overcoat; dressed in suit and tie, he makes his offering and a short speech afterwards. He is followed by other similarly dressed officials and the silk-robed *kannushi*.[3] The ritual remains the major focus of attention. Some onlookers lose interest and wander away, but within the confines of the site and unquestionably among the actual ritual participants, the ritual is the center of attention.

The two situations illustrate aspects of formality in Yuzawa. In the first of the two speeches on the walk, positional identity was invoked when the city official was introduced in his formal capacity. The speaker maintained code consistency, particularly noticeable in his dress: the participants were dressed informally for the hike, but he wore a suit. Association members, by ceasing activity and orienting themselves visibly to the speaker, effectively stilled all other activity. Ancillary effects also came into play: rather than slouching or sitting on their packs, hikers stood at attention and faced the speaker; children were hushed. Thus, part of the walk, a leisure activity but also an event relating to local pride and history, was converted to a ceremonious occasion.

In the guide's talk at the lookout point the same aspects did not apply. Many individuals did not recognize the guide's talk as a focus of attention. Other reinforcing qualities of formality were not evident: the guide was dressed casually, association leaders did not orient their body stance toward him, and he had no official position as far as the hikers were concerned.

The *dondo-yaki* ritual manifests other aspects of formality. Code behavior was minutely regulated during the ritual, and those participating performed a prescribed set of motions. There was a clear central focus, personal statuses were invoked, and code consistency was maintained. The *dondo-yaki* appears the more formal of the three rituals not because it was a religious event, but because more ceremonial behavior was apparent. Degrees of formality can be created by the combination and number of the aspects invoked. Skorupski implies that ceremonial action is not a distinct state but one end of a continuum. All and any aspects of formality may be, and often are, utilized. The more formal the situation, the more aspects utilized, and the social devices used to make a situation formal can vary extensively.

The presence of extremely high-ranking individuals is one manifestation of a formal situation. The visit of a high-ranking teacher to a club of which I was a member was the occasion for a display of great formality, not only in the interaction with the teacher, but between the members of the group as well. Club members abjured the usual jokes and noisy

byplay. The members who met the teacher at the train station wore suits for the occasion, although they were to change their clothes for a special lesson later. Interactions were generally more restrained.

As the teacher's visit demonstrates, important events may make people deem formality appropriate. The converse also appears to be true. Great formality marks an event as important. Ground-breaking ceremonies for public and private buildings are an example. In one such ceremony in Yuzawa, the white-collar participants wore suits, regardless of whether they wore them daily, and the workmen, including those without a role to play in the proceedings, wore clean uniforms and spoke in lowered voices using *keigo* (polite language forms). Formality serves an important function in rituals. It makes the ritual actions overt, as Skorupski has said, but it also makes rituals noticeable. In other words, formality is one means by which rituals are marked.

Marking

Ritual actions are intended as consequential acts; they are overt and on-the-record. The overtness often expresses itself in unusual actions and objects that set ritual apart from the ongoing flow of life. A ritual's most salient characteristic is its function as a frame that sets off otherwise unremarkable activities (Myerhoff 1977, 200). Formality is one behavioral way of marking and creating the frame, the use of special objects, another.

Kannushi and some Japanese who are not ritual experts will hesitate for a second before pouring the first cup of sake for a guest. The first time I saw a *kannushi* hesitate in this way, I thought he did so because he could not see the cup without his glasses. Observing the same behavior on other occasions, I questioned another *kannushi* and learned that the hesitation was purposeful. He was touching the cup three times, effectively filling the ritual requirement of "three cups,"[4] marking the frame by his behavior. A *jichin-sai* (ground-breaking ritual) involves ritual actions and special objects. A barrier of rice-straw rope festooned with paper streamers is erected around the site. Special items and brand-new tools are used if possible, and the ritual, like many others, is marked by a musical interlude before and after.

The separation of rituals from daily life is an inherent quality of all ceremonial and of ritual in particular. It can be extremely subtle, like the *kannushi*'s pouring, or very obvious, as at the *dondo-yaki* when the deputy mayor took off his warm overcoat. The behavior of the Historical Association members before the deputy mayor's speech is also a clear

40 Matsuri

marker of the beginning and end of behavioral periods. Entering the ceremonial period is shown by orienting to a single focus, the speaker; leaving that period is marked by splintering to several foci of activity. Markers are rarely isolated, and they include acts of formality as well as elaborate items and acts. The components of what transforms actions into ritual actions may fulfill several functions at once. The framing of rituals as separate events is made possible by marking the event, and such marking is a combined pattern in which formality, elaboration, and liturgical order compound their effects.

Liturgical Order

One significant way in which religious ceremony differs from social ceremonial forms is that it has liturgical order, an invariable order within a ritual (Rappaport 1979, 176). As an illustration of what is meant by "invariable order," consider the differences between the religious and the nonreligious formal practices described earlier. When the deputy mayor spoke at the hike, there was no protocol to speak, nor was there a prescribed set of actions for the participants, aside from the general forms of formality used in Yuzawa. In the *dondo-yaki,* however, as in other *kannushi*-run rituals, there was a prescribed order of actions integral to the formal situation: bows, claps, manipulation of objects, and set verbal exchanges. These were similarly prescribed in all rituals run by *kannushi* in Yuzawa. The actions of the *kannushi* at the *shichi-go-san, dondo-yaki,* and taxi rituals followed a clearly recognizable, invariant order. Such an invariant order is a liturgical order. The liturgical order expresses a set of canonical messages that "make reference to processes or entities . . . outside the ritual in words or acts that have, by definition, been spoken or performed before" (Rappaport 1979, 179). The invariance of a ritual is not the performer's choice, but, rather, a product of historical and immediate circumstances, as well as of a concern for the proper modes of conduct.

Attending a ritual, "itself the basic ritual action" (Bocock 1974, 40), strengthens the import of liturgical order in rituals. By attending and participating, the participant acquiesces publicly (at least insofar as the relevant audience is concerned) to the ritual and, by implication, to the contents transmitted in the ritual (see Rappaport 1979, 192).

Formality, which puts a liturgical order's sequence of acts and the invariance of the event on record, has two effects on liturgical order. First, because formality is serious, it makes of the order a serious matter. In

other words, it adds weight to the invariance. Second, it acts reciprocally to make the invariable and thus unusual order a part of the marking process of the ritual. A participant in a ritual implies that he or she acquiesces to what the ritual states. Participants acquiesce to the seriousness of the occasion because it is a formal occasion. They are also acquiescing to claims that its canonical messages are true or at least implying by their participation that they are not prepared to challenge the ritual's premises. In a broader sense, this acquiescence also implies acquiescence to the form of social order espoused in the ritual in general terms. Participants in a Yuzawa ritual are stating publicly and on the record that, whatever their private feelings may be,[5] they are part of a particular social system in which the *kami* are at the head, followed by high-status individuals and common people. Such acquiescence is circumscribed. An analogy is to be found in such ceremonial practices as the tea ceremony and certain types of fencing. By participating in the activity, the tea or fencing practitioner follows an invariable order, and by performing that order acquiesces publicly to certain canonical messages. (See, for example, Kondo's 1985 discussion of the tea ceremony.) The canonical message in these two examples is that the practice will lead to spiritual improvement.[6]

Ritual as Social Interaction

"The action in ritual is social, that is, it involves groups of people who share some sets of expectations in common" (Bocock 1974, 36). Rituals are performed as interactions between one or more performers and one or more moot entities. When several humans are involved in a ritual, that ritual may become a locus of social as well as religious action. Ritual is also collective; that is, it is an aggregate of the simultaneous activity of several actors. There can be no monologue; a person must "assert whatever his message is through acts fully embedded in a flow of interaction and simultaneous expression" (Barth 1973, 208). The characteristics of the groups involved in Yuzawa rituals greatly affect the nature and form of festivals. Such groups form the most obvious links between rituals and the festivals that surround them. It is important to understand rituals as social events, as well as the social and behavioral context in which they occur, to understand the rituals' ties to festivals.

Social interactions in Yuzawa often are to one degree or another ceremonial. The interaction code includes rules for behaviors that are "outward signs of states that stand in need of signs, being socially significant,

but not themselves directly and publicly visible" (Skorupski 1976, 114). These outward signs, ritualized behaviors such as bows and facial expressions, are de rigueur in interactions in Yuzawa. Conventional expressions of personal regard frame these interactions. The behaviors are formal, they involve specific behavioral rules that specify increased code-structuring, and their precise expression invokes the social identities of those involved. These behaviors are marked by specific gestures, vocal tones, and word uses and patterns.[7]

In dyadic interactions in Yuzawa, the following will occur, particularly if there are status differences between the parties. Both parties will bow, with the lower-status persons bowing more deeply. Each will utter a stock phrase, usually *"Dōmo,"* *"Kono aida, dōmo,"* or *"Ii tenki dasu be?"* perhaps followed by some moments of conversation. They will part again with one bow or several. In more formal situations, formality will be expressed by greater restrictions on behavior as well as by the introduction of other aspects of formality. Thus, when meeting one's boss alone on the street, it is possible to stand in a somewhat relaxed fashion after bowing, to venture comments and ideas, and to take notice of passing friends. When meeting someone of much higher status, one might wear special clothing, stand more stiffly, and speak only when spoken to.

In addition to indicating presumed internal states, that is, their "meaning," these conventional signs also mark the status of those involved and the degree of the interaction's formality. Because formality is a composite of four possible usages, there can be gradations in formal occasions as usages are added and combined. The more of the features present in any given interaction, the more formal it is. These signs indicate the gradations of "polite behavior."

Politeness is composed of deference—the quality of appreciation of someone conveyed to that individual—and demeanor—the statement of personal worth and qualities made through comportment, dress, and bearing (Goffman 1956). The forms of politeness, like those of liturgical order, are conventionalized expressions whereby a performer acquiesces to a generally accepted set of rules, implying a certain accepted reality and a supposed inner state. Politeness shares with formality an increased code-structuring and invocation of positional identities. In contrast to formality, politeness does not involve code consistency and a single focus; if these are introduced, the situation becomes formal. Empirically, politeness and formality often appear as the same or contiguous phenomena. Polite behavior, which is sometimes formal, but often not, is part of daily interaction in Yuzawa.

The differences between the two speeches during the Historical Association walk can now be seen in different terms. Both speeches were polite, as were all interactions at that time. Only one of them, the deputy mayor's speech, was also a formal occasion, made so because of the interjection of other aspects of formality. Because politeness is such a common element of Yuzawa social life, it is a familiar aspect of behavior. Very formal occasions are encountered less frequently. Nevertheless, all rituals, which are very formal occasions, "make sense" to Yuzawa participants because they share some aspects with other polite interactions.

Multisided social interactions follow a set pattern that marks them off by the behaviors involved. The proceedings of the final yearly meeting of a club I belonged to in Yuzawa are typical. The club has four officers and ten untitled members. The most junior officeholder cajoled and maneuvered the senior officeholders and a high-status guest to the positions of honor at the far wall of the room. Everyone found a place, amid conversation and banter. The junior officer, whom I shall call the introducer, said, "Let us begin." All the members moved to sit in *seiza*. "This is the final meeting of our group. Mr. Sato will say a few words." Mr. Sato, the guest, began his speech with "My name is Sato. Thank you for coming. I will now begin . . ." Following Sato's speech, the introducer announced the senior officer of the club, who also preceded and ended his speech with stock phrases. The introducer then proposed a toast, after which people relaxed, abandoning *seiza* to sit cross-legged or to lean against the wall. After about thirty or forty minutes of drinking, eating, and conversation, the club's officers quietly excused themselves and left with the high-status guest for more drinking elsewhere. The party then got livelier, and the remaining members drunker and less inhibited. This pattern—a formal start, commensal eating and drinking, departure of the senior members—is reiterative at any formal party or group gathering.[8] It is also the model followed for rituals and festivals.

In rituals, great deference is directed at a high-status guest with a formal, bounded set of behaviors. This deference behavior is followed by a looser, social-party atmosphere of equals, called a *naorai,* during which participants eat, drink, and talk in a relaxed atmosphere after the high-status guest (the *kami*) has left. Festivals, which are wider replications of this same pattern, involve a formal event—a ritual—and a relaxed, unbounded set of events—the festivity.

The "honored guest," a high-status individual who is not a part of the group, is often singled out in some recognizable way. He will, as in the case cited above, be seated in the place of honor. He may have a corsage pinned to his lapel or a bouquet or pot of bonsai placed before his seat. By analogy, moot entities are extremely high-status guests who are treated accordingly by participants at rituals.

Jinja Rituals

Shinto rituals, the rituals that are part of the majority of festivals in Yuzawa, consist of two identifiable and distinct types. Individual obeisance, called *hairei,* is practiced by people on their own, sometimes during group rituals. Group rituals—colloquially, *harai*—subsume, as we shall see, a special form of *hairei* that is integral to the group ritual. A ritual in Yuzawa is a ceremonial act: it is elaborate and very formal. It is also polite: participants express by their actions a deference toward one side of the interaction, the moot entity. Extreme formality also separates rituals in obvious and identifiable ways from other behaviors: rituals are much more formal than even the most formal interactions in daily intercourse. In line with the increased formality, rituals also tend to be more elaborate.

On most mornings, one of my neighbors would awake early and walk to our neighborhood shrine, Kumano-jinja, to perform *hairei.* Feet together and hat off, he would stand before the small, unpainted wooden structure. He would ring the bell attached to the cluster of bellpulls hanging from the *jinja*'s roof beam and then toss a coin into the offertory box. Clapping his hands twice in a measured cadence, he would close his eyes and bow his head over his joined hands for a few seconds and then repeat the claps. Finally, he would bow deeply and walk off. Kumano-jinja is small, and the trickle of people who come to perform *hairei* is slow but steady. *Hairei* is the religious equivalent of the social dyadic interactions discussed in the previous section. It expresses deference to a very high-status individual, a moot entity. It is a quintessentially personal ritual. It is, and can be, performed in public or private; in one case observed, it was actually performed in a shrine in the middle of and unrelated to a *harai.*

For their practitioners, *jinja* rituals are analogies, extensions, if you will, of polite and commonly known forms of social interaction. Exchanges between individuals in Yuzawa are generally polite, the more so the greater the difference in status between participants. Many situations in Yuzawa, such as the deputy mayor's speech and the teacher's visit, are both polite and formal. Very formal, very polite occasions are uncommon in Yuzawa, as elsewhere, because individuals of very high status rarely appear. Nevertheless, Yuzawa residents are able to make the transition between familiar and relatively unfamiliar forms of interactive behavior such as rituals. Because rituals are unfamiliar formal occasions, the elaboration and formality of rituals require that someone serve as "introducer." The need is dictated by common practice in other ceremonial interactions and by the necessity of avoiding social solecisms. Such an introducer is a ritual expert, a priest who performs *harai*.

Most group rituals—those characterized by the participation of more than one individual and the activities of an officiant running the ritual—occur in *jinja. Jinja* rituals take place in a part of the shrine called the *haiden,* or before the shrine if the shrine building is too small to allow entrance. Before a ritual starts, the participants sit in *seiza* facing the altar. Usually, when more than one participant group is present or represented, the different groups sit slightly removed from one another. The officiant, also seated in *seiza* but at the far right of the room (see Figure 2), formally announces "We will now start," and bows to those present. A drum, flute, or full musical ensemble plays, if available. Divisions in *jinja* rituals are marked by the *kannushi* clapping twice and bowing two bows at the start and end of each segment. The segments are named, though few except the *kannushi* know the names or use them.

The first segment is *kōjin* (invocation). After announcing that the ritual is to start, the *kannushi,* moving in straight lines and turning only at right angles, goes to sit directly in front of the altar (see Figure 2 for positions and movements). After bowing to the altar he chants, in a deep and throaty voice, a formula inviting the *kami* to join the assemblage. This ritual segment ends, as do all others, with claps and bows.

Following immediately is *harai* (purification), a term often used to mean Shinto ritual in general. The *kannushi* takes a *harai gushi* (a wand or evergreen twig tied with white paper streamers) from a stand near the altar and waves it three times from side to side over the altar. He repeats the motions over the seated participants and finally over the *jinja* entrance. He then restores the *harai gushi* to its place in the stand. His movements are smooth and deliberate. The *harai gushi* is held with both hands at all times. At the end of each sweep, which is performed with hands outstretched and body bent slightly from the waist, the officiant twitches the wand slightly to impart a swirling motion to the streamers. The start and end of each motion are clearly identifiable.

Norito (prayer) follows. The prayer is read from a scroll prepared by the

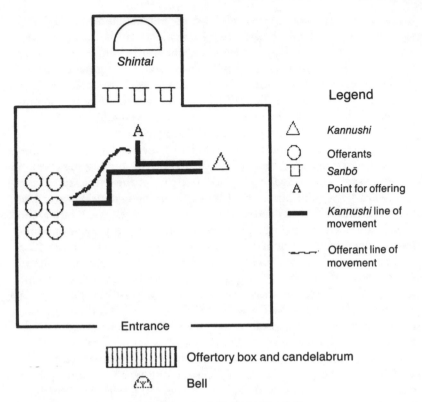

Figure 2. Positions and movements in a *jinja* ritual

kannushi from a standard formula. It contains praises of the *kami* and requests for the *kami*'s blessing on those participating in the ritual. The *kannushi* unfolds the scroll and reads, holding it at arm's length in both hands (Sadler 1974). His tone is the same throaty, chanting voice used for *kōjin*.[9]

Then comes *tamagushi hōten* (offering *tamagushi*). In this segment the *kannushi* takes a sprig of *sakaki* adorned with paper streamers from a tray near the altar. He offers the sprig to a participant and then returns to his original seat. The recipient of the *tamagushi* sits in *seiza* before the altar and places the *tamagushi,* stem end toward the altar, on a small table. He claps hands twice, bows deeply, then claps his hands again before returning to his place. If he represents a group, the entire group will clap and bow in time with his actions. A final *tamagushi* is offered by the *kannushi* himself.

The fifth segment is *guji aisatsu* (officiant's greeting). Once the last *tamagushi* has been offered at the altar, the *kannushi*, from his seat at the side, bows to the assembled participants and thanks them for having attended the ritual. If there has been a musical prelude to the ritual, music will be played again at this point. In very large rituals there may also be a *kagura*, an entertainment of traditional ritual dances for the benefit and pleasure of the *kami* and other participants.

The final segment of ritual is *naorai*. After the music, the officiant goes to the altar and removes the sake container and cups. He offers an empty cup and then pours a sip of sake for each of the participants, finally accepting a cup himself from a participant. Strips of dried squid or seaweed and sometimes a morsel of cooked rice with beans may be offered at this time. In some instances the sake and food from the altar are followed by a feast either in the *jinja* itself or nearby.

Several generalizations can be extracted from the above description. They are valid for any ritual performed by any officiant in Yuzawa. First, a ritual is formal because extra rules and restrictions apply to actions and speech, because these rules occur together with elaborate dress and special settings, and because a ritual event has a single focus.[10] A multitude of rules regulate such actions as movement, speech, and seating. *Kannushi* move in straight lines and right angles as much as possible. The participants all sit rigidly in *seiza* during the ritual. The language used during the ritual is extremely formal. The tones used in reciting the *norito* are uncommon in daily address. The *kannushi* wears robes, and sometimes the participants wear special clothes. All the participants sit facing the altar and react to what is going on in front of it. Moreover, only one set of actions takes place at a time; the actions of the officiant and offerants are always sequential, never simultaneous. Next, the boundaries of a ritual's segments are clearly marked, isolating and separating each segment. Moreover, the ritual itself is set off from outside events by the same means. These rules, markers, are kept as consistent as possible. Finally, the officiant plays a major role in a *jinja* ritual. His actions are the focus of attention, except during the *tamagushi hōten* segment. In contrast, the introducer in the party described previously played a minor role.

The similarities between *tamagushi hōten* and *hairei* are self-evident. In both, an individual communicates directly with the *kami* in a formal and polite manner. During the exchange, the human makes an offering to the *kami*. It is significant that the *kannushi* removes himself rather ostentatiously from before the altar during *tamagushi hōten*;[11] the encounter is between the offerant and the *kami*. But *tamagushi hōten* and *hairei* differ in one very significant way. A participant in *hairei* stands as an individual. In *tamagushi hōten* the individual offering the *tamagushi* and approaching the altar is a member—actually, an extension—of a group. The group as a whole is making the offering through one of its members.

Just as the multisided *jinja* ritual has an invariable liturgical order, so too does the dyadic ritual, the *hairei*. Like a *jinja* ritual, *hairei* is a formal act. However, because *hairei* is dyadic, there is no need for an intermediary, an officiant. *Hairei* is less elaborate. By analogy, even more formal personal dyadic interactions in Yuzawa tend to be less elaborate than ceremonial actions involving more people. The *tamagushi hōten* segment within a *jinja* ritual represents an elaboration of *hairei*. Both *tamagushi hōten* and *hairei* are unmediated interactions between human and *kami* participants. But because *tamagushi hōten* occurs within the context of a larger and more elaborate event, it too becomes more elaborate.

Festival rituals, then, are but a subset of Shinto rituals in general, which in turn are related to the set of polite, formal behaviors that provide the framework in which the normal, daily interactions of individual Japanese take place. A theoretical frame proposed initially by Skorupski and elaborated here identifies *matsuri* rituals as formal-behavioral activities and relates them to social issues in Japanese society. The analysis suggests that it is possible to deduce how the Japanese view their relationship to important moot entities—the *kami*—within their total social viewpoint. In subsequent chapters we shall see how this particular vision affects the relationships between personae in ritual and in festivals.

4

Parades

THE CUSTOM of circumambulating holy objects is not unique to Japan. It can be seen in China (DeGlopper 1974; Wang 1974), in Latin America (Vogt 1969; Robert Jerome Smith 1975; Buechler 1980), Spain (Christian 1972), and Malta (Boissevain 1969), to name a few. Parades, which occupy an intermediate place between formal and informal events, are major parts of many festivals. The high visibility of parades makes them into effective devices for manifold uses. Parades mark off specific local areas (Bestor 1985), display individual or group positions or power (Yanagawa 1974; Booth 1982), or signify and embody challenge (Dundes and Falassi 1975). This is true in Japan (Sadler 1972; Sonoda 1975; Yanagawa 1974) as well as elsewhere (e.g., Robert Jerome Smith 1975; DeGlopper 1974; Brandes 1980; Grimes 1976). All parades require a degree of formality simply because, without some imposed order, they have the potential to become riots. On the other hand, parades often encourage, by the paraders' intent and with the connivance, active or passive, of the parade managers, a great deal of informal participation. As we shall see, in Yuzawa's major parade, all these factors are brought into balance and are allowed expression.

Those who watch a parade are drawn into participating in it in a variety of ways. The mere existence of a crowd lining a parade route is a measure of the parade's success and a part of the parade itself. Less formal parades may, however, do more than create a one-way interaction with the spectators. In some, crowds are drawn in, or parade marchers may break ranks and mix with the audience. Because of their visual impact, parades may draw great numbers of spectators who may participate in either the parade or in related festive activities.

This chapter therefore deals with parades, the most visible of a *matsuri*'s many parts. It will be necessary to distinguish performative from managerial aspects, because, even though these two aspects interact within a parade, they are analytically separate, and their consequences differ considerably.

Shinkō shiki

In most festivals in Japan, a special ritual object, usually shaped like a miniature shrine and said to contain some aspect or all of the *kami,* is paraded through the *kami*'s parish. The parade is called *shinkō shiki* and is considered by laypersons and ritual experts alike to be a review of a parish by its *kami.* Parades throughout Japan differ in content, in the behaviors permitted, in the degree of formality, and in the kind and amount of participation. The column of marchers, sometimes limited to certain categories of individuals who walk or ride along a prescribed route in a parade, is the most visible part of *matsuri* and often serves as the main attraction. Parades require organization and, consequently, a group to manage them. Elaborate parades involve the significant mobilization of resources. In Yuzawa, as elsewhere in Japan, parades are most often organized as adjuncts of a shrine's ritual or related to it.

Shinkō shiki, like other parades, also serve (see Bestor 1985; Davis 1977a) as affirmations of social boundaries. Individuals and households affirm their membership in a particular neighborhood or area by contributing time and resources to its parade, by participating in the parade's organization or performance, and by publicly affirming membership— displaying signs, posters, jackets—in the group whose parade it is. *Shinkō shiki* are those parades associated specifically with the visit of a *kami* to its parishioners. But even here, as we shall see, there is great variation in performance and interpretation. In contrast to *shinkō shiki* in Tokyo and its environs, which are generally noisy and rowdy (Sonoda 1975; Yanagawa 1974; Akaike 1976; Sadler 1972, 1975b), *shinkō shiki* in Yuzawa are generally quiet. Yuzawa residents often comment in amazement at the drunken behavior of the *mikoshi* (ornate miniature shrine) carriers brought from Tokyo for one of Yuzawa's festivals. This custom from Japan's metropolitan areas has gradually been penetrating Yuzawa, and we shall examine some of the reasons for and effects of this change.

Parades in Yuzawa

Many, though not all, of Yuzawa's *matsuri* include a parade. The largest and most impressive, that of the Daimyō Gyōretsu, is discussed below. Smaller neighborhood shrines also have parades. Before World War II, these were often managed and performed by adults, usually members of the *wakamono-kai*. Today, Yuzawa's neighborhood parades are usually managed by adults but performed by children. Of eleven neighborhood shrine parades observed in Yuzawa (excluding the Daimyō Gyōretsu and parades in shrines outside the town proper) only one was performed by adults. All of these parades center on some specific object. Although a parade may be its own justification, an object of some sort seems to offer a better focus, particularly in small neighborhood affairs. The paraded object is often a *mikoshi*. There are several recognized styles, but generally it is made of lacquered wood fitted with brass beam ends, wind chimes, and a brass phoenix on the roof. A *mikoshi* being paraded is recognized as the temporary abode of a *kami* (Herbert 1967; Sadler 1975b), and the *kami's shintai* or *taima* (slips of paper with the *kami's* name) are ritually installed in the *mikoshi* before the circumambulation starts (Sonoda 1975). The Atago-jinja *mikoshi* has been in use since 1766, when the Satake lords began supporting the shrine (Yuzawa-shi 1981, 78–80). Other objects are also paraded. In Wakayama prefecture, Davis (1977a) reports the use of a dried fish and a sake barrel. In other places in Akita, decorated poles *(bonden)* are the focus of many parades. In Yuzawa a common parade object is a rice bale called Ebisu *dawara*.[1] Decorated with colored streamers, it features masks of Okame and Hyottoko, characters from *kyōgen* (ritual plays) who represent country simplicity, good humor, and plenty.

The contrasts between *mikoshi* and Ebisu *dawara* are significant, although both forms of the palanquin are carried only in festivals. *Mikoshi* are expensive, whereas Ebisu *dawara* are relatively cheap: the straw bale *(tawara)* is readily available, the streamers are vinyl, and the masks are of paper or plastic. Also, the *kami* is not ritually installed in the *tawara*. Most of the shrines in town make Ebisu *dawara* if they have a parade.[2]

Before World War II, Ebisu *dawara* were made and carried to the shrines by neighborhood young men's associations.[3] After the war, most Ebisu *dawara* parades were apparently canceled, although the *mikoshi* of Atago-jinja continued to circulate. In the middle or early 1970s (informants are vague on the precise time) Ebisu *dawara* began to be revived. By 1979, three neighborhoods had organized Ebisu *dawara* parades. Atago-chō is large and divided into numerous subunits *(kumi)*, several of which had organized Ebisu *dawara* parades for both the spring and the summer festivals of Atago-jinja. By 1980 two other *machi,* all of Atago-chō's *kumi,* and the retired citizens' home[4] in Atago-chō had started Ebisu *dawara* parades.

In all cases the custom is the same. The bale is made the night before by the local young men's association. The *chō's* circulating notice board and some handwritten signs inform residents of the parade. Happi coats (light cotton jackets, tied with a sash) with the names of the neighborhood and the sponsor (usually a sake brewery) are prepared. On *yoi matsuri,* the first day of the *matsuri,* the neighborhood children assemble under the guidance of the young men's association members. One child carries a tray and bag (for donations) and another a bottle of sake for *naorai.* The children carry the Ebisu *dawara* through the neighborhood, stopping at houses along the way to sing a congratulatory song. At most houses someone comes out, offers some money in an envelope or a bag of sweets, and receives a sip of sake. After covering the neighborhood, the procession makes its way to the neighborhood *jinja,* where the children sing their song again in front of the shrine. The bale is then hauled into the middle of the shrine. If a priest is present, he performs *harai* for the carriers. The children are then taken for a party at the neighborhood community hall, the money previously collected being used to help defray the party costs.

In Kanaike-machi and in Yunohara-chō Ebisu *dawara* are not used. The Yunohara-chō children insisted that they have a proper *mikoshi.* The reason given was simple: "The children saw *mikoshi* on television and wanted one, too. We got together and agreed to have one made." Kanaike and Yunohara commissioned carpenters, who were residents of the neighborhoods, to make child-sized *mikoshi* (the common size of 1.5 meters square requires about forty adult porters). The *mikoshi* were then lacquered at a neighboring town that specializes in lacquer craft. One of Yunohara-chō's residents, a practicing *kannushi,* took it upon himself to perform a ritual over the Yunohara-chō *mikoshi* and install a *taima* before the *mikoshi* was paraded. He performed the ritual while the *mikoshi* was held overnight in the neighborhood hall. Few of the people involved were aware there was a *taima* inside. In Kanaike-machi, whose *jinja* is serviced by a Buddhist bonze, there was no ritual before the *mikoshi.*

Most informants view the neighborhood parade as a social act, designed to entertain and teach the children the values of neighborhood solidarity. *Shinkō shiki* parades are a part of the festivities following a ritual, but many are also an extension of the ritual. While an officiating *kannushi* may be involved, palanquins are more likely to be the result of local initiative and will, and on the whole, people see the ported objects as an aspect of festivity. The palanquins are often explained by neighborhood residents responsible for them in terms of the need to preserve local culture. In Okachi-machi I was told, "We could have had a *mikoshi,* but preferred the old-fashioned Ebisu *dawara.*" Kanaike-machi, in contrast, chose to have a *mikoshi* because of pressures deriving from metropolitan culture. That neighborhood parades in Yuzawa today are performed almost exclusively by children is in contrast with the period before World War II, when they were performed by the young men's association. Only one neighborhood, a *kumi* of Maemori-chō, still preserves an adult parade, which is used to raise money for a new boundary hawser (*shimenawa,* a thick rice-straw rope that is tied across a *torii* below the cross beam) for Atago-jinja.

Parades were generally dropped during and immediately after the war largely because of adverse economic conditions and partly perhaps because the neighborhood associations that ran them were in bad repute from their wartime function as agents of government control. When economic and political conditions improved, *tawara* quickly returned within the confines of the Yuzawa festival system. Some of the palanquins were re-created in a form that had not been used before in those *machi*—in the shape of a metropolitan import.

Mikoshi and Ebisu *dawara* are part of the festival entertainment for the children, who consider it slightly rowdy fun. Not incidentally, it is also touted as something uniquely Japanese, "something only we Japanese do," as one child put it. The Ebisu *dawara,* within the narrower context of Yuzawa, has the same sort of connotation: "something we Yuzawa people do." The *mikoshi* is a marker, a focus of community solidarity. Bunting hanging from the *mikoshi* and children's happi coats are usually dyed with the neighborhood's name. Whatever the object used, its route covers only the neighborhood that owns the palanquin. In many areas (Bestor 1985), violation of neighborhood boundaries is considered enough of an offense to create a great deal of interneighborhood bad feeling. Ported objects appear to serve partly as devices by which adults, who manage and build them, try to instill a sense of neighborhood solidarity in their children. Children do not, after all, associate solely with children from their own neighborhood. On the contrary, school life tries to foster city and national spirit, not neighborhood awareness. Whether or not hauling a *tawara* together creates a communal solidarity among the children is arguable. It seems clear, however, that the adults feel it is a way to create the same sort of local spirit in their children that they themselves perhaps feel they should have.

The Daimyō Gyōretsu Parade

The multifarious aspects of parades in Yuzawa are illustrated by Yuzawa's largest parade, the Daimyō Gyōretsu. Of all Yuzawa's parades, the Daimyō Gyōretsu exhibits the greatest variety of parade phenomena. Because of the size and complexity of the Daimyō Gyōretsu, it is useful to describe the entire parade and its various aspects.

Atago-jinja, the largest *jinja* in Yuzawa, is the *chōnai-jinja* of Ōmachi as well as of several of Atago-chō's *kumi*. It is maintained largely by the five core *chōnin* neighborhoods—Maemori-chō, Yanagi-machi, Ōmachi, Tamachi, and Fuppari-chō—who rotate the management of the Daimyō Gyōretsu, Atago-jinja's main festival. Atago-jinja is one of only two *jinja* in Yuzawa to have a resident *kannushi*. During the Edo period the shrine was supported by the local Satake *daimyō,* who donated the shrine's *mikoshi*. After the Meiji Restoration the shrine was endowed by several rich Yuzawa families with rice fields and a considerable maintenance. The endowment enabled Atago-jinja to attain the rank of *kensha* (prefectural shrine)[5] before World War II.

The Daimyō Gyōretsu combines the lord's parade of Yuzawa with the *koreisai* (main ritual) of Atago-jinja. In the following discussion I will use "Daimyō Gyōretsu" to refer to the whole festival, *"daimyō gyōretsu"* to the lord's parade section, *"mikoshi* parade," to the shrine parade section, and "parade" to the whole parade. The *daimyō gyōretsu* commemorates the yearly passage of the Yuzawa *daimyō* to Edo, the shogunal capital in the Tokugawa period (1600–1868). The trains of *daimyō* performing this yearly requirement of residence in Edo were minutely regulated (Tsukahira 1966). The present lord's parade roles are copies of the *daimyō's* train. The *mikoshi* parade is part of the *koreisai* of Atago-jinja, which dates from about 1611, the date the Satake clan arrived after being forced to relinquish their fief in Mito. The Atago-jinja *koreisai,* originally celebrated in July, has since been shifted twice: once when it was merged with the Daimyō Gyōretsu at the insistence of its supporters and again when the Daimyō Gyōretsu was moved from August 24, its formal date, to the third weekend of the month.[6]

The Daimyō Gyōretsu's Divisions

The lord's parade reenacts the Yuzawa *daimyō*'s train. The *mikoshi* parade involves Atago-jinja's *mikoshi* and its attending functionaries. There are 155 fixed roles in the lord's parade and 45 in the *mikoshi* parade. All the roles are supposed to be filled every year. The permanent roles of the two parades are followed by floats carrying dioramas called *"kazariyama."* The subjects of these dioramas vary from year to year, but they are generally drawn from Japanese mythology and history. Together these three sections form the body of the parade. The tail of the parade is composed of a number of lantern-bedecked trucks that carry groups of children, dancers, and floats with papier maché figures.

The central figures in the parade are three horsemen: *nakanori* (representing the *daimyō*), *bugashira* (representing the commander of the guard), and *atonori* (representing the chief of the household). Each is accompanied by personal attendants carrying his gear. Each horseman is preceded and followed by blocks of functionaries: bowmen, musketeers, lancers, falconers, and samurai (personal bodyguards and officers). The *nakanori* is also followed by a tea master, tea equipment, a doctor, and body servants who carry his personal standards and badges of rank.

All the formal roles are filled by children. In addition, each child-rider

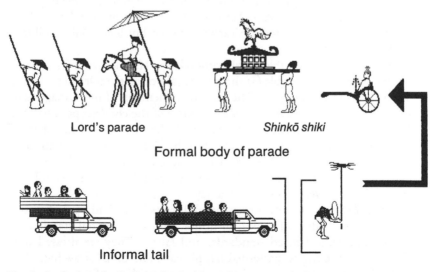

Lord's parade   *Shinkō shiki*

Formal body of parade

Informal tail

Figure 3. Order of march in the Daimyō Gyōretsu parade

is accompanied by functional assistants, adults who are there to handle the horse, carry the heavy umbrella over the rider's head, and make sure the child has someone familiar with him. Though not part of the cast of fixed roles, these adults too are dressed in costume.

The expenses of the three riders, estimated by Yuzawa respondents at between three and ten million yen, are borne by their families. Costs include the hire of a horse, the horse's transportation and keep, groom's fees, and the cost of making the rider's rich costume. The name of the donor, usually a grandparent, is stenciled on all equipment, and it is in the donor's name that the child rides. The financial burden cannot always be borne by a resident of the *chō* responsible for that year's festival, and many parades do not have a full complement of riders. In some years there are only two riders; one rider is not unusual. Maemori-chō was proud of the fact that when it came their turn to run the festival, "their" Daimyō Gyōretsu was the first one in ten years to have had all three riders.

The parade authorities supply the equipment and costumes for the other participants. With the exception of the *yakkofuri* (the *daimyō*'s body servants) and the riders' attendants, the roles are filled by children from the neighborhood designated to run the parade that year. Each house in the neighborhood with children of the appropriate age is requested to have its child or children take part. Parents assume responsibility for dress and makeup. Younger children are given roles, such as falconers, that do not require carrying heavy burdens. Older children carry lances or muskets.

In 1980 the responsible neighborhood was Maemori-chō. The *wakamono,* who are responsible for the parade, allocated the roles in a series of meetings at the end of July. (The seventeen members of the management of Maemori-chō's *wakamono-kai* know most of the children personally, if they are not in fact related to them.) With the exception of members of Sōka Gakkai (a militant, exclusivist Buddhist lay organization) and some children who were sick, I heard of no refusal to play a role. Those roles that cannot be filled for lack of candidates are filled by high school students hired at seven thousand yen a day.

The *yakkofuri,* the only consistent adult roles in the lord's parade, carry the *daimyō*'s badges of rank:[7] an armor box, a rooster-tail standard, a folded umbrella, fringed standards, and lances. They are dressed uniformly in white shorts, patterned happi coats, and broad straw hats. The *yakkofuri* are all residents of Atago-chō, two residents of which, as heirs to families that claim to have served in the same position for generations, train and lead the *yakkofuri* and have sole discretion on recruitment. The *yakkofuri* perform a dance at set points on the parade route: before Seiryoji, the temple where the Satake lords are buried; before the municipal hall; before the neighborhood halls of each of the Go Chō (the five neighborhoods that rotate Daimyō Gyōretsu management); before the *mikoshi*'s midday resting place; and before the Yuzawa train station. The *yakkofuri* "dance" consists of sliding side-to-side steps; the movement makes the fringes of the standards swirl gracefully. Each performance is short, lasting about three minutes.

The *mikoshi* part of the parade, the *shinkō shiki*, consists of the *kami*'s badges of rank, attendants, paraphernalia, priests, escort, shrine maidens, and the *mikoshi* itself, which carries the *kami*'s *shintai*. The *mikoshi* of Atago-jinja is a massive structure carried silently through the streets, in contrast to rowdy Kantō practice. It is preceded by boys carrying baskets into which spectators put offerings of bags of rice and coins. The *mikoshi* is followed by the *mikoshi* guardians, two representatives from each of the Go Chō, dressed in *montsuki* (formal traditional dress), and the representatives of the first families who worshiped the *shintai*.[8] The *guji* (chief priest) of Atago-jinja and his assistant, a *guji* in his own right of a neighboring village shrine, ride in *jinrikisha,* and the other officiant *kannushi* for the ritual follow on foot. The shrine maidens ride flower-bedecked carts, and *sakaki* carriers, *sanbō* (footed trays for offerings) carriers, and porters march on foot.

Following the *mikoshi* parade come the *kazariyama*. These floats, mounted on the backs of trucks, depict scenes from Japanese mythology: Ushiwakamaru and Benkei, Kintaro, Taira generals, and so on. One or two children portray the title figures; the scenery and other decorations are made of papier maché and plastic. In the tableau vivant, the actors do not move, but anxious mothers sit with the younger children and fan their heavily costumed darlings for comfort. The heat and the inaction cause many of the child actors to fall asleep during the parade.

After the body of the parade comes the nonformal tail. The atmosphere in the tail is completely different. Here there is room for participation by other organized groups in Yuzawa. Neighborhoods and villages in Yuzawa-shi send a truck, a *mikoshi,* or a band to participate. There are no set themes for this segment: decorations, music, and roles are up to the imagination of those responsible for the truck. The themes are usually more contemporary and the decorations less exactingly made than the *kazariyama*. The children and some adults on the trucks beat drums, dance, dispense sake. There is a sense of movement and performance. On most of the trucks, the children are supplied with musical instruments, cold drinks, and ice cream. Costumes are not formal; children and adults wear *yukata* (light summer robes) or shorts, happi, and *hachimaki* (headbands). The children in the tail are encouraged to be noisy, and loudspeakers on the truck blare *matsuri* music. All of this is in contrast to the conspicuous silence of the formal body of the parade—the lord's and *mikoshi* parades and the *kazariyama* section.

The tail of the parade is explicitly intended to be fun for all involved. The Maemori-chō *wakamono-kai* supply a truck for the children of each *kumi* of Maemori-chō, and local shops donate drinks and snacks. *Wakamono* control the passage of the trucks, and mothers accompany the children. In contrast to the formally clad *wakamono-kai* members directing the body of the parade, the *wakamono* in the tail wear shorts and happi coats that bear the neighborhood's crest and the name of the large sake brewery in Maemori-chō that donated them. Other neighborhoods in the town and villages nearby did the same. There were some thirty trucks and floats in all.

That this part of the parade is intended for amusement is demonstrated by my own participation. I was drafted during the afternoon to be part of the Maemori-chō contingent in the tail. I was told by the *wakamono-kai* headman and subsequently overheard other members saying that it would be hugely amusing to have a foreigner walking in the parade dressed in the traditional *matsuri* costume of shorts, brightly colored happi, headband, and straw sandals.

The parade starts from the grounds below Atago-jinja at eight in the morning. Two-way radio communication ensures that the *mikoshi* and ritual participants at Atago-jinja arrive in time to assume their places. The radio is used throughout the five-hour parade to coordinate movement of the long column. The parade route differs slightly from year to year depending on the neighborhood running it. There is a two-hour break at midday during which the *mikoshi* rests in a *mikoshi-shuku* (a house designated as the official resting place). When the parade resumes it goes straight down the main street back to Atago-jinja, where it disperses.

The parade is part of a Yuzawa civil ceremony, an extension of the main ritual of Atago-jinja, and also a major component of the festivities of the Daimyō Gyōretsu festival. At the same time the parade itself is a performance involving performers and spectators that in part is motivated by the desire to be entertained (Hymes 1975). The body of the parade is formal, elaborate, and clearly marked. The lord's parade serves as a display of economic power and as a claim for primacy by the Go Chō. The *mikoshi* parade is a continuation of the *jinja*'s rituals. It is much more elaborate than any other *shinkō shiki* in town and displays Atago-jinja's claim to primacy among Yuzawa's *jinja*.

The parade must be seen from three perspectives. First, it is a ceremonial event, part of which is an extension of Atago-jinja's ritual. Second, it is an attraction, a performance. Local residents, tourists from other parts of Japan, and even foreigners come to see the town of Yuzawa, their neighborhood, or their child put on a show. Third, parts of the parade are festivities in their own right. In the tail, observers and paraders are participants, not just performers and audience. Those who ride the trucks interact with spectators by offering sake, smiling, laughing, and waving at people lining the roadway. Adults and children are in this portion not only to perform but also to be entertained. The formality that characterizes the body of the parade is nowhere in evidence.

The contrast is explicit between the formal body and the informal tail. The former has numerous rules dictating what to wear, how to walk, and how to behave. It is minutely organized, and the advisory group to the *wakamono-kai* maintains checkpoints along the route to ensure that costumes are correct, distances kept, and formations maintained. The tail, on the other hand, is informal and loosely organized.

Another dimension of the difference between the body of the parade and the tail is no less important. The lord's parade is intentionally a local affair. Every *daimyō gyōretsu* in Japan strives for uniqueness. Different costumes, equipment, and orders of march are maintained. The items and activities in the tail of the parade, in contrast, are national: nationally famous folk dances, well-known *matsuri* music, and TV cartoon figures predominate. The tail section of the parade replicates any of hundreds of *matsuri* parades mounted elsewhere in Japan.

The parade as a whole is a multivalent event. It is also, as Abrahams has noted, a "dramatic technique for announcing . . . celebration" (Abrahams 1982, 175). Analytically, the ritual and formal parts are distinguishable from the festive, informal part. In addition, different participants have different perceptions of the parade. The *kannushi* say the *mikoshi* parade is a continuation of the rituals held for Atago-jinja's *koreisai*. Only circumstances cause it to be overshadowed by the lord's parade. For the *wakamono-kai* who run and organize the lord's parade, the tail is an unimportant addition to the parade; for them the formal lord's parade and the *mikoshi* parade are the Daimyō Gyōretsu of Yuzawa. Some *wakamono* told me that the tail section is there "just for entertainment." Festival-goers, including tourists and Yuzawa residents not involved in managing the parade, rarely distinguish between the parts of the parade and do not usually care about these differences. For them, the parade in its entirety is the main event of the Yuzawa Daimyō Gyōretsu festival.

Mikoshi in the Daimyō Gyōretsu

The different *mikoshi* in the parade exemplify the contrasts between the body and tail of the Daimyō Gyōretsu parade. They also exemplify some contrastive elements that go into the makeup of the Daimyō Gyōretsu.

The *mikoshi* of Atago-jinja is a massive structure requiring close to twenty porters hired by the shrine *guji* to carry it along the route. The porters are dressed in laborer's clothes of the Heian period (794–1185): black gauze hats, loose white shirts, and short blue breeches. They carry the *mikoshi* in complete silence, with none of the yelling and shoving that can be seen at festivals in the Kantō area. The *mikoshi* is purified by a *kannushi* before being brought to the shrine, and the *shintai* is ritually installed before the parade.

In the tail section of the parade, where any neighborhood may participate, several neighborhoods and villages of Yuzawa-shi bring along *mikoshi,* some carried, some mounted on trucks. In both cases the neighborhood's children accompany the *mikoshi.* The carriers wear happi emblazoned with the village or neighborhood's name. The *mikoshi* are carried to the accompaniment of cries of encouragement and a certain amount of bouncing around, a Kantō custom. To my knowledge, few of these *mikoshi* had been purified by ritual before the parade.

Hirashimizu-machi has hired a group of *mikoshi* carriers from Tokyo every year since 1978. In line with Edo tradition, they drink, carry their own Edo-style *mikoshi* at a jog, bounce it on their shoulders, sing and chant loudly, and wear little but loincloths, happi, and headbands. In the evening they serve as entertainers, parading their *mikoshi* through the neighborhood that has hired them. This "Edo *mikoshi*" is an acknowledged part of the evening entertainment and listed as such along with the fireworks show in Omachi and the *karaoke* show of Minamishin-machi.

Obviously these different kinds of *mikoshi* do not represent the same thing. *Mikoshi* are associated with the transportation, or the presence, of the *kami*. But more than that, partly because of the spread of metropolitan culture, they represent festivity and, to most participants, something uniquely Japanese. The presence of the various sorts of *mikoshi* indicates tensions inherent in the parade. On the one hand is the seriousness and ritual quality of the statement made by carrying Atago-jinja's *mikoshi* solemnly through the streets. The *shinkō shiki* is, after all, a religious ritual of tremendous importance for the shrine, its priests, and the parish. The Atago-jinja *mikoshi* is paramount, but only in a local sense. The Edo *mikoshi*, in contrast, is not a ritual device except inasmuch as it celebrates the "Japaneseness" of the event. Other *mikoshi* in the parade are national cultural symbols employed in a local context; by using them, those neighborhoods not running the Daimyō Gyōretsu indicate their adherence to a commonality, that of Yuzawa as a unit and that of Japan as a cultural unit in which a broad set of commonly used devices indicates common membership.

Costumes, Old and New

The costumes worn by the participants in the Daimyō Gyōretsu help the observer to understand important aspects of the parade. Clothes are a primary presentation device in all societies. In the case of parades, though, they express social and group imperatives within a given culture. A close examination of the costumes worn points out, to a limited degree, what a group (in this case, Yuzawa) thinks about itself and what it is interested in displaying to the public. These costume decisions extend well beyond the Daimyō Gyōretsu. As is common in other *matsuri*, some festivalgoers (the percentage is usually small) wear traditional *yukata* as they enjoy the festivities. In the parade, however, we find that both choice and public preference play a role.

The costumes worn in the parade can, like the Daimyō Gyōretsu itself, be divided into more formal and less formal. Strict rules and uniformity govern the former, particularly the costumes worn by those who have the roles in the Daimyō Gyōretsu. The rules for these costumes are set and maintained by a group of retired *wakamono-kai*, officially an advisory group, that monitors all aspects of a parader's performance. This oversight extends to the proper way to carry a sword or lance, the provision of straw sandals for all marchers, and the preservation of all costumes and equipment. Marchers in these groups, whether in the lord's or *mikoshi* parades, present a uniform appearance, one that enhances and underscores the traditional nature of the event.

The formal parade, is, however, a *show*. In other words, unlike the original passage of vassals to Edo, the various positions in the parade are roles rather than functions: the *bugashira,* for example, is in no position to give orders to members of the military bodyguard, for obvious reasons. The real management of the parade is vested formally in the *wakamono-kai.* Thus the *wakamono-kai* members who take part in the formal body of the parade are dressed in the most formal of modern Japanese dress, *montsuki. Montsuki* consist of wide ankle-length culottes worn over a robe and a thigh-length black surcoat over that. The surcoat bears small circular crests at nape, on both breasts, and on the backs of sleeves. While in traditional Japan there was a variety of dress standards for different occasions (some exemplified in the parade),[9] the most formal mode of dress today is the five-badge *montsuki.* Thus the managers of the parade demonstrate by the costume they wear how serious is their role, and how serious, as well, is the parade they are marching in.

Another level of parade management is the Daimyō Gyōretsu Preservation Board, which has the final say in all aspects of the parade's performance. Interposed along the line of march, they stand, in drab Western suits or everyday wear, correcting role-bearers and formal managers alike. Here, too, over and above practical concerns we witness an aspect of Japanese society brought to the fore. Management in Japan has often been by *inkyo,* individuals who, though formally retired, exercise de facto authority. Starting with emperors in the Heian period and continuing on to "retired" company officials today, Japanese culture is conscious of the hand of management, often not officially recognized but nontheless widely known.

The children riding the horses are rarely trained horsemen. Moreover, role demands are sometimes such that children are unable to carry them out, such as carrying one of the heavy umbrellas that shades each rider. A small group of adult males therefore surrounds each rider. These include one or two horse handlers, an umbrella carrier, an equipment box carrier, and the child's father or other male relative. Except for the child's father (who dresses in *montsuki*) these adult attendants are all dressed in Edo-period costumes. One major difference between these adults and the others participating in the parade in costume is that the short happi coats they wear bear the name and often the crest of the role's sponsor (usually the child's grandparents). The wearing of the patron's crest distances the attendants from the body of the parade. The costume signifies that they are the servants of the rider, but, no less important, employees of the individual who hired them.

Finally, among the formal costumes is one of particular interest. Most of the roles in the formal body of the parade are undertaken by children, whose participation, not unnaturally, is a source of concern for their parents. The day of the parade may be hot or rainy, the parade route, long and tiring. It is therefore not uncommon to see a small Edo-period samurai accompanied by his mother, who carries a bottle of juice, a small parasol or umbrella, and often a small folding chair, all for the child's comfort. Noticeably, however, all mothers wear Western dresses, quite often very expensive ones, along with high heels and full makeup. In other words, this role too has performative requirements. Not being part *of* the parade, the mothers are not obligated to wear role costumes, but being *in* the parade, thus part of the show, they must demonstrate their formal participation by dressing appropriately.

Informal costumes are important particularly in contrast to those worn in the formal part of the parade. There are, of course, very few roles associated with the informal part of the parade except for those assumed ad hoc by the participants. The functional managerial roles are indicated by fuller wearing of traditional festival clothes: straw sandals, shorts, happi, and headbands. Children wear, in whole or in part, some variation of the above. Mothers accompany children in this part of the parade too, but they dress informally, often in sweatsuits or slacks or other varieties of daily wear. The elder managers are not in evidence at all.

Festival clothing therefore emphasizes or deemphasizes aspects of the parade. Clothing indicates how various parts of the parade are perceived. The degree of flexibility in dress is one facet of the degree of flexibility evident in the various parts of the parade (and the festival) as a whole.

Summary

Parades exemplify events midway between rituals and festivities. To a degree, and provided we do not take the analogy too far, they "mediate" between the two, being formal in their performance and organization and informal and festive in their interaction with the audience that lines the parade route. This situation is highlighted by Yuzawa's major parade, the Daimyō Gyōretsu. Here the body of the parade is ritually ordered, serious, and uncompromising in its roles. At the tail, in contrast, formal roles are nonexistent, and interaction with the public is the order of the day.

Something no less important emerges in all parades. The managerial

sinews that, I claim, must underlie even the most exciting and wild festivities show very clearly in the hands that guide and manage the parade.
Because this issue of management is much wider than parades and affects
all aspects of *matsuri,* I will return to in a later chapter.

The need to be *in* the parade, for pragmatic managerial or maternal
reasons, but not *of* it requires individuals in specific roles to manage their
appearance in order to avoid incongruity. Parents and sponsors in the
main body of the parade dress formally according to the impression they
want to make; in the tail they dress informally, even clowning and performing. Insofar as these "rules" pertain, in the body a parade is ceremo-
nialized. Yet paraders must and do interact with a heterogeneous audience, which they do at the tail, and therefore a parade is also part of the
festivities, because the audience expects, at a minimum, to be entertained, to take part.

Another element only hinted at in the Daimyō Gyōretsu is discord.
While parades are explicit statements of unity, the Daimyō Gyōretsu,
with its multiplicity of organizational roles and groups and its overt dis-
crimination between primary and secondary participants, demonstrates
that at least the seeds of conflict are present. That such conflict is suppressed, or at least does not erupt publicly, has to do with a number of
factors that will be examined later.

5

Feasts and Festivities

THE PRECEDING two chapters have started with the most formal of festival events—rituals—and then proceeded to examine other events that exhibit lesser formality. This chapter will continue the theme of less-formal events, proceeding through feasts, an inescapable part of any festival, and then describing and discussing various other festivities and their implications.

The discussion of "festivities" as a phenomenon on its own helps in understanding the total phenomenon of *matsuri*. For most participants festivities *are* the festival. They are certainly the most visible and most sought after part of a *matsuri*. It is necessary, therefore, to take into account not only the constituents that make up "festivities" but the nature and qualities of "participants" in this particular context. In this chapter I first examine the feasts and eating that accompany *matsuri*, then address the issue of festivities and their nature.

Food is almost always associated with street and public events in Japan, and no *matsuri* takes place without the complements of food and drink. Food in *matsuri* comes in two forms: as a more or less formal meal restricted to particular participants, and as street food. The latter is available to all comers and is consumed without many formalities. Like the food events, *matsuri* festivities range from the organized to the unorganized, with its consequent loosening of structuring and ordering rules. As with festival food, we find that in festivity, many of the rules, even those of ordinary, daily life, are relaxed. As with food, multiple events may take place side by side and may include various participants who involve themselves voluntarily. These two very similar ranges of festive activity, feasts and festivity, are addressed here.

Food and Feasts in *Matsuri*

It has been argued by Douglas and Gross (1981), Douglas (1982), Khare (1980), and Murcott (1982), among others, that "food

events"—occasions when food is consumed by humans—have a significance that goes well beyond nutrition. In effect, the methods of preparation, presentation, consumption, and disposal of foods constitute a system of meanings for any given culture. Here I am concerned with food
and eating only as an aspect of *matsuri*. We have seen that a small morsel
of food and some drink—*naorai*—are offered all participants. This is only
one aspect of food in festivals.

Food—as display, as communion, and as a center of social relations—is
prominent in all *matsuri*. Food offerings run the gamut from formal
feasts at the ritual *naorai* to snacks offered by booths along the fairway in
larger festivals. The context and nature of food offerings range from the
formal and structured events of *matsuri,* the rituals, to informal and
unstructured events in the festivities.

The Shoichi Yuzawa Inari-jinja in Ura-machi holds one of its festivals
in summer. Its shrine building also serves as the *chōnai kaikan* or neighborhood hall. After the ritual, the *tōban* (those responsible for managing
the shrine for the year) arrange the tables and bring out food. *Eda mame*
(green soya beans), soup, and some other items are prepared in the
shrine's kitchen. Sushi, grilled chicken, beer, and sake are ordered from
neighboring shops.[1] The *naorai* starts with a toast by the head of the
tōban and then everyone helps himself to food, and his neighbor to
drink. The conversation gradually becomes louder. The matters discussed
are generally not related to the festival. The men move from their places
at the table to offer a drink and engage in talk elsewhere, so that by the
end of the event everyone has had at least one drink with each of the
other participants. After about an hour, their plates almost empty and
their bellies full, the feasters clear away the debris (remains are wrapped
up and taken home) and disperse to their sundry occupations.

At a festival in Yunohara-chō, the *wakamono-kai* sold draft beer and
skewers of grilled chicken. There was ice cream for the children, who also
enjoyed a cartoon film in the Yunohara spa's parking lot nearby. Drivers
of cars passing by stopped and dropped in for a beer. More men than
women were present, but the event was by no means exclusive. The
composition and number of feasters shifted constantly.

In a previous chapter I made an analogy between drinking parties and
rituals. In a drinking party, the start is characterized by the presence of
high-status guests and leaders of the group. The atmosphere is formal,
and people sit in *seiza*. Later, after the higher-status individuals leave, the
participants relax, get drunk, and play games. Most adult males attend
such parties several times a year. The similarity between entertaining a

guest and receiving a *kami* in a ritual was pointed out to me by several *kannushi* in Yuzawa. It is also discussed by Yanagawa (1974). An analysis of a famous Tokyo *matsuri* in terms of receiving a high-status guest can be found in Sonoda (1975). My interest here is slightly different from his, however. Rituals are complex sets of behaviors, many of which are not seen often by any given individual. This similarity between rituals and parties appears to help make rituals comprehensible to participants in Yuzawa. People refer to feasts associated with rituals as *naorai*.

Actually there are two distinguishable *naorai*. One is the offering of *miki* (consecrated wine) to those present at a ritual (see Chapter 3). The officiant pours the *miki* from containers that have been previously offered at the altar. The drink is accompanied by some food; a strip of *surume* (dried squid) or dried salted laver is most common. To add to the significance of the commensal nature of this *naorai*, participants are urged to share some of the food with their families at home. Ritually this represents the community's shared feast with the *kami*.

Naorai is also a feast, although a kind of feast that occurs only in rituals that are part of festivals. Its name—*naorai*—associates it with the ritual, but it is also a part of the festivities; drunkenness, singing, and other lighthearted activities are expected. Inevitably there are different views of the *naorai* and its significance. Priests state that the sharing of the *kami*'s food that has actually been offered at the altar (*miki*, *surume*, and cooked rice) is the real *naorai*; it relates individuals and groups to their *kami*. The participants' concern is more social. They accept their share of the *kami*'s bounty and recognize that the morsel of food is part of the ritual's formal requirements, for which the priest is responsible. However, they state openly that for them the important *naorai* is the feast that follows. For many individuals this substantial *naorai* is the heart of the ritual. "The meaning of the ritual is entirely social," one individual said. "It is an opportunity for us to get together and do something as a community. Drinking and eating together, even getting drunk, is for us Japanese a special way of feeling togetherness. Socially we are often very isolated from one another—there are so many formalities in the language—so getting drunk together is a good way of getting loose and reinforcing our feelings of solidarity for one another." Other informants expressed the same sentiments, although often less eloquently. The difference in views is not surprising, nor are the two contradictory. The difference derives from the different responsibilities of priest and participants and from the fact that the priest is usually an outsider and thus does not share the community's concerns. Priests are nominally concerned with the propriety and formality of rituals. The community and its members are more concerned with their feelings and with maintaining their group relationships.

Commensal feasts have a special meaning in festivity. The feast at Uramachi appears to have been intended consciously to strengthen group solidarity within a neighborhood represented by the feasters and within the group of *tōban*. The individuals who run a festival are compensated for their efforts with this feast. In Ura-machi, which is lined with shops, the feast also serves as an unofficial forum for discussing trade problems and business.

Added to the informants' view that feasts create and reinforce solidarity in a group or community is another analytical point: food at festivals does not constitute a meal. Rice, the definer of a Japanese meal, is often not served. No matter the size of a *naorai*, it is by nature a snack. In this a festival is similar to a drinking party, implying greater freedom, greater levity, less formality—entertainment, in other words. Festival stalls offer only snack foods: noodles, pancakes, candy. This food, too, by its nature —alcohol, sweets, finger foods, nonstaples[2]—is informal, associated with relaxation. Food is thus a major component of festivity.

Festivities and Entertainment

Festivals are primarily visible public events. The festivities, that part of the festival that allows for the participation of a mass of people, distinguish a festival from a performance with an audience. "Festivity" in a festival consists of those events and activities that are generally nonformal and yet, paradoxically, can have a strong meaningful content: "Festivity . . . is symbolic action carried out with spontaneity, confusion, and a great excitement" (Sonoda 1975, 3).

Early attempts to analyze festivity relied primarily on the disjunction between daily life and festivity (e.g., Jensen 1963) and on the similarity between festivity and play (e.g., Huizinga 1955, 21, and Caillois 1979). Others emphasized the disjunction between the seriousness of religious ritual and the seemingly irreducible component of play and festival (e.g., Caillois 1950, and Cox 1969). None of these approaches is truly satisfactory as none explains the mechanisms by which festivals or festivity do whatever they do. Max Müller's observation (1882) about religion—that we all know there is something there, though we disagree about its precise nature—seems true for festivity as well.

On the whole, festivities are now more often viewed as an important category of human behavior on their own. Serious analysis of festivity is something of a contradiction in terms; the idea of festivity embodies play, which is often unconfined, "paidillic," if one can paraphrase Caillois (1979). What is important is that the play in festivals is confined and limited to the festival itself.

The distinction between ritual and festivity is sharpened by their obvious differences. Ritual is rule-bound, festivities appear not to be. Festivities, because they are playful, often invite us to make believe, whereas ritual insists that we must believe (Handelman 1977). But perhaps the most important characteristic of festivities is one articulated by Abrahams (1982 and 1988): Festivity contrasts with the everyday working world; it uses the devices of the daily world to make fun, to emphasize points, to upset and disorganize things within an area of license. How much license is actually granted depends very much on the degree of license the local authorities and, more importantly (because more basic), local cultural preferences are prepared to tolerate. The wild, uncontrolled erotic festivities of a Rio de Janeiro *carnaval* (Turner 1983a) would horrify and embarrass the townsmen of Yuzawa.

One final point: festivals are community affairs. They conjure up, in their performance and vocabulary, ideas of openness, of the community and its constituent elements putting themselves on display. Japanese notions about privacy severely limit openness, however. As we shall see, there are displays of private areas during Yuzawa *matsuri*, but they are confined to the public spaces of houses. All this is to say that there are distinct limits to the generic analysis of the term "festival" or "festivity," and such terms must be understood in the local context, notwithstanding the general similarity of such categories of events.

Japanese scholars have sometimes been reluctant to consider the festive elements of *matsuri*. Sonoda divided events within *matsuri* into two classes: "shrine events" and "lay events." Shrine events emphasize formal programs, what have been called here rituals. Lay events feature a variety of entertaining events such as "parades of mikoshi, . . . feasts, *kanda bayashi* (festival music), . . . and the like" (Sonoda 1975, 12). Sonoda dismisses other activities carried out within shrines during *matsuri* as irrelevant. There are naturally a great many forms of festivity. Their sheer variety, within a given pattern, indicates quite clearly that festivities are indeed significant phenomena. Some examples from Yuzawa give a flavor of the complexity of Japanese festivals.

Early on the first day of the Daimyō Gyōretsu the *tekiya* erect their stalls on the main streets of the town. The *wakamono-kai* of the various neighborhoods, assisted by other organizations such as the Parent-Teacher Association, start erecting their own booths. The *wakamono-kai* put up markers and decorations such as lanterns at the entrances to their neighborhoods and put the finishing touches on their floats. By evening, the *tekiya* are in business. Children scoop for goldfish and light sparklers; young men try their hands at the shooting galleries. Bars and food spots stay open. In 1980, Omachi sponsored a half-hour fireworks show. A folk dance club annually arranges a public Bon dance in the space before the municipal hall; the Chamber of Industry arranges a show of Yuzawa products: pickles made from sake lees, wooden dolls, lacquerware, sake, fruit. The sword dealer on the main street, whose shop is also the Yuzawa Sword Appreciation Society headquarters, displays the members' best blades. The Tamachi *wakamono-kai* installs play equipment near the neighborhood hall. The streets are closed to traffic, and thousands of people watch the displays, frequent the booths, and join in the dancing. Many family groups stroll dressed in matching *yukata*. Groups of young men, many in *yukata* worn *aragoto* style—chests bare and one corner of the skirt tucked in the sash—swagger along the streets and drink at the booths. The following day, after the parade and a short rest, the festivities start again.

Hirashimizu-machi, aided and abetted by the Edo *mikoshi* carriers and liberal amounts of drink, had what was by all accounts a wildly successful *shinkō shiki* (the term is used here loosely; there was no association between the neighborhood shrine and the Edo *mikoshi*) through the streets of the neighborhood, during which many ribald songs were sung and the sake and food flowed freely. Omachi set off more fireworks. Fuppari had a folk dance on the main street in which the loop of dancers extended half the neighborhood's length. Other neighborhoods have similar events, and residents of outlying neighborhoods gravitate to the town center to join the fun.

Three specific examples taken from different festivals in different places in Yuzawa-shi will help to characterize the image of festivity that can be, and is generated in different festivals. Tanabata is one of Yuzawa's three main festivals. In contrast, the annual festival of the shrine of Hirashimizu-machi, a residential and industrial neighborhood near the Yuzawa railway station, is that of a medium-sized, undistinguished

neighborhood. The festival of the main shrine of Sekiguchi, a small township in Yuzawa-shi, just south of the town, is somewhat between those two extremes.

Tanabata is a festival observed by the majority of households in Yuzawa. The main streets of the town, where the entertainment is held, are lavishly decorated; and outlying neighborhoods put up decorations of their own as well. Tanabata, the Star Festival, is of Chinese origin. It commemorates a Chinese legend in which the weaver girl and the cowherd, two demigods, are separated by the wrath of the heavenly emperor, only to be reunited once a year on the seventh day of the seventh month. In some places Tanabata is celebrated as a public holiday. During Tanabata, the streets of Yuzawa are decorated with varicolored paper streamers, papier maché balls and figures, large painted lanterns, and green bamboo fronds. Colored paper slips with poems or requests written on them are attached to the fronds. Always there are fireworks.

In the evening the lanterns are lit and the residents and guests come out to view them. Between nightfall and ten in the evening the streets are packed. In the warm summer weather many people wear light cotton *yukata*. Toddlers and girls of marriageable age wear the most attractive *yukata*. People stop to admire the paintings on the lanterns, chat with acquaintances, or make candy animals at a *tekiya*'s stall. At garden tables set out in the street by a large dry goods store, people sit to talk and drink beer or soft drinks. Although there are a few lanterns displayed on the side streets, most people crowd around the lanterns on Yuzawa's main street. Bars and food stands do a brisk business. Children light sparklers and hunker around lit candles used for setting off the fireworks. A samisen player shows off his skill in front of the furniture salesroom sponsoring his performance. Toward midnight the police clear the streets and reopen them to motor traffic. The lanterns that had obstructed the road are taken down, to be hung up again the following morning.

The Hirashimizu shrine, hidden in a jumble of narrow streets behind a factory, consists of a row of stelae and tiny shrine structures in front of the neighborhood association hall. On a wooden platform erected especially for the festival, the neighborhood children play singing games. Two *tekiya* stalls are patronized by children who want to catch the goldfish in the plastic tanks. Inside the hall a number of elderly women cheerfully prepare snacks: mounds of *eda mame*, slices of raw fish, *oden* (a kind of stew), and vegetable soup. Neighborhood residents bring sake, some of

which is consumed by the cooks, and greet the neighborhood officials sitting at the far end of the hall. New arrivals are helped to food and drink. A small group at one of the long tables sings ballads.

The composition of the group changes with time as new people arrive and others leave. There is always at least one official in the hall, sometimes drinking with people, sometimes talking to one or two residents in the corner. The children keep to themselves in the yard, fortified by an occasional plate of *oden* or rice cakes. Toward noon and again toward evening, the hall fills with people coming to join the fun. Again and again I am assured that "this is a real Japanese-style festival." Late in the evening even the most stubborn festival-goers head for home.

Singing, usually to *karaoke* (recorded music), is a popular modern form of group entertainment in Japan. The festival at Sekiguchi includes a *karaoke* event. Hopeful singers, most in *yukata*, proceed to the microphone one after the other. Their friends, many with faces red from drink (supplied by the neighborhood association), cheer them on, some waving banners in encouragement. The crowd laughs with the singers when they forget a line and claps and yells enthusiastically. Spectators occasionally join in when the emotion generated by the nostalgia-evoking *enka* (popular ballads) overpowers them. The singing goes on for several hours until the *enka* fans have had their fill of both songs and beer. The children, in the meantime, are visiting the ubiquitous *tekiya* booths, some screaming loudly as they play the games. Neighborhood groups have together acquired several casks of sake, which are being broached, and the sake is being drunk out of square cedar cups; the smell of fresh cedar mingles with that of the freshly brewed liquor and grilling squid. Before the Sekiguchi *jinja* a troupe of dancers in dragon costumes dances a *tatsu-mai* (dragon dance); the adults applaud, the children giggle or stare wide-eyed. Not until late in the evening does the noise die down as the last of the festival-goers shout their final farewells.

Performances and Fun

Festivity as a whole is hard to characterize, in no small part because it is generally unstructured. Moreover, anthropology, which attempts to generalize "rules" from observation of behaviors, finds it hard to examine concepts such as "fun," which are critical for understanding festivities. On the one hand, "fun" is not concrete enough for generalization; on the other, festivity activities are highly individualistic.

A major part of festival participation can be credited to the lure of entertainment, of fun, of enjoyment, that participants feel to some degree. While many actions in festivals "mean" something else or can be interpreted as masking or serving as extensions of other, more important, cultural issues, the prospect of fun and entertainment is what brings people to festivals. The promise of a good time is probably not so pertinent in festivals in small societies. Buechler (1980) gives an idea of how much social pressure there is on Andean villagers to participate in and give fiestas, and how much anxiety this involves. Even in modern urban societies, there are many for whom the importance of festivals is in their social impact, their managerial function, or the like. Still, for most casual participants, whether they are locals or outsiders, it is the recreational value that counts. But festivals need people as much as people need (or want) festivals. Without mass participation, a festival will be a failure, simply because, as has happened in some of Yuzawa's neighboring townships, there are no crowds to create a real sense of festivity. We turn, therefore, to an examination of how festivity is generated.

As a city, a single community, Yuzawa celebrates three major festivals: Daimyō Gyōretsu, Inukko, and Tanabata.[3] Each of these is characterized by the presence of large masses of people coming together to participate in the public event. Several neighborhood festivals display the same characteristics, although they tend to have fewer participants. Here we discuss the three major festivals in greater detail.

The locus of Tanabata and Daimyō Gyōretsu festivities is the main street of the city and the city industrial hall about fifty meters away on another main street. In contrast, since the 1950s the Inukko festivities have been concentrated on the wide baseball field next to the city office.

The Daimyō Gyōretsu's festivities consist partly of organized activities and performances and partly of booths, shops, and exhibits. The organized activities are often participatory: drumming teams, the parade (which includes ribald songs, drink, and dancing) of the Edo *mikoshi,* folk dancing in the main street. The exhibits range from a fireworks display through a display of local industry and crafts to the inevitable booths of the itinerant *tekiya.* So long as these activities are taking place, the festival goes on. As they die out, because of the hour or for lack of interest, so does the festival itself.

Tanabata and Inukko festivities are more highly visible and concentrated than Daimyō Gyōretsu festivities because they depend less on activities than on the preparation and "consumption" (by observers) of artifacts that signify festivities. In Tanabata, as we have seen, the main street of the town is decorated with lavish and elaborate bunting, and almost all houses in the center of the town and many on the peripheries indicate their participation by erecting bamboo fronds to which colored streamers have been tied. The centerpieces, however, are the colored lanterns. Wooden frames from one to ten meters square are covered by papers on which traditional illustrations (some original) have been drawn and illuminated from within. With nightfall, festival participants stroll down the street and look at the decorations. Food and drink are available, as in all the three festivals, from coffee shops and stalls.

Inukko, like Tanabata, relies on artifacts to both focus and circumscribe the festivities. In this case, however, the focus is on snow sculptures of dogs and small snow shrines in which offerings are placed. Unlike Tanabata, Inukko has a ritual core, but like Tanabata, events are dependent upon a display. In both Tanabata and Inukko, pragmatic concerns of modern society must be kept in mind. Tanabata decorations must be down before traffic resumes the day after the festival and thus must be coordinated with the police. Inukko sculptures, traditionally erected before each house, are now erected in the Inukko concourse, where they do not interfere with traffic. Inukko festivities, like Tanabata, consist of people coming to observe their own and their neighbors' efforts. Various activities are offered (for example, a dance troupe sponsored by a store in Tanabata, *mochi* [sticky rice dough]-pounding, and a photography contest featuring a lightly dressed and thus half-frozen model on an *inukko*), but these come about as a result of the focus.

The Image of Festivity

While it is difficult to assess the feelings of those engaged in festivities, it is possible to examine their actions. Festivities are not so much characterized by confusion or uncontrolled excitement (though these, too, are much in evidence) as they are by an atmosphere. This atmosphere derives from the image the festivities generate, which is perceived by local participants and outside visitors. The image is generated by some central event or events, although a central event is not sufficient, by itself, to create an atmosphere of festivity. The event must stimulate public nonstructured activities that are usually associated with recreation and entertainment. It is therefore impossible to dismiss the exhibitions and other performances in festivals as Sonoda has. These peripheral activities generate involvement among the festival's participants.

As seen from the examples cited, festivities rely for their success on the presence of a mass of people. The mass is not static; its composition constantly changes. Festivities are essentially fluid and unbounded, in contrast to rituals within a festival, which are formal and well-bounded events with a limited cast. The types of activities that people engage in define the festivities. Activities of individuals surround and permeate whatever events or shows are offered. They mark a situation as festive and by their presence induce festivity. This continuous interaction of activities creates festivity.

Individuals and groups engage in these activities as a response to events that take place in the festival, in response to other individuals' activities, and in response to their own inclinations and interests. To mark their participation in festivities, many Yuzawa residents wear *yukata* rather than Western attire. Everyday etiquette, which discourages eating or drinking while walking in the streets, is relaxed. People snack as they stroll or simultaneously drink and throw quoits at targets in a *tekiya*'s stall. A drum band may give a performance and then invite spectators to try their hands with the sticks. Participation in a *mikoshi* parade may be restricted, but onlookers may be urged to lend a hand to generate a more festive air.

Festive events include parades, performances of many sorts, and promotional and commercial events. They may be commercial activities by *tekiya* or local merchants or they may be organized by neighborhood association groups, whose aims are not strictly commercial. Some events in festivities, such as public folk dancing and *mikoshi* parades, can be seen only in festivals. They mark festivity and indicate that a festive situation is in progress and at the same time are major components of festivity.

The issue of *fun,* people entertaining themselves, is harder to come to grips with in an anthropological analysis, perhaps because it seems to be an irreducible concept: enjoyment requires no explanation. While no easy generalizations can be made about the nature and genesis of fun—in other words, about what activities or items contribute at any time in any culture to an individual's having "fun"—the variety of phenomena and effects that constitutes fun can be observed and determined. Certainly fun is "infectious": being a member of a group or crowd having fun may be its own reward, and it certainly encourages the individual to enjoy him- or herself likewise.

Performances

Events with a performer or performers, some expressive form, an audience, and a setting—what Bauman (1975) defines as a performance—constitute one distinct element of festivities. Parades and dance exhibitions and even parts of rituals (even though rituals are distinguished here from festivities) are performances. In these performances the audience expects the performer to display an appropriate level of competence. Performances can be the centerpiece that attracts the public to festivities. They can also shift from spectator to participatory events. Drummers can invite listeners to drum with them; *mochi* pounders are helped by the children crowding around; and a circle of dancers can be enlarged as bystanders join in. In festivity the boundary between performative and participatory events is often very thin. A formal performance such as a ritual is separated from the festivities, just as ritual participants are separated from and ignore those who are not participating. In contrast, nonformal performances acknowledge and sometimes even encourage participation by spectators. An amateur dance group in a Yuzawa festival acknowledges applause from the audience after a number and later encourages the crowd to join in: their performative competence having been established, the dancers are then easily able to bridge the gap to a participatory event. It is not always possible, therefore, to categorize a festivity event as distinctly participatory or performative. The more formal a performance is, however, the less likely it is to turn into a participatory event. This is particularly true of performances, such as rituals, that have a liturgical order. Because ritual performance requires a high degree of competence, free participation unbounded by rules would, by definition, lower the formality of the event, in effect "deritualizing" it.

Commercial and Promotional Events

Because of the large number of people they draw, festivities also become loci for commercial activities. *Tekiya*, who establish their booths at festivals, sell toys and games of various kinds as well as food, drink, plants, and household articles. The *tekiya*, who are organized into territorial groups (Sadler 1975a), operate on the fringes of the law (Iwai 1974) and often have ties to *yakuza* (organized crime) gangs (Raz 1987). Their booths are a recurrent and permanent feature at all *matsuri*. Discount sales by business establishments are also common during festivals. In addition, businessmen may contribute to the festivities (and promote their businesses) by hiring performers as part of the entertainment or by supplying food or drink.

During the Inukko *matsuri* festivities I observed, four different booths near the entrance to the Inukko concourse[4] vied for the attention of passers-by. The owner of a *tekiya* booth, half frozen from the cold, called out to passers-by to warm themselves with his "fresh, good, warm hot-dogs-on-a-stick." Further along, an elderly farm wife sold small, varicolored dogs made of rice dough; they were placed in snow shrines or eaten hot, according to preference. The Women's Association sold hot *amazake* (sweet fermented rice gruel) from a tent. Because of the subzero weather, the tent was full during the entire festival. The undoubted star of the sales booths was that of the Rice Cooperative. Outside a large tent, a young man extolled the virtues of Akita rice: "Guaranteed to make you strong. Good for men and women. Give some to your husband, lady, and tell all your neighbors about the difference it makes the following morning." Inside the tent a team of young men and older women busily pounded *mochi*.[5] The resulting hot, sticky cakes made from the dough were immediately snatched up and devoured by the children and adults who watched the pounding.

While the first three booths were concerned primarily with direct economic profit, the Rice Cooperative's effort was a promotional exercise intended to boost the local product against the inroads of bread and other nonlocal consumables. It relied for its appeal on a local idiom—*mochi* pounding—that is a traditional sign of happy and propitious occasions in Japan. The economics of display in *matsuri* are part of a range of commercial-promotional activities that are not open, on the whole, to nonlocals.

Marking and Display

Marking and display are two festival qualities exhibited in rituals and festivities. I have discussed marking within the context of ritual and will expand on it and on a related factor, display, in this section, since both are prominent, in fact necessary, components of festivities. Markers, either objects or actions, set off events within festivals as well as the festival situation itself. Markers may be obvious—that is, they may stand out and attract attention; they may be ubiquitous—that is, they may be frequently in evidence; sometimes they are both. The sound bombs—5,000 yen a shot—that signal festivals are probably a *matsuri*'s most obvious and ubiquitous markers. The number of bombs rises in direct correlation to the resources allotted to a festival. Markers label a festival situation as such to its participants. They are used in combination to enhance the effect, the atmosphere, and the image of festival as well as for display.

Among the various methods used to mark festivals are stencil-dyed vertical banners held by poles, usually ordered from one of the town's dyers.

Atago-jinja's banners, in keeping with its status as the town's premier *jinja,* are about eight meters high. The banners of other less important *jinja* are usually smaller. The day before the Daimyō Gyōretsu, the residents of the five neighborhoods who rotate the management of the festival erect posts hung with lanterns along the route of the parade. *Shimenawa* are stretched between the posts. In addition, most households hang out a painted cylindrical lantern.[6] The entire route of the parade through the organizing neighborhoods is so marked. In small neighborhood festivals the markers are generally less elaborate. The *jinja* of Nishi Tamachi Number 3, one of the smaller neighborhoods, is a two-mat structure open on one side; two banners mark the approach to the shrine, but the neighborhood itself is unmarked.

The festivities also offer opportunities for individuals and corporations to engage in display. This display helps, in turn, to create the festival atmosphere and to mark the festival space and thus shapes the festival in many ways. Display is the exhibition of elaborate markers to make social and economic claims. The promotional activities of the Rice Cooperative in Inukko *matsuri* are an example of display. The Rice Cooperative not only supports its general aims of promoting rice,[7] it also promotes local community spirit: It is not *any* rice that is so good, it is *our* rice.

During Tanabata and the Daimyō Gyōretsu, the Sword Dealers Association exhibits members' treasures. Included among the many fine blades is a valuable antique sword guard. There is a sufficient leavening of aficionados in the general populace to make of the display of this single, rather small item an object of conspicuous consumption, a claim to economic worth and aesthetic connoisseurship by its owner, a local restaurateur.[8]

Many households in Yuzawa prepare an altar during Daimyō Gyōretsu. Such an altar faces the street and is designed to be fully visible, either by setting it in a front room with the rain shutters removed or by erecting it in the entryway. The altar display is as elaborate as the household can make it: a scroll with the name of the Atago *kami,* some expensive fruit, perhaps family heirloom sake sets or vases. Wealthier households and households that participate in and finance the *matsuri* (or parts of it) may display a valuable set of armor, gold-washed screens, or an expensive tea bowl, all with long provenances. On nonfestival occasions such as weddings, household altars may be erected, but they are never made visible to passers-by.

Displays such as these fulfill at least two purposes. On the one hand, a display indicates certain economic or social claims that an individual, household, or group is making vis-à-vis others. The Yanagi family's display of an antique screen said to have been owned by a famous historical personage is a claim that the Yanagi family is rich, has taste, and by extension is one of the foremost *chōnin* families of the town.[9] On the other hand, the display of such objects marks a commonalty: a community having a festival. The territorial area of a *matsuri* is marked by these displayed objects. Thus, while the exhibition of a similar class of objects —lanterns, valuable objets d'art—marks a commonalty, the individual choice, that is, the discrete unit of the class used—a unique object such as a rare suit of armor—is an item of personal display.

Claims to individual worth and to community feeling can be displayed together. The Daimyō Gyōretsu is the primary example. It is a part of Yuzawa's culture, something that distinguishes Yuzawa not only from other towns of its size but also from its neighbors. Some of Yuzawa's neighbors have *daimyō gyōretsu* parades, but none of them has survived in as complete a form as Yuzawa's. The Daimyō Gyōretsu therefore serves as one focus of the town's identity as a community. The Daimyō Gyōretsu also displays the financial power of the "old families" and the merchants of the Go Chō. They finance the festival, and their house badges and business trademarks are prominent in the parade. The members of the young men's associations that manage the Daimyō Gyōretsu are Go Chō residents, and their permission is necessary to join the parade.[10] The festivities of the Daimyō Gyōretsu festival take place in their streets, which are also the main streets of the town. Whether calculated or not, such a display serves as a concrete reminder that the merchants and businesses of the Go Chō are Yuzawa's major economic asset.

In a larger Japanese perspective, festival markers can make claims for Yuzawa against the whole of Japan. During festivals a community can promote itself as a commercial and social entity (Inoue et al. 1979, 183–185; Bestor 1985). Groups within a community can do the same: they can display characteristics they think valuable or important or drum up support for a local product. Because of the large numbers of visitors, a successful *matsuri* is an excellent forum for such a display.

Display in the Daimyō Gyōretsu

Several weeks before the Daimyō Gyōretsu, as before Tanabata and the Inukko *matsuri,* posters announcing the event appear in Yuzawa, neighboring cities, and Tokyo. These posters are sponsored by and advertise the town's largest sake-brewing companies. In the Daimyō Gyōretsu parade, many of the floats and trucks carry colored promotional lanterns marked with the trademarks of the town's brewers. In Japan arrays of these lanterns *(chōchin)* are recognized markers of entertainment and fun, bars and *matsuri* alike. Most floats in the formal part of the parade are wrapped in indigo bunting stenciled with the name of the village or *chō* and the badge of a sponsor. The sponsor is always local, usually a shop or other commercial enterprise.

The area and time of a *matsuri* are marked by the presence of objects such as lanterns, bunting, elaborate altars, and family treasures. The bunting and the posters announcing the festival are a form of advertising, but the advertisers are all local concerns. Large companies with plants or offices in Yuzawa but headquarters elsewhere do not take part in the *matsuri* display. The festival is Yuzawa's festival, and what makes it so, what makes it Yuzawa's unique event, are the money and effort Yuzawa people devote to it. A major part of the financial resources that support it as well as the manpower[11] that manages it derive from in-town commercial activities. Besides being a source of neighborhood pride, the festival provides a way for local small shops and firms in Japan to counter the constant and growing threat posed by metropolitan-based marketing and manufacturing firms who enjoy broader sales and manufacturing networks.

The display these local merchants put on presents Yuzawa as a unique entity in contrast to the rest of the world. What the merchants display is a claim to the unity of Yuzawa, to its performative and festival health and, by extension, its commercial health. They demonstrate that elaborate and complex *matsuri* such as the Daimyō Gyōretsu are possible, but only as result of the combined resolve, purpose, and financial ability of the people of Yuzawa. *Matsuri* are elaborate and costly, and without cooperative effort—a characteristic highly valued in Japanese society—they could not be mounted. When the economy declines, this effort cannot be made, and these festivities decline as well.

The display of local economic interest is not the only theme expressed by the Daimyō Gyōretsu. The *mikoshi* of Atago-jinja is an extension of the *jinja*'s ritual. It fits the conservative image many residents have of the region as relatively stolid and staid. Being part of the ritual, the Atago *mikoshi* parade is a formal affair, carried out in a straightforward manner. To give the festival broader appeal, the raucous Edo *mikoshi* has been imported into the Yuzawa festival.

The formal body of the parade—the lord's parade and the *mikoshi* parade—is conventional and manifestly local. The tail reflects the national festival system. Neighborhoods and hamlets in Yuzawa-shi that are not part of the Go Chō participate in the tail of the parade. This part of the parade has little that is specifically Yuzawan about it. Because modern communications in Japan have spread metropolitan culture everywhere, the flowers, dances, music, clothes, and decorations in the tail, which accepts all local comers subject to the primacy of the organizers, can be seen in any festival in Japan. Metropolitan culture is gradually infiltrating Yuzawa's culture and breaking down some of the barriers between Yuzawa and its neighboring communities. The tail of the parade is no longer the parade of a relatively small and exclusive section of the populace, the Go Chō, but of Yuzawa-shi, a much broader area. Not only do outlying communities participate in the festival, but their display uses national themes instead of specifically local ones.

Thus we see that displays serve various purposes. The municipality contributes to the Daimyō Gyōretsu as a matter of local pride. The Go Chō maintain the parade as their traditional prerogative. Local companies support it because they are managed by men who see a virtue in maintaining local traditions and because the parade is a useful vehicle for their promotional activities. Outlying communities join in because it is an opportunity for entertainment and community involvement and because the idiom used is national, rather than just local.

Summary

The three themes that make up this chapter—festivities, food, and displays—are closely related. In each theme, directed activities are intertwined with hidden or at least nonovert intentions. Food and festivities are of course irreducibles, enjoyable for their own qualities alone, yet they can be manipulated for other reasons and intentions. The intentions of an individual or group when displaying itself are more complex, perhaps, but the display itself serves to pass a number of messages, some of them contradictory.

As in many other public instances, individuals define and redefine for themselves what is going on. This definition does not hinder the basic enjoyments available for the individual in the performance or participation in a *matsuri*. The word "voluntary" used earlier to identify festive participation was intentional: people can, and indeed some do, withdraw from festivities.

It is important to understand that even within the nonstructured, often blurred confines of a festival, there are structured and bound events whose integument is differentially permeable. Rituals separate themselves almost entirely from the festivities surging around them. Performances and *naorai* do so to a lesser extent; other performances do so almost not at all. All, in their great variety, help lend texture to the festival.

6

Organization, Management, and Ritual

IN YUZAWA, as elsewhere in Japan, festivals are run by groups that maintain the physical body of their *jinja*, each sustaining and benefiting from the rituals of their particular shrine. The nature of the organizing bodies of Yuzawa's festivals, their relationship to festivities and events in festivals, are important for understanding how such groups affect the nature of Yuzawa's festivals. During Japan's Edo period (1600–1868), the growing complexity of events in *matsuri* encouraged a division of labor in festival management antecedent and similar to the one existing today (Davis 1976, 28). Such physically tiring activities as *mikoshi* carrying (Sadler 1972), drumming, and running errands were left to the *waka-shu* (youth gangs), the forerunners of today's *wakamono-kai* (Wakamori 1963). The activities of such groups today run the gamut from total responsibility for some festivals through managing only parts of others to merely putting on a show in still others.

The basic and most pervasive organizational feature of groups that maintain *jinja* is a system of rotating responsibility called *tōya* by Harada (1973) and *shinji-tonin* by Hagiwara (1963), in which "family heads of a community rotate the duties of performing Shinto rituals and conducting festivals" (232). In Yuzawa *tōya* are called *tōban,* and the same word is used to refer to the group as a whole and to individuals fulfilling the duty.

Until about the middle of the twentieth century, an exclusive form of *jinja* management group called *miyaza* (shrine guild) was common. *Miyaza* were "socio-religious monopolies" (Davis 1976, 25). In the form described by Davis as well as by Bernier (1975), members of a *miyaza* restrict access to resources—religious, political, and economic—by monopolizing membership in shrine affairs and, through their interaction in the shrine, in other areas as well. Shrine membership both validates the exclusion and maintains its focus. Many types of *tōya* restrict participation on the basis of property or residence (Higo 1942; Ando 1960) or lineage membership (Chiba 1970). *Tōya* that are restricted to members of certain lineages, called *ujiko,* are more common in Tōhoku than are other forms, according to Chiba. Occasionally *ujiko* may be divided into a senior and a junior group of lineages with different rights and responsibilities in the shrine (see Bernier 1975 for an example). Even though the basic characteristics of shrine support groups—rotating responsibility and membership by household or family—are similar, the actual organizational forms differ quite extensively and, moreover, change with time (Davis 1977b). Thus Ando claims that *ujiko* as non-property-based support organizations (in contrast to *kabuza,* a group whose members each hold a share in some common property, such as a *jinja*) developed only during the Meiji period. More recently Chinnery (1971) reports on cooperation between traditional support organizations and a New Religion group in maintaining a village *jinja* festival, an indication that the support forms are, or have become, reasonably flexible.[1] A range of different affiliation forms for *jinja* membership can be observed in Yuzawa. As I will show, however, there is a significant pattern of change from an exclusive and hierarchical form based on lineage to an egalitarian one based on neighborhood residence.

Shrine Support Organizations in Yuzawa

While it has become a commonplace in the literature on *jinja* support to refer to territorially based support groups as *ujiko,* I intend here to follow Yuzawa practice to more clearly identify the three common types of shrine support organizations there.

An *ujiko* in local usage is a shrine support organization nominally restricted to or composed of representatives of one or more *ie* (households). These may or may not be kin. The basis of their ties to a shrine is ancestral practice.[2] Responsibility for the shrine may rotate among *ujiko* households or it may rest in the hands of a more restricted group called *ujiko sōdai* (*ujiko* committee) whose positions are often inherited.

A *tōban* is a territorial, usually neighborhood, group responsible for maintaining a shrine and its festival. Its membership is based on residence or other territorial criteria. One *tōban* in Yuzawa accepts as *tōban* proprietors whose shops are in the area even if their residence is elsewhere. Responsibility for maintaining the shrine rotates among the households in the *tōban.* Several households are responsible for a shrine or ritual for one year, then transfer the responsibility to the next group of households on the list.

A *kōjū* is an association whose members undertake to support a particular shrine. The members may be residents of the same area or of different areas. Unlike the *ujiko* and *tōban,* membership in *kōjū* is individual rather than by household or family. In all three types certain group members, either individuals or households, assume financial and managerial responsibility for *jinja* maintenance for a period of one year in rotation. In *tōban* and *ujiko,* as in most instrumental associations in Japan, membership obligation "is customarily limited to one person for each separate household" (Norbeck 1967a, 187). In practice, some specific examples tend to be intermediate between the forms, and I have drawn the lines dividing the types somewhat more sharply than they in fact are in each and every case. The typical distinctions and labels will, however, prove useful in later discussion.

The *Ie* and Shrine Support

Japan is often pictured as a group-oriented society whose minimal units are not individuals but *ie.* In some authoritative descriptions of Japanese society, the household is described as the basic unit and as the model for all Japanese groups: "The primary unit of social organization in Japan is the household. . . . Its composition varies according to the specific situation such as the stage in the cycle of the domestic family, and the economic situation of the household" (Nakane 1967, 1–2).

The picture of a group society whose structural forms replicate the household is somewhat overstated.[3] *Ie* as defining corporate units are declining in importance. Many households in Japan today neither have nor pretend to have any continuity with the past. Japanese law no longer recognizes the corporate concept of traditional *ie,* nor does the law require membership in it as it did during the Edo period. A primary requirement for the establishment of an *ie* is a house building (Nakane 1967, 2). This is no longer within the reach of many Japanese in the cities. Economic and demographic conditions are such that in the crowded metropolitan centers of today where population mobility is relatively high, a group whose existence relies on the lengthy physical possession of a house is no longer practicable or useful.

In the traditional *ie* system a household was considered a perpetual unit consisting of the living, the dead, and the unborn (Plath 1964). The living had special usufruct rights and stewardship obligations. Upon the retirement or death of the househead, the entire property was passed on to a single heir (Befu 1962). The household was a self-perpetuating unit following certain specific aggregation and recruitment rules (Bachnik 1983). Usually the eldest son in each generation succeeded his father as head of the household. The property belonged to the *ie* (Dore 1978, 128). All of these customs changed to some degree during and following the American Occupation. Nonetheless, certain customs and official requirements such as the compulsory household registry *(koseki)* tend to reinforce the Japanese view of society as a collective of *ie* units. This view is held notwithstanding evidence to the contrary in modern Japan. As an ideological concept, the idea of *ie* still has great force in some areas of life as a customary practice (Fukutake 1974, 33–34).

In small, self-consciously traditional towns like Yuzawa, the *ie* is still a viable concept. Yuzawa families descended from the *bushi* (warrior) stratum of the Edo period retain their elitism and pride. "Our house is descended from a *bushi* house serving the Satake as bodyguards," a farmer told me. "We are the *honke* [main house] of our surname. Others are our *bunke* [branch houses] or have just acquired the name somehow." Some merchant families, particularly those who live in the town's core, also retain long genealogy lists to demonstrate their houses' origins and usually their ties to the Satake.[4] The same is true of traditional professional households of priests and doctors, some of whom have handed down the profession for generations.

Hsu (1975, 46) notes that *ie* rather than individuals are registered as members of temples and shrines.[5] This is true in Yuzawa shrines as well. Financial contributions to shrines, particularly for construction, are recorded on boards attached to the shrine walls. Largest contributors are listed first, and the household, not the individual, is given as the contributor; the house, therefore, is the beneficiary of the *kami*'s benevolence. Households rather than individuals are assessed for contributions to a neighborhood's *jinja,* and *tōban* rotation is by household, not individual.

Neighborhood Associations

In the prewar years, neighborhood associations—I use the term *chōnai-kai*—were considered the lowest level of government, combining the functions of sanitation, fire protection, and internal police. They transmitted messages from higher authorities and passed along the rare complaint permitted against those authorities (Steiner 1965). The power of these associations was severely curtailed after World War II, partly because of their association with the prewar and wartime police state.

Yuzawa is divided into residential neighborhoods, the distinguishing characteristic of which is the sharing of a *kairanban* and the election of a headman. *Chōnai-kai* affairs consist of three sets of matters: sanitation, social affairs, and shrine maintenance. Disinfectant distribution, pest control, and, in those *chō* bordering Yuzawa's canals, a yearly cleaning of the canal bed[6] are major *chōnai* functions. Social relations in the *chō* include a range of services in which the neighborhood supplements some of the functions of the municipality. Uwa-machi, for instance, has a yearly trip for the mothers and children and fishing expeditions for the men. Both occasions are followed by a communal meal and, in the case of the fishing outing, the award of prizes. In Yuzawa as elsewhere (Dore 1978, 222), these occasions are rather more frequent today than they were before the war. The Uwa-machi *chōnai-kai* also has a "beautiful garden" competition; photographs of the winning entries are posted near the neighborhood hall. In the winter, the *chōnai-kai* erects an *inukko* and shrine from snow for the children and distributes sake and *amazake*. Shrine maintenance includes maintaining the physical structure and materials of the *jinja* and running and financing the *jinja*'s festival. Although there are legal strictures against the intervention of public bodies in religious affairs, in practice running the neighborhood festivals is considered part of the neighborhood association's civic functions. The American Occupation authorities attempted to disentangle neighborhood authorities from the running of Shinto shrines (Steiner 1965), with no great success (Akaike 1976). At least such is the case in those areas where there was a preponderance of families long resident in the neighborhood. Morioka (1975) studied a bedroom community in Mitaka, outside Tokyo. In that community, many residents objected to contributing to the neighborhood festival because they did not expect to remain long in the neighborhood. In Yuzawa and in Chichibu (Akaike 1976), where the population is more stable, there is less opposition to spending much of a neighborhood's budget on a festival insofar as all the residents presumably benefit equally. In a few cases where residents have grumbled about festival expenses, alternatives were quickly found for raising money.

Corporate Groups and *Tamagushi* Offerings

As is still common in Yuzawa, the name of a household is composed of the family name and the personal name of the househead followed by the character for house *(ke* or *ie)*. Running around the wall just below the ceiling of the neighborhood shrine of Ura-machi is a long strip of paper containing fifty-seven names in order of residential proximity and the year those households are expected to serve as *tōban*. One of the participants in the Ura-machi festivals the year I was present was a quiet young man who was obviously, by his manner and the kinds of work assigned to him, the most junior of those present. His surname, however, was not that of any of the households listed. In fact, the young man was not the household recorded on the list, nor was he a relative. He was one of the assigned man's employees, detailed to serve in lieu of his employer, who was too busy to attend to his shrine duties. In other festivals, an adolescent girl replaced her father at a ritual and a mother stood in for her son. In the Daimyō Gyōretsu, high school students are hired by households that are assigned roles but are unable to fulfill them.

As a general rule any individual of a group may substitute for any other individual in the same group. The principle is a continuation of traditional practice in which the *ie* as a unitary group could be represented by any of its designated members. The rule does not necessarily apply to all forms of association: *wakamono-kai* membership is individual, PTA membership by family; fishing expeditions are exclusively for males.

The principle of substitution, most noticeable in festival and shrine affairs, has several implications. First, it helps demonstrate the context in which festivals are seen as traditional activities operating on traditional principles. Second, the management of festivals is greatly influenced by this principle; substitution of personnel is common. Third, understanding that such a principle operates helps in understanding certain aspects of festival rituals. It is useful to conceive of each group that supports a festival in Yuzawa as a corporate group.

> Corporate groups . . . despite important differences in their bases, scale, organization and other qualities, all share certain common features, being presumptively perpetual aggregates with unique identities, determinate boundaries and memberships, and having the autonomy, organization and procedures necessary to regulate their exclusive collective affairs. While some corporate groups or publics lack corporate subdivisions and may or may not form parts of larger groups, others often contain two or more such divisions, which may or may not differ in their bases, scope and organization. . . .
>
> To organize and administer their collective affairs routinely, all but the smallest and most intimate corporate groups require special-

ized regulatory structures of corporate character, which must thus be determinate, unique, and presumptively perpetual. *Colleges* provide one possible agency of such public regulation, *offices* provide another. (M. G. Smith 1974, 176–179)

Ie are presumptively perpetual and include within them a single office: the househead (Nakane 1967, 1–2). Other groups in festivals such as *ujiko* and *wakamono-kai* have the same character. The concept of *corporate group* is useful for comparative purposes. A neighborhood shrine festival is run by a single corporation, the *chōnai-kai*, composed of a number of small, intimate corporate divisions: the neighborhood's *ie*. In some neighborhood festivals, other corporations may also play a part—*ujiko*, for instance. Other festivals are run by corporations with large and complex corporate divisions such as *wakamono-kai*, still others by corporations that do not have internal corporate divisions such as *kōjū*.

Officiants—those who perform as ritual experts in rituals, whether qualified priests or not—may also be accounted for in these terms. An officiant is a corporation sole—an office—and several officiants acting together constitute a college. Any officiant with the proper qualifications may, and in fact often does, substitute for any other. What is important is that a qualified officiant perform the ritual.

Festival rituals in Yuzawa always recognize the corporations responsible for the festival. In other rituals, while responsible corporations are often named and requested to offer *tamagushi*, these offerings are usually made by individuals. In *shichi-go-san,* for instance, the children themselves offer the *tamagushi* even though the families clap with them to indicate they are of the same unit (household/family).

The foregoing discussion of corporations points out the great variation in festival management. That each managing complex is composed of corporations that are internally autonomous does not matter, so long as it performs its expected functions within the complex. At the same time, it is to be expected that closely associated corporate groups will display a certain amount of similarity because of their association, as we shall see in the discussion of officiants in the following chapter.

The discussion of substitution can now be put into context. Substitutions of participants in rituals take place within the boundaries of a single corporation. Corporations may substitute for others when all are corporate divisions of a larger corporate group. Individuals may substitute for other members of the same corporation. The definition of who is a member of a given corporation may be quite broad. The office worker substituting for his employer was not a member of the other's family in the strict sense, but he was a member of his house in the accepted Japanese use of the term.[7]

Group Representation and Substitutability in *Tamagushi Hōten*

The priest conducts the *tamagushi hōten* segment of *jinja* rituals from a seat along the side wall of the shrine. One after another participants come forward to place sprigs of *tamagushi* on a small offering table before the altar. Groups of participants at a ritual are separated spatially, and in most cases one individual from each such separate group offers *tamagushi*. As the individual approaches the altar, the officiant instructs all members of that person's group to clap together with the person making the offering. At the altar, the offerant places the *tamagushi* on the table, claps his hands twice, bows, and claps again. As the sprig is offered, the members of the designated group (and only they) copy the actions of their representative. Those who offer *tamagushi* represent the corporations that are responsible, sometimes complementing one another's functions, for the maintenance of a shrine's ritual and its festival.

In the two successive rituals of one of Ura-machi's festivals, representatives from the following were to have offered: *chōnai-kai, ujiko,* outgoing *tōban,* incoming *tōban,* and the priest. Each of these corporations has a different relationship to the shrine. The *ujiko* are descendants of the original builder-worshipers of the shrine. The *chōnai-kai* accepted financial responsibility for the shrine from the *ujiko,* which was unable to maintain it. The *tōban,* who are members of the *chōnai-kai,* function in the shrine as a college delegated to maintain the shrine physically—they oversee repairs for the year, prepare the equipment, and clean the shrine—and form an autonomous corporation. The neighborhood association of the fifty-seven households in the neighborhood was represented by one individual, the *chōnai-kaichō.* The *tōban* of both years, eight individuals for each group, were all present, but only one individual offered *tamagushi* for each group. The *ujiko,* composed of ten households, most still resident in the neighborhood, were represented by the four members of the *ujiko sōdai,* the college that manages the affairs of the *ujiko* as an autonomous entity. The officiant, a Shinto priest, offered for his office as ritual expert. As the representative of each group offered *tamagushi,* the rest of the members of that group echoed his bows and claps.

In the second ritual the following day, the *chōnai-kaichō* failed to appear. After waiting a while, the participants consulted among themselves, and the ritual was started with a substitute. The head of the *ujiko* was, as it turned out, also the deputy headman of the neighborhood. He promptly moved away from his fellow *ujiko sōdai* and offered "for the neighborhood," refraining from clapping and bowing with his erstwhile group. Another member of the *ujiko sōdai* offered in his stead.

Thus we see that individuals may and often do substitute for other individuals within the same corporate group. Moreover, an individual may, if necessary, shift from acting for one group to acting for another, provided he or she is a member of both groups. The ritual being collective, the collaborative motif is expressed in various concrete ways. Much effort is made to involve those who are not physically offering. Those present at a ritual clap and bow with their representative; households that contribute financially to a festival are usually given a concrete symbol of their participation such as *mochi* cakes or chopsticks that have been placed on the altar.

A neighborhood association in Yuzawa may be conceptualized as a corporate group composed, in turn, of corporate divisions. At the lowest level are the *ie* that comprise the neighborhood. There may also be corporate units intermediary between the neighborhood association and the *ie*. Maemori-chō, for instance, is subdivided into *kumi*. Other corporate units may exist as well; these usually confine themselves to a limited scope of affairs. PTAs and women's associations are examples of this specialized type. A major concern of most neighborhood associations is support of *jinja*. The support is accomplished by a rotative system—the *tōban*—that involves households rather than individuals. The household representative, usually but not strictly the househead, performs the functions of his *ie*. In this manner, shrine affairs become, in effect, civil affairs. The *chōnai-kai* does not restrict itself to civil-administrative matters. In those neighborhoods where the population is largely shopkeepers, shrine meetings are foci for coordinating business matters and for discussing issues that range from taxation through social control of members.

The grounds of a shrine are often the only open area in a neighborhood. Land is expensive, and shrine locations in Yuzawa (as elsewhere in Japan) can be and are converted for a number of public uses. In some cases the shrine itself serves as a hall for the activities of the neighborhood association. In others, a small shrine is built into a neighborhood hall. In many cases shrine grounds may be converted to playgrounds by the addition of swings and slides.[8] In addition to being provided with a safe space for recreation, the children are expected to benefit from the protective interest of the shrine *kami* in its neighborhood residents.

The relationship between a shrine and the neighborhood attached to it is intimate and pictured by all concerned as mutually beneficial. This relationship is exemplified in the *tamagushi hōten* segment of the shrine's ritual. The number and relative status of the corporations involved are reflected in the number of *tamagushi* offered and the order in which groups approach the altar.

At the rituals of Atago-jinja, for example, several corporate units offer *tamagushi,* and their order reflects certain social and economic realities about the relationship among them. Atago-jinja is not only the main shrine of Yuzawa; it is also the neighborhood shrine of several Yuzawa neighborhoods: Omachi and several *kumi* of Atago-chō. Its social and managerial relationships are particularly complex, and no other shrine in Yuzawa has as many groups in attendance. The number of *tamagushi* offered in other shrines is correspondingly smaller.

In addition to the Daimyō Gyōretsu, Atago-jinja's main festival and the most elaborate one in Yuzawa, the shrine has a number of minor festivals, including the *hatsu matsuri* (the year's first ritual). After describing the shrine, I will compare these two rituals.

Atago-jinja is built on a spur of Atago Hill in the southernmost neighborhood, Atago-chō. The shrine structure has three units: a small, windowless *honden* (main hall) raised on tall piles, which enshrines the *shintai;* a large hall, the *haiden* (offering hall) in which rituals take place; and a covered bridge connecting the two halls. Mythical animals in high relief —leopards, lions, elephants, and dragons—peer out from under the eaves. Painted flowers cover the ceiling of the *haiden.* A narrow veranda runs around three sides of the twenty-four-mat-sized *haiden.* Two rows of pillars trisect the *haiden,* forming a central gallery from the bridge to the exit, with two alcoves flanking it. The shrine is reached after climbing a steep stairway and passing underneath a gatehouse. From the gatehouse one can see the southern neighborhoods of Yuzawa and across the Omono River valley to the volcanic cone of Mount Chōkai, sixty kilometers away. In the twenty-meter space between the gatehouse and the *haiden* is a garden with a small pond and a washbasin for the use of worshipers. Gnarled, cedarlike cryptomeria cover the rest of the hill. A number of smaller "guest shrines,"[9] mainly the *ujigami* shrines of families and associations, dot the grounds.

The first ritual of the *honsai* (main festival day) of Atago-jinja's main *matsuri* started at 7:30 A.M. while the Daimyō Gyōretsu was being assem-

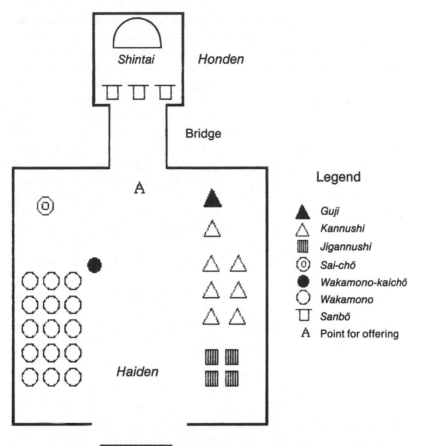

Figure 4. Atago-jinja seating during the festival's main ritual

bled in the football field of the high school at the bottom of Atago Hill. The *wakamono-kai* representatives from seven *chō* (the Go Chō plus Minamishin-machi and Hirashimizu-machi, which are traditionally associated with them) were in the shrine. The rest of the Maemori *wakamono* were with the parade. Minamishin-machi and Hirashimizu-machi, settled by servants of households in the Go Chō in the Edo period, once belonged to the *tōban* and took their turns at managing the festival, but now they only assist.

The *montsuki*-attired *wakamono* were grouped at the near left corner of the *haiden*. The *tōban* chief was the head of the Maemori-chō *waka-mono-kai*, which was head of the entire *tōban;* he sat slightly to the fore. Representatives of the four *ujiko* families of Atago-jinja, called locally the *jigannushi*, sat at the near right corner, formally attired in *sode-ginu:* blue, stiff-shouldered *haori* (jackets) with matching *hakama* over white kimono. The *sai-chō*, titular festival chief and first offerant, was on this occasion an eleven-year-old surrogate, the grandson of the *sai-chō*. The boy, dressed in white robes and a black sugarloaf hat similar to a *kannushi*'s, sat on a slightly raised dais in the left alcove. In the far right alcove, partly hidden from view by a hanging brocade curtain, sat the *guji* (chief priest) of Atago-jinja in full regalia: a red over-robe, and black *kanmuri* (a flat cap with a raised protrusion at the back to accommodate a topknot and a long black gauze "feather"). The assistant *guji*, attired likewise, sat somewhat closer to the entrances. The other *kannushi*, some of them *guji* in their own shrines, wore regular priestly garb of brocade *kariginu* (brocade overrobe) and *ebōshi;* they were grouped between the *guji* and the *jigannushi*.

The beginning and end of the ritual are signified by one of the *kannushi* beating a drum in a gradually accelerating staccato, the same rhythm that signals the start of many traditionally oriented public events in Japan. The assistant *guji* proceeded to the front of the bridge (marked "A" in Figure 4), faced the *honden* sitting in *seiza*, and read *kojin* (a request for the *kami*'s attendance). All heads bowed during the chanting. After the assistant *guji* had finished the *kojin* and returned to his place, two *kannushi* approached the altar, one to take up a *harai gushi*, the other a small bowl of salt to purify the premises and those present. After the two *kannushi* had resumed their seats, the *guji* rose, approached the entrance to the bridge, and bowed to the *honden*. He then returned to his place while a *kannushi* placed a small mat at the same spot. The *guji* rose again, knelt on the mat, and bowed to the *honden*. During this last action, one of the other priests left his place to direct the carriers who had fetched the *mikoshi* from the gatehouse, where it had been placed earlier in the morning. A *kannushi* handed the *guji* a scroll from which he read the *norito* while all the other participants bowed, the officiants with their faces to the floor. When he had finished, the *guji* returned to his place. Two *kannushi* then brought a small table and placed it at position "A" for *tamagushi* offering.

Tamagushi were offered in the following order: *guji* (all other *kannushi* bowed and clapped with him), *sai-chō*, *tōban-chō* (all other *tōban* members clapped and bowed), and finally, one *jigannushi* (the rest clapped and bowed too). One *kannushi* played a drone while *tamagushi hōten* was being performed. The offering table was then removed, and a *kannushi* unrolled a long mat from the bridge to the shrine entrance. The *guji*, bearing the *shintai* in its case, walked on the mat toward the waiting *mikoshi* to install the *shintai*. On approaching the *honden*, the *guji* was careful not to step in the middle of the bridge, walking instead along its sides. Once he had the *shintai* in his hands, however, he proceeded straight down the path, exercising the privilege of the *kami* he was now carrying.[10] The drone was played again while the *shintai* was being moved, and the rest of the *kannushi* uttered *keihitsu*, a long, drawn-out "ooooooo." As soon as the *shintai* was installed in the *mikoshi*, the bearers shouldered the *mikoshi* and all present descended with it to the parade below. The ritual was repeated later in the day after the parade had dispersed, with one difference: the *shintai* was reinstalled in the *honden* before the ritual began.

To underline some of the issues that derive from the description, it is useful to contrast *tamagushi* offering in the Daimyō Gyōretsu with another one at the same shrine, the *tamagushi* offered at Atago-jinja's *hatsu* (first of the year) *matsuri*. The *hatsu matsuri*, despite its name, does not have any festivities associated with it. As the first ritual of the year, in March, it marks the start of the work of preparing in earnest for the *honsai* in August. The order of the ritual segments is the same as that of the main festival in August, the Daimyō Gyōretsu, except that the *shintai* is not moved to the *mikoshi*.

In the *hatsu matsuri* that I observed, the *tōban*, as in the main festival, sat at the near-left corner. Most wore *montsuki* (one over a pair of jeans); others, including the *tōban-chō*, wore business suits. Only one *jigannushi* was present, and he too wore a business suit in preference to *sode-ginu*. The officiants wore full robes. The *sai-chō* was absent, and no place was prepared for him. The *guji* sat in the alcove, but there was no assistant *guji*. Instead, one *kannushi*, dressed in *kariginu*, sat slightly apart from the others.

The *hatsu matsuri* ritual has the same segments as the Daimyō Gyōretsu. The ritual starts with drum beating. One priest sits before the entrance to the bridge and chants the *kojin* by heart. That done, the priest returns to his place; two *kannushi* perform the purification, using a sprig of *sakaki* for *harai gushi* and a bowl of salt. The purification completed, the *guji* seats himself on the bare floor at the entrance to the bridge (point "A" in Figure 4), produces a scroll (rather than having it handed to him), and intones the *norito*. After finishing and returning to his seat, he rises once again, crosses the bridge, and opens the *honden* doors. The other officiants, barring the two who play instruments, form a queue and pass *sanbō* laiden with *osonaemono* (mainly food) to the *guji*, who places them before the open *honden* doors. The queue *kannushi* intone the *keihitsu* "ooooooo." All the *kannushi* then return to their places.

At the start of *tamagushi hōten* two *kannushi* rise and prepare the table for the offerings. The *tōban-chō* offers first, then the *jigannushi*, then the *guji*. As in the summer festival, members of each offerant's group clap and bow along with their representatives. Following the ritual there is a *naorai* for all present, and the ritual ends.

Compared to rituals in other shrines in Yuzawa, all the Atago-jinja rituals are elaborate: there are numerous *sanbō* of altar offerings, participants wear formal clothes, and many officiants and several corporations take part. Consider, however, the differences in the *kojin* segment in the two examples. The *kojin* invokes and requests the presence of the *kami*. In the *hatsu matsuri*, an officiant who is not a *guji* recites the *kojin* by heart. In the Daimyō Gyōretsu, the *kojin* is read from a scroll by an assistant *guji* dressed differently from his colleagues. The *norito* segment, too, differs. In the *hatsu matsuri*, the *guji* reads the *norito* from a scroll he provides himself, and he sits on the bare mat like everyone else. In the Daimyō Gyōretsu ritual, another officiant hands the *guji* the scroll, and he sits on a special mat. In the Daimyō Gyōretsu, offerings are placed before the *honden* in a separate "opening-the-shrine" ritual performed the night before, on *yoi matsuri*. This ritual is followed by a *kagura* performed by four young *miko* "to entertain the *kami*," as the *guji* at the ritual I observed said.

The Daimyō Gyōretsu ritual's activities are broken down so that more officiants participate. There are more participant corporations. Dress and actions are more restricted and rule-bound. The Daimyō Gyōretsu is elaborate in the sense used by Skorupski: exceedingly complex and done on a large scale. Lavish amounts of energy, money, time, and other resources are expended in its production.

The lord's parade and the accompanying *mikoshi* parade are complex affairs too, requiring many individuals and groups to serve managerial functions and secure the necessary resources. The requirements of the lord's parade are fixed and set out in a formal and recognized document (although the option to cut out parts and make the parade smaller or less elaborate, if less "authentic," exists). The *daimyō gyōretsu* of Yamada and of Iwasaki (the first a village, the latter a town in Yuzawa-shi), both of which had resident lords during the Edo period, have become much less elaborate. The residents call the Yamada parade a *"hoido matsuri"* (beggars' festival) because "when we lost our status as an autonomous fief and became an administrative part of Yuzawa-shi, all the rich people and the elegant samurai abandoned the parade, and now only the poor people are left to commemorate it." Complexity and power, it is obvious, are clearly associated. The original *daimyō gyōretsu* was a display of power: the power of the shogun in being able to compel the expensive practice and the power of the *daimyō* vis-à-vis the townspeople. Though the *daimyō* is gone, the parade, which by the late Edo period was already financed directly by rich townspeople, still marches. It still serves at least partly as a display of wealth and power: the power of individual families and their ability to muster resources to equip a rider, the economic ability of the *sai-chō* to guarantee the finances of the festival, and above all the power of the *tōban,* who are the representatives of the community acting in concert.

Among other things, the set of individuals managing a festival demonstrates their ability to mobilize people and resources. There is a congruence between this ability and the ability of the *kami* to command an appropriately elaborate ritual. Where human participants can mobilize and demonstrate considerable power, it would be incongruous if the *kami* were unable to do the same. *Kami* differ in rank, although the differences do not necessarily correlate with *jinja* ranking. In prewar Japan the ranks were assigned by the national government, and throughout Japanese history, *kami* have been promoted (and demoted) to serve national interests. Historical association, wealth, and number of support groups were criteria for shrine ranking. Healing, miracle working, political considerations, or imperial favor were criteria for promoting *kami*. In a historically famous case, for example, the *kami* Tenjin in the Heian period was promoted several times to end the disasters he was supposed to have caused. The Atago *kami* was promoted several ranks when the *jinja* received the rank of *kensha* (prefectural shrine).

Since 1945 no official ranks have been assigned. Few lay people, in any case, care. The *kami* of Atago-jinja ranks relatively low in the official hierarchy formed by Jinja Honchō theorists and their predecessors, yet the shrine of Atago-jinja is larger and its festival more elaborate than those of the two Yuzawa shrines dedicated to Amaterasu-Ō-Mikami, officially the highest-ranking *kami*. *Kami* rank and shrine importance do not correlate since each shrine is autonomous. The most important area of autonomy is the form and number of support groups, and these indicate the popular importance of a shrine.

Elaborate festivals reflect popular importance; if there is to be a ritual with such a festival, the ritual too must be elaborate.[11] No less important, an elaborate ritual cannot be sustained without the commitment of financial and human resources.

A single group may be responsible for all aspects of a ritual and festival (Moriarty 1972, 133). Some examples will be given in the following chapter, when we discuss officiants. However, it is more common to find several corporate units operating in concert. Such cooperation is not surprising because the primary requirement for putting on a festival program is manpower. And, as I have already shown, ritual elaboration, number of participating corporations, and size of festivities are closely related. Where there are several corporations operating in concert, there will be corresponding recognition of their role in *tamagushi hōten*. Each of the groups offering *tamagushi* at a ritual has a distinct relationship to the *jinja* and to its festival. Atago-jinja illustrates this point.

1. Officiants are responsible for the proper performance of ritual.
2. The *sai-chō*, in addition to his ritual role as chief worshipper, is the underwriter. He is a prominent individual who offers his name and sometimes his purse to assure the execution of the festival.
3. The *tōban-chō*'s post complements that of the *sai-chō*. The *tōban-chō* is responsible for managing the festival's manpower requirements. In other words, he manages the affair sponsored by the *sai-chō*.
4. The *tōban* constitute the group actually running the festival and supply its manpower. They are an extension of the community, acting for it and in its name.
5. The *jigannushi* have a responsibility to the shrine itself, to the *shintai* that is their ancestral heritage because they are the *ujiko* of Atago-jinja.

Atago-jinja is unusual in that all of these functions are separate and carried out by easily identifiable and formally separate corporate units. This is not the case for most shrines in Yuzawa, and presumably elsewhere in Japan. Smaller shrines in Yuzawa (and this accounts for most of the neighborhood shrines and all the *ujiko* shrines) are required to "collapse" functions. That is, most, and in some cases all, of the five functions enumerated above are carried out by a single corporate group. In one extreme case a *kannushi* has accepted responsibility for a shrine for which there are no other supporters and himself carries out all functions.

If responsibility for a shrine is transferred, residual rights are maintained for a time, particularly if the collective of corporate units that make up a shrine feels an obligation. This is the case in Kumano-jinja, where a *tamagushi* is put aside for the landowner on whose land the shrine is built. Neither the landowner (who lives in a different neighborhood) nor any representative has attended the ritual for a number of years, but, as the *chōnai kaichō* said, "We prepare for the possibility, just in case."

Rights in a shrine are not retained in perpetuity, however; they must at some point actively be exercised. In Kumano-jinja no *tamagushi* is prepared for the former owners of the *shintai* because "there is only one member of the family left; he is ill and will certainly not come." Effectively, therefore, in the offering of *tamagushi* it is the contribution that is being recognized and not some abstract principle.

Operating Responsibilities

The operating monies required by a *jinja* and its festival are in most cases raised by contributions solicited from the neighborhood residents. All contributions are recorded. Since a shortfall is common, it is expected that those in charge—the *tōban,* the *wakamono,* the *ujiko sōdai*—will make up the losses. A shortfall in a small *jinja* is easily covered, not so in a large festival such as the Daimyō Gyōretsu. When there is a shortfall in a large festival, the *sai-chō* can become crucial to its success or failure.

Rituals require certain physical preparations; parades and other components of festivity require even more. Some, like cleaning the *jinja* grounds, can be performed by hired help. Others—offering *miki* to visitors, arranging offerings, collecting *kifu* (donations) for rituals, managing a parade, preparing decorations—can only be done by volunteers because they rely on personal relationships and a show of personal concern among the people involved.

In some cases, *ujiko* associations maintain their local shrines. However, in many cases in Yuzawa, *ujiko* have relinquished their rights and duties to the broader-based neighborhood *tōban* groups. The increasing use of *wakamono-kai* to run festivals in Yuzawa is a response to the need for managerial personnel. The young men have the necessary stamina and enthusiasm (Wakamori 1963). Alternatively, particularly in smaller neighborhoods where there are not enough youths, each household is expected to contribute one able-bodied worker once every three to ten years. The size of the *tōban* group depends on the neighborhood's population, and the elaboration of the festival is partly a function of that size. In addition to size, a community's managerial ability and will determine its ability to put on a festival. By forming a *tōban* people often consciously feel they are contributing to the social solidarity of their community, notwithstanding Norbeck's contention (1970, 105) that they are rarely aware of festivals' social integrative function.

The order in which *tamagushi* are offered reflects the distinctive contributions of each component corporate unit to the festival. In most cases, the officiant offers *tamagushi* last. As *kannushi* say, "It is more polite this way, even though, properly speaking, a *kannushi* should offer first." The Atago-jinja rituals are an exception. The Atago-jinja ritual officiants prefer to obey the order of ritual they feel is right (the order taught and practiced by Jinja Honcho[12]) rather than cater to local social conditions, as they do in less elaborate, less formal rituals. The difference derives from the greater elaboration of Atago-jinja rituals. It is also possible that *kannushi* in Yuzawa are conscious of, and to some degree resent, the primacy given to the lord's parade in the Daimyō Gyōretsu.

The relations between corporate units responsible for a festival are complementary. The internal affairs of each corporation, however, are a matter of internal arrangement. The Daimyō Gyōretsu *tōban* bear the largest burden because they are able to mobilize a great number of people for the festival. The *tōban* of Atago-jinja as a whole is recognized by its right to offer a *tamagushi* in the ritual. The *tōban* of Atago-jinja consists of five autonomous divisions, one from each of the Go Chō. The *tōban* of the Daimyō Gyōretsu are nominally the *wakamono-kai* of each *chō*, but the label *"wakamono-kai"* conceals a number of different organizational patterns.

An example is the *wakamono-kai* of Maemori-chō, which is composed of men resident in the *chō* who are under the age of forty-two. Those who maintain an interest in shrine affairs after retirement from the *wakamono-kai* may elect to join a group of advisers. In Maemori-chō, management of the Daimyō Gyōretsu is intimately tied to the management of Maemori-chō's neighborhood shrine, Yunohara Hitachi Inari-jinja. Formally, at least, the Maemori-chō neighborhood association is separate from the organization that supports its shrines. In practice, since many of the financial channels run through the *chōnai-kai*, personnel and financial affairs are operated in tandem. The *gojikai* (shrine support group) of Yunohara Hitachi Inari-jinja was formally incorporated as a religious

juridical person (Maemori-chō jinja gojikai n.d.) after the Religious Juridical Person Law went into effect in 1951.[13] The purpose of the Yunohara
Hitachi Inari Preservation Association is to "give thanks for our revered
ancestors' outstanding virtue; to pray for the household prosperity of the
members in and out of Maemori-chō; to maintain and manage the *jinja*'s
assets; and to support the mutual friendship of the members (Yunohara
Hitachi Inari Gojikai bylaws n.d.).

All residents of Maemori-chō are eligible for membership in the shrine
support group and they appoint representatives[14] to a committee that
selects trustees and managers. These appointees in turn select the execu-
tive officers of the *gojikai*. The committee also appoints a group of advisers who serve as the *ujiko sōdai* and advise the committee on *jinja*-related
issues. Another group serves as advisers to the *wakamono-kai* in the management of the Daimyō Gyōretsu. The resident *kannushi* of Hitachi
Inari-jinja serves as adviser ex-officio. Some individuals sit on several
committees and serve at all functions.

Once in five years the *wakamono-kai* of Maemori-chō are responsible
for Daimyō Gyōretsu preparations. Their functions are also tied intimately to Maemori-chō and its neighborhood *jinja*. During the spring
festival of Yunohara Hitachi Inari-jinja the *wakamono* solicit donations
by parading through the neighborhood with new *shimenawa* for the
jinja. Firecrackers are set off, and the *chō*'s children are offered sweets.
The festival also allows the officers of the *wakamono-kai* to start forming
their ideas on preparations for the upcoming Daimyō Gyōretsu. The
finances of Yunohara Hitachi Inari-jinja are the main topic of conversation during the *naorai*, but the managerial and financial details of the
Daimyō Gyōretsu—expected revenues and expenses, assignment of major
roles, and so on—are also discussed. Minor practical details are firmed up
privately between the *wakamono-kai* advisory committee and the *wakamono-kai* officers and between the advisory committee members and
potential large contributors, who are expected to furnish a rider or a *jinrikisha*. Final details of the Daimyō Gyōretsu plans are decided in July at
Kashima-jinja, the last Maemori-chō festival, which the *wakamono-kai*
also run and which includes a picnic and film for the neighborhood children. As the *wakamono-kaichō* said in his toast before the *naorai*, "This
is the last round. From now until the end of the Daimyō Gyōretsu we
must all give it all we've got." From that point on, the *wakamono-kai*
meet every evening, first to assign parade roles, later to attend to myriad
other details of the Daimyō Gyōretsu.

The interdependence of the Maemori-chō *jinja*-related corporations is

acknowledged in the rituals of Yunohara Hitachi Inari-jinja but not in
any of the rituals of Atago-jinja. Each of the groups named above is
expected to, and does, offer a *tamagushi* at the rituals of Yunohara
Hitachi Inari-jinja and Kashima-jinja because these corporations together
make up the support system of Maemori-chō's neighborhood shrine. Different corporations, however, are responsible for the rituals of Atago-
jinja. The Maemori-chō *wakamono-kai,* which is part of Atago-jinja's
tōban group (the Go Chō) who run the festival, is acknowledged, but the
rest of Maemori-chō's groups are not, because the internal affairs of the
groups within the *tōban* are not relevant to the Atago-jinja festivals. For
the same reason, a child may substitute for his grandfather in the *sai-chō*
role. The *sai-chō* is a corporation sole—what M. G. Smith (1974) calls an
"office"—and its internal arrangements are part of its internal autonomy, something outside the scope of the other corporations' affairs.

The degree to which different corporate units, even within a given corporation such as the *tōban* of Atago-jinja, are autonomous can be seen by
comparing Maemori-chō's arrangements with those of two other of the
Go Chō, Yanagi-machi and Fuppari. The *wakamono-kai* of Yanagi-machi
contrasts strongly with Maemori-chō's structured and differentiated
organization. Yanagi-machi is a small neighborhood situated between
Omachi and Maemori-chō. It is lined with shops whose owners live on the
premises, several out-of-town companies such as banks and department
stores, and one operating sake brewery. The current members of the
wakamono-kai are relatively young men. Most own or operate their or
their families' shops in the neighborhood. While there are formally
about twenty members, only a smaller core group regularly attends the
functions. These functions include leisure activities. The members of the
group are obviously quite close and the relationship of long standing.
The Yanagi-machi *wakamono-kai* does not have an advisory group of
elders to help them run the Daimyō Gyōretsu because, the *wakamono-
kaichō* said, "We are good friends. We are a small group, and we all do
this [working on the Daimyō Gyōretsu] every year, so everyone knows his
job when we are responsible for the festival."

Before World War II, a group of men from Yanagi-machi formed a
consortium and bought the forestry rights to Mount Mitake, northeast of
the town. One man had a shrine transferred to the mountain top, and the
consortium members formed themselves into a support group to maintain the shrine.[15] Worshiping at the shrine means a one-hour climb from
Yanagi-machi carrying all the paraphernalia needed for the ritual. As the

original group of purchasers grew older, they suggested that the Yanagi-machi *wakamono-kai,* some of whom were their own sons, assume the maintenance of the shrine. The *wakamono-kai* and *chōnai-kai* consented and adopted the shrine as Yanagi-machi's neighborhood *jinja.*

There are two festivals on Mount Mitake during the year. In both, the *wakamono-kai* spend a night on the mountain in a hut. While the expressed reason is that such attendance is a ritual requirement, there are some unexpressed reasons too. The core group of the *wakamono-kai,* close in age and good friends, help one another in their shops and go fishing and drinking together. The festivals of Mitake-jinja are an opportunity for a group of friends to get together twice yearly for a camp-out. They equip themselves with a sufficient quantity of beer to supplement the sake for the shrine, a great amount of food (some of it from donations, the larger part from their own funds), mahjong and card sets, and sleeping bags. They spend the night engaged in those pursuits that entertain them best, including a great deal of talk (only some of it obscene). The rituals, if not an afterthought, are approached as part of the party. The head of the *wakamono-kai,* one of the old consortium members (as *ujiko*), and the *chōnai-kaichō* of Yanagi-machi offer *tamagushi.* The priest is a middle-aged man who has taken over from another, older priest, who found the climbing hazardous as years went by.

The Yanagi-machi *wakamono-kai* has little formal internal organization. When, every fifth year, it is Yanagi-machi's turn to run the Daimyō Gyōretsu, the responsibilities are divided as convenient. Little of the formality and discipline displayed by Maemori-chō are in evidence.

Fuppari-chō, the southernmost of the Go Chō, borders Atago-chō near Atago-jinja. There are several small industries in the neighborhood. Most residents are either self-employed businessmen, farmers, or white-collar workers. The *chōnai* has no real *jinja,* although there is a small and neglected shrine inside the *chōnai kaikan.* That shrine has offerings placed before it during spring equinox (when a sign outside the hall invites people in to pay obeisance) and during the Daimyō Gyōretsu.

The Fuppari-chō *wakamono-kai* includes those adult males resident in the neighborhood who care to join as well as several men from neighboring Atago-chō, where land was once owned by Fuppari-chō landowners.[16] Except for the preparation and execution of the Daimyō Gyōretsu, none of the neighborhood association's activities (which are few in any case) take place within the framework of the *wakamono-kai.* The same men run the traditional market for Obon (day of the dead) decorations in the

neighborhood's street, but the armbands they wear proclaim them officials of the *chōnai-kai*. This is true also of the *chōnai* cleanup campaign.
The Fuppari-chō *wakamono-kai* is therefore merely the title of the *chōnai-kai* when acting within the framework of the Daimyō Gyōretsu.

Individuals in the Fuppari-chō group may be friends, and many are.
Some have an interest in festival activities; two are members of the
Daimyō Gyōretsu advisory committee. However, Fuppari-chō as an organized unit does not function in the same way or for the same purpose as
does Yanagi-machi or Maemori-chō. In Fuppari, various volunteer organizations are available for those who wish to engage in public activities
within the *chō*. Fuppari-chō has a *chōnai-kai* with several officers and a
volunteer fireman organization like other neighborhoods. In Fuppari-chō
the same individuals change hats, acting sometimes as members of one
group, sometimes of another. Any of these groups, under a specific
name, may act in a *matsuri* or may be utilized for *matsuri* purposes.

In addition to management, the Daimyō Gyōretsu, like all public
events, requires financing. The overall expenses of the Daimyō Gyōretsu
are hard to estimate, because many of the costs are hidden within other
items or not accounted for. For example, there are no reliable data on the
expenses involved in financing a rider, since the managing committee
does not include such in its calculations. Moreover, while the finances of
Atago-jinja, its *honsai,* and the Daimyō Gyōretsu are separate on the
books, in practice, there is a fairly free flow of money from one item to
another. Much of the expense of the parade is collected through donations by households, individuals, and businesses. The largest donations
(from companies) amounted to about 50,000 yen in 1980; the smallest
sum was the 600 yen assessed on every household in the Go Chō. During
the 1980 Daimyō Gyōretsu, the busiest man in the Maemori-chō *wakamono-kai* was the treasurer. While others spent part of their time in the
tōban office drinking, sleeping, playing mahjong, or chatting, the treasurer had his head buried in his books the whole time. The *chōnai-kaichō*
of a small neighborhood confided that the financial aspects of the festival
were the most bothersome: "People want to know exactly what you do
with their money all the time." Once all the bills have been paid, a balance sheet is drawn up and filed with the other *jinja* documents. Some
neighborhoods distribute this balance sheet through the *kairanban* to all
member households; others merely have it available for perusal by any
interested neighborhood resident.

After the Daimyō Gyōretsu, a series of meetings at various levels assesses the success of the past festival and starts planning for the next year's. Each group involved in the festival performs a postmortem on its performance. In these *hansei-kai*,[17] new officers are chosen and introduced to their duties, the performance of the particular body—*chōnai-kai, wakamono-kai,* or the whole *tōban*—is evaluated, and each participant is given a chance to have his say. The final activity is a party; there is a feast after each meeting and, after all the meetings have been finished, a party for all the organizers at a local spa.

Hansei-kai, under a variety of names, take place at every level. The constituent *kumi* of a *chōnai-kai* meet separately and then together. The *wakamono-kai* of each neighborhood meet separately, then together, and finally all the bodies involved with the festival meet together. At the last meeting, where the heads of all the groups meet to discuss overall performance, a senior representative of the municipality—the mayor or his deputy—is also present because the city contributes money to support the Daimyō Gyōretsu as a *shi bunkazai* (city cultural treasure) and because the festival is a major public event.

The web of acquaintanceships based on the festivals constantly expands as individuals pass through the festival system and rotate in and out of various functions. The system is also a closed one, since participation is based on residence and open to Yuzawa residents alone. Areas contiguous to Yuzawa have similar limits. The geographical boundaries of a particular set of festivals—a festival system—will be discussed in the final chapter. Residents of Iwasaki (a township within Yuzawa-shi) manage their own *daimyō gyōretsu*. Individuals may fulfill a variety of festival roles during their lifetimes in Yuzawa, and many do. Those individuals who do so are socialized into the "Yuzawa way of doing things."

Festival preparation in Yuzawa is intimately tied to shrine support. Although it is a form of group action, individual motivations and interests also come into play. It is possible to examine the corporations that manage festivals in Yuzawa in light of these premises.

Plath (1969, 76–86) suggests that there are four premises of group action in Japan: (1) groups are oriented toward achievement; (2) they are oriented toward *group* achievement and group goals and not the goals of particular members; (3) tasks and rewards are allocated by status (all members must perform and all performances are essential, though some may be more visible than others); and (4) where group goals are not endangered, groups are prepared to satisfy the human needs of their members. Shrine support groups exhibit these characteristics.

The primary goal of a shrine support group is to maintain a festival and its shrine. Some of these groups also satisfy their members' social and emotional needs. Some utilize commonly accepted slogans ("the good of the *chōnai*") to persuade people to participate in achieving the group's goal: putting on the *matsuri*. Although the group may coerce some individuals to participate in an activity they do not really care about, such coercion ensures maximum possible participation and maximizes the possibilities of success. Individuals who are so coerced participate "to keep good human relationships" with their neighbors. The structure of these groups is designed to meet certain performative requirements. So long as these requirements are met, however, there is great variety in actual group structure. Once these groups are viewed as corporate groups with internal arrangements that respond to their specific conditions, it is possible to compare their functioning without worrying about developmental typologies, as Davis (1977b) has. It is obvious that if such groups are internally autonomous, as I have demonstrated, their internal arrangements will tend to differ as they react to specific local neighborhood conditions. Moreover, the corporate analytic model helps explain how social change and social continuity are possible at the same time.

Change occurs within each corporation. It is a response to individual needs and preferences and to particular social constellations that emerge within a given corporation. Members grow old, new ones join, the outside impinges in myriad ways. Yet the boundaries of the corporation are maintained, and they are such that as long as the given corporation's relations with the other corporations in a system of local, related *matsuri* remain unchanged, the system can be maintained. The system can therefore encompass great variety and scope of change within its component corporations without significant alteration to itself. On the other hand, change that affects intercorporate relationships in a case where several corporate groups cooperate, as in the Daimyō Gyōretsu, will greatly influence the ability of the groups to maintain a festival or achieve some other group goal.

This view is also applicable to Japanese society as a whole. At a collective level, Japanese society can be viewed as a set of nesting corporations, any of which can change internally. Changes that overcome the entire society are graduated, with some corporations responding quickly, and others more slowly. Traditional elements as well as new ones can exist side by side with little disorganization, and the functioning of the total system can appear to be relatively unchanged. In fact, whole constellations of corporate units can change internally and even change their relationships to one another while other corporations and constellations of corporate units remain unchanged or change at a different pace. Change thus spreads through a system at different rates, with different corporate units being able to make their own internal adjustments in their own time. Thus we have the apparently paradoxical phenomenon in Japan of very traditionally organized groups functioning side by side with newly developed ones. Since each corporate unit can make its own adjustments, it is possible to find corporate groups changing in some ways but not in others in response to their own specific conditions and requirements. These conditions differ from group to group, and thus we find corporate groups with very similar scopes of affairs but very different internal arrangements.

Groups in Japan often overtly support and publicly espouse "human values," what the Japanese call *ninjō*. As Plath's proposition implies, human values are often sacrificed to achieve the goals the group has set for itself. Festivals are often portrayed as means rather than as ends in themselves. The "true" goal of *matsuri*, I was assured again and again, is "neighborhood/group solidarity." This view is, of course, only one level of the "native" understanding of festive events. It is valid in itself, even if it is not the only goal of *matsuri*, but only one among many. The same individuals who supplied the group explanation would, on other occasions, state that *matsuri* are for enjoyment, or that they help educate the people in Japanese values, or even that they are a religious practice. Nonetheless, the conception that actions undertaken in a group are undertaken to support the group and its values is prevalent and very important in Japanese culture. Still, even though a great deal of superficial attention is devoted "human values" in Japan, support for those values is rarely allowed to interfere with performance. Like Japanese companies, which are no less goal oriented than their foreign counterparts, notwithstanding lip service to ideals such as "serving humanity," *matsuri* support groups are involved in the creation of a festival.

A related question is why so many people invest their time in festivals. Because things are done within group frameworks in Japan, there is little room for self-promotion. The group-oriented solution is also the easiest one to entertain given stated Japanese preferences. Besides the motivation supplied by religion, which is explicitly weak, and the need to conform to group demands, which is strong, what motivations do individuals have? There is no hard and fast answer. Obviously individual motivations do count, and, just as obviously, they differ from one individual to another. I would hazard, however, that one important motivation for participation is individual satisfaction. Participation in *matsuri* affairs in Yuzawa is only one of many options for public activity. There are other public groups in any town to which one may belong, according to taste. In Yuzawa these range from sports, through a hiking club run by an elderly teacher who is also the steward of an *ujiko* shrine, to a Noh chanting group whose president is the steward of another shrine. Such groups are generally interneighborhood. Depending on factors ranging from personal taste to social pressures exerted by neighbors or friends, an individual might decide to devote time to composing haiku rather than working on a *matsuri*.

On the whole, people in Yuzawa, as elsewhere, are conscious that useful personal benefits might accrue from working on the *matsuri* (although this is far from a major, or single, consideration). Business connections can be made, better custom assured. For the younger members, working on the *matsuri* provides an opportunity to exercise managerial skills in frameworks larger than those ordinarily available to them and an opportunity to enlarge their circle of acquaintances, a critical matter for local businessmen. Locally powerful individuals who might not be so easily accessible otherwise might also be working on the *matsuri*. Akaike (1976) seems to feel that political involvement and support is the main motivating factor. I would suggest that it is only one among many. Some of the elderly and wealthy residents of Yuzawa have emotional commitments to festivals and encourage participation by younger men in festival affairs. Many other individuals profess to be totally uninterested in festivals. Indeed, some of them even avoid participation if they can. The combination of pressures exerted by public opinion demanding a show of communal solidarity and by wealthy businessmen who in other circumstances are one's neighbors, suppliers, clients, and often relatives is formidable persuasion.

One might well ask what might happen when human values and goal orientation clash. In the instances cited above, and during lengthy observations in Yuzawa, there were no instances of overt conflict. Does this imply that the organizational system manages to balance the two in perfect harmony?

The fact that the organizational form works in Yuzawa is indisputable. Moreover, Japanese culture has evolved a series of mechanisms to avoid conflict, and, if that is not possible, to mute or transform it (see, for instance, Lebra 1984 and Eisenstadt 1990, and, for the specific case of Yuzawa, Ashkenazi 1990). In other cases, where conflict is avoidable, it undoubtedly works as well. What makes it work, apparently, is the tremendous variability of the managerial form and managerial process. As the data in the chapter show, this variability is built into the system. At the same time, it allows different organizational forms to interact and to function cooperatively with a common purpose. The data also show that the structure and the interrelationships of these groups hold together not only each *matsuri* as a unit, but also bundle all Yuzawa's *matsuri* into an integrated system, a system that nonetheless allows for a great deal of autonomy to each of its constituents.

7

Officiants and Rituals

To understand Yuzawa's festivals it is necessary to understand how the entire set of festivals holds together. A major factor in the system is the priests who perform at festival rituals. Rituals are not performed only in festivals, however; in fact, most rituals are not festival rituals. Moreover, as has already been noted in passing, *kannushi* are not the only ones who perform rituals. Previously I have contrasted *hairei*, individual obeisance at a shrine, with collective shrine rituals. In this chapter I will address the entire range of rituals commonly performed in Yuzawa. To discuss this fully, it is necessary to make a terminological distinction. I define as "officiant" any individual who is performing a ritual on behalf of himself and others. Professionally trained officiants include in Yuzawa Shinto priests *(kannushi)* and Buddhist bonzes.[1] However, other individuals may also serve as officiants.

The role of an officiant is analytically similar to that of a performer in a public performance, with the participants in the ritual serving as the officiant's audience. There are, of course, differences. For one, a participant in a ritual *participates* rather than taking a passive role as an audience does, but the rules of competency apply to both performer and officiant. "Competence" is the acceptance by relevant others—an audience or a group of ritual participants—of a performance or of its adequacy. A performer may be more or less competent. In rituals, specifically in shrine rituals in Japan, the basis for the judgment of competence is local, not global or national, standards. A ritual is compared to other ritual performances observers have witnessed. "Other ritual performances" often means almost exclusively the performance by local officiants, because those are the ones an individual is likely to interact with.

The interaction between the participating audience in a ritual and the performer-officiant explains the particular forms that a ritual assumes in a given social context. This relationship is explored here. The audience

110

affects the performance by its expressed expectations and satisfactions—
or dissatisfactions. These are based on and related to the audience's experience in other rituals. The performer maintains or changes a ritual
because of his own understanding of how a given ritual should be performed and how rituals should be performed generically, but he is also
affected by the attitude of his audience and his fellow experts. The outcome of specific pressures produces different effects, depending on the
forces in operation and their relative influences.

An audience that becomes more knowledgeable or experienced with a
class of performances forces the officiant to perform more competently.
Performers in other occupations in Japan—Noh theater (Bethe and Brazell 1978) and storytelling (Hrdlickova 1969), for example—are subject to
the same principle. In Yuzawa rituals, the participants can and do comment on the quality of a ritual performance and on the performer's abilities.

An officiant's competence is also honed by his relationship with other
officiants. Besides satisfying participants, an officiant in Yuzawa must
also satisfy his peers—other officiants with whom he might have to cooperate in elaborate rituals—as to the competence of his performance. He
must meet a standard of excellence set by other experts; his possible range
of deviation therefore depends on his relationship with them as well with
his "audience."

Ritual Performers—
Kannushi, Carpenters, and Laypersons

In Shinto practice, as I have been repeatedly assured by both laypersons and experts, anyone can perform a ritual, whether a registered
kannushi or not. Whether the individual can perform a ritual *competently* is another question, the most important question to many.

Some of the rituals in Yuzawa are private, performed for or by individuals or limited and closed groups such as households, ritual associations,
or commercial firms. Other rituals are public, effectively, those for neighborhoods or the city. What is common to all these rituals is that they
require an individual or individuals to run them and perform the ritual
actions. As noted in the previous chapter, officiants are substitutable, the
limitation being, of course, their relative competence. A trained *kannushi,* although able to replace the head of a household, is unlikely to do
so. Likewise, the head of a household is highly unlikely to replace a *kan-*

nushi in a public ritual. Like performing a magnificent ritual in a poor shrine, the results of such a substitution would be ludicrous, spoiling the event.

Kannushi run all public and open rituals and many private ones. Non-expert officiants perform only in private rituals. This distinction is not ideologically or theologically motivated. *Kannushi* are not "ordained" but merely trained. According to many *kannushi* any individual who knows the forms and is able to carry them out may officiate at a ritual. There are no prior ritual objections to a layperson performing any ritual. The sole determinants for performance are knowledge of the complex rules involved in performing the ritual properly and a willingness to perform.

Rituals run by *kannushi* have already been described in previous chapters. In comparison, it is worth examining those run by a sample of other officiants. Two categories of nonexpert officiants that commonly perform rituals are househeads (usually the senior male of a household) and carpenter-foremen responsible for the construction of wooden dwellings. The differences between expert and nonexpert officiants illuminate the nature of expertise and the question of variance and invariance in rituals.

A Carpenter-run Ritual

Three stages in the construction of most residences and other structures in Yuzawa are marked ritually: the ground breaking, the completion of the roof (called *mune age*), and the end of construction. About 70 to 80 percent of all construction in Yuzawa is marked by these rituals, which is probably not unusual for Japan as a whole. Roof-raising rituals are performed by the senior carpenter-foreman of the construction crew. To become chief carpenter, an individual must serve an apprenticeship for a number of years and have become accepted as a master craftsman for a few more. During the time spent working up the professional ranks, a carpenter inevitably participates as one of the participants in a number of *mune age*. The ritual also has an economic function, as it marks the payment by the client of part of the construction expenses. At the roof-raising ritual, the house owner also provides the workers with a meal and several bottles of sake.

The officiant-carpenter performs in work clothes. *Tamagushi* are neither made nor offered, although sometimes one of the carpenters may prepare *gohei* (paper streamers) and a stand for them. The altar is usually a very simple affair: some raised trays brought by the client or perhaps a low folding table otherwise used for snacks or playing cards. The altar paraphernalia and offerings are provided by the owner of the structure being erected, and the elaborateness of the offerings and altar is the owner's decision. (Usually, however, the owner seeks the advice of the master carpenter.) On most altars there is a sake bottle and a cup, a plate piled with uncooked polished rice grains, some seafood, a plate of salt, carpenter's tools, a straw sandal, a candle in a candlestick, and one or more trays or large plates loaded with *manjū* (small rice cakes stuffed with bean jam).

As the ritual is about to begin, crowds of children gather near the site, waiting eagerly for its conclusion. The officiant kneels before the altar, bows twice, claps, then picks up the salt plate and strews salt to the four corners of the construction. The tools are then raised to the officiant's forehead and replaced. All the participants then bow and clap their hands. The officiant takes the hammer and knocks several times on a corner post of the construction, then ties the sandal to a roof beam, returns to the altar, and bows again. The moment the children have been waiting for arrives. The officiant and the owner rise and throw handsful of the cakes to those outside. After they have been assured that all the largesse has been distributed, the children amble away, their pockets and mouths full of cake. The participants in the ritual are regaled with a meal and sake.

Performances by different carpenters vary, as do the offerings and the altar. In some cases the carpenter knocks on the *daikoku bashira,* the main pillar of the house near which the house altar will be placed. Sometimes one mutters a *norito* after bowing. In general, however, the pattern is as described.

The Househead and the Honorable Moon

September 15 is moon-viewing night. The moon is usually full, the weather good, and the *susuki* grass in bloom. Many Yuzawa households prepare a small altar before an open widow or on a porch with offerings to the moon. The altar includes plumes of silvery *susuki* grass, some sort of round seasonal fruit (watermelon is preferred), a sake bottle, and some cups. In many households, the household head performs a ritual before the altar, with members of the family in attendance. The residents of the household kneel facing the full moon and the altar. The head of the house, sitting directly before the altar as the officiant, waits for a moment when the moon is not obscured by clouds. He bows, claps his hands, then bows again, encouraging all those present to do likewise. Sometimes the househead adds a short sentence of greeting such as "Thank you, Honorable Moon, for looking over us and for favors received." Finally, everyone is offered a sip of sake from the bottle on the altar. Not every household performs this ritual, and there is great variation in the altars. Even the ritual formula varies considerably at the discretion of the officiant.

Summary

The three types of rituals—those by *kannushi,* those by carpenters, and those by household heads—display similarities, but it is with their differences that we are concerned here—primarily, the ways in which the ritual differences indicate significant differences between the three types of officiant. Anyone may attend public rituals, which are intended for the benefit of a broad audience of participants, whether they are present in person or through representatives of corporate units of which they are part. This feature characterizes most *kannushi*-run rituals. Other rituals are more private, being limited to the membership of a single unit. This feature characterizes rituals run by household heads and by members of small *ujiko.* Carpenter-run rituals are intermediate. They are for the benefit of one group, the household, but participants include members of another group, the construction workers. A third public is also involved, albeit peripherally, and that is the neighborhood children.

A second point of dissimilarity is in the gradation of elaboration and the amount of rigidity of the rules of procedure. Even simple rituals run by *kannushi* adhere to strict rules of elaboration and performance. Moreover, rituals performed by *kannushi* vary little so long as they are performed for the same type of social group. A *kannushi* performing a given type of ritual for one household will perform the same ritual actions, with little variance, for another; carpenters or househeads, in contrast, may vary their presentations.

Third, the less public a ritual, the greater the differences between performances of one officiant and another. One carpenter may omit the hammering on the pillars. Another may raise the food to his head, but not the tools. Still a third may disagree with the house owner about the proper order of acts in the ritual. There is even greater variation in the domestic moon rituals. Some households do not perform the ritual at all. In others only part of the family gathers for the ritual: perhaps a female member will perform it with the children. The verbal formula varies from household to household, just as it varies from year to year in the same household. There is, in other words, no agreed-on procedure or formula; where a form is fixed, it depends on the inclinations of a member or members of the household.

Fourth, in the household and roof-raising rituals the authority of the officiants usually extends to matters outside the ritual, depending on their other societal roles. In public rituals where the officiant is a ritual expert, authority in nonritual matters is nonexistent.

Kannushi as Ritual Experts

There are basically three types of circumstances in which *kannushi* perform rituals: cyclical events, purifications, and transitions. The annual festival rituals are cyclical events. These, as we have seen, are normally performed at neighborhood or group shrines. Purification rituals are performed as needed, to ensure that no pollution will affect the lives and doings of individuals or groups. New objects—houses before and after construction, taxicabs, equipment—may be purified by rituals specially commissioned by their owners. A *kannushi* may urge the performance of such rituals when he has performed them previously for an individual or group, but the final choice is up to the owner of the object or the sufferer from affliction: in other words, the one benefiting from the performance. Transition rituals include, in addition to rites of passage, rituals that indicate and purify regular changes in patterns of work and life. Birth and marriage are obvious examples of the former. More rare (because they are normally the province of Buddhist priests) are funerals and memorials. Other less obvious occasions include, for example, the start of the logging season at a sawmill and the onset of snow at a city snowplow depot. Some individuals in Yuzawa perform transition rituals of their house once or twice a year, at the ends of winter and summer.

Purification rituals are often private, whereas cyclical rituals are mainly public. Transition rituals may be either public or private, depending on the nature of the group commissioning the ritual, but are usually private. The differences among the three types extend to the elaboration of the performance. Although *kannushi* take as many pains for private as for public rituals, the scale of the performance is in almost direct proportion to the size and economic importance of the group or groups ordering the ritual. A ritual for a single household is small and simple in terms of altar decorations and *tamagushi* offerings, that for a public corporation much larger and more elaborate.

Six *kannushi* regularly perform rituals in Yuzawa. Five are residents of the town; the sixth resides in a nearby community. One of the six, son of the incumbent of Atago-jinja, is employed as a salaried worker and performs only in major festivals or as a replacement for his father. Another limits his performances to rituals in one specific shrine. Four of the six have had academic training, two at Kokugakuin University, the other two at a training institute that was run by the Bureau of Shrines until 1945. These four have certificates attesting to their expertise that are recognized by Jinja Honchō. All the *kannushi*, academically trained or not, have undergone lengthy apprenticeships, usually under a relative—father, uncle, father-in-law.

Practically speaking, the position of a *kannushi* is inherited. The duty to officiate at the rituals of a particular shrine is passed from a man to his heir. The inheritance essentially consists of two elements: the right to officiate at a particular shrine and a set of social relationships with groups who require the *kannushi*'s services. Theoretically, individuals or groups may turn to any *kannushi* to perform rituals for them. In fact, *kannushi* succeeding to an office acquire the previous incumbent's "practice." Long-lasting relationships are formed between a *kannushi* and the members of the shrine he serves. The members in turn feel obligated to have the same individual perform their annual rituals. Some of these relationships persist for generations: one *kannushi* is the seventeenth incumbent of his family to hold office in the same shrine (Yunohara Hitachi Inari-jinja Gojikai n.d., 10). *Kannushi* without a son are likely to secure a successor by adopting a son-in-law. Although there are cases of daughters succeeding to the office of *kannushi* in the Yuzawa area, in Akita, and throughout Japan, there are no such cases in Yuzawa itself.

The most important factor in the *kannushi*'s role is the proper performance of ritual. Ritual actions are prescribed by the complex rules that are a major component of the formal and elaborate behaviors that constitute a ritual. *Kannushi* often volunteered the information that their position is analogous to that of a master of ceremonies. Although not directly one of the interested parties in the intent of the ritual, they must nevertheless ensure that the proper decorum and forms are observed by other participants.[2] The concentration of *kannushi* on ritual affairs, and their lack of interest in doctrine or faith, can be traced to the emergence of national Shinto in the late nineteenth century (Hardacre 1988). Certainly, with one exception, none of the *kannushi* in Yuzawa or its vicinity was in any great measure as concerned with the ideology of Shinto as with the propriety of ritual behavior.

Beyond that basic agreement about the importance of proper performance, *kannushi* give various explanations for their role. One of the
Yuzawa *kannushi* sees no separation between Shinto as a religion and the
Japanese nation. A common response, which was recorded elsewhere as
well as in Yuzawa, is that rituals bring out the *kami* nature in the participants' hearts, and the *kannushi*'s role is to ensure that this outcome is
accomplished according to the most efficacious practice. A third response
sees the *kami* as beings with empirical existence with whom proper social
relationships must be established and maintained. It seems that two
mechanisms are at work here: on the one hand is the *kannushi*'s desire to
ensure that opinions they voice about the *kami* are acceptable to the public with whom they interact. The ideas of Shinto nationalism (the first
response, above) are prevalent, though not dominant, in Japanese society
today. So too is the second response, a "spiritualistic" one that also bears
some relationship to Japanese ideas of purity *(hare)* and pollution
(kegare; see Namahira 1977). The third view, which sees *kami* as actual
entities, is one to which probably all *kannushi* would subscribe *in private*.
Given the tenor of the times in modern Japan, however, this last
response, voiced openly, would be likely to cause Japanese who see themselves as "progressive" and removed from the "superstitions of the past,"
as Hori (1968) calls them, to exclude themselves from ritual. As the *kannushi* well know (as do other ritual specialists, such as Taoist priests; see
Saso 1978), so long as lay people attend and rituals are performed, it does
not matter whether the officiant's and the participants' beliefs coincide.
Notably, whatever explanation is given for performing rituals, anchored
as it is in an individual's perception of ritual and of the *kami,* the major
concern for officiants and participants is the proper and timely performance of the rituals.

Being a *Kannushi*

In addition to their function as ritual performers, *kannushi* also function
as ritual experts. Most of the *kannushi* in Yuzawa are regularly consulted
by people suffering from illness or other afflictions. The truth of Evans-
Pritchard's observations about Azande cosmology (1969) seems to be
borne out here: People are aware of mechanical agents of misfortune,
whether these be viruses and microbes or faulty constructions, but they
are also interested in ultimate causes and in dealing with them, something doctors cannot do. Consultations with *kannushi* therefore usually
deal with persistent illness or physical afflictions or with afflictions that
smack of the supernatural. Killing a snake, the servant of Ryujin the dra-

gon *kami,* or some other accidental pollution is often diagnosed as the cause. Because people are reluctant to admit they have consulted a *kannushi* and the *kannushi* refuse to allow observation or interviews of consultees, the data are far from complete in this regard. It is apparent that the *kannushi* complement the varied and extensive system of divination and shamanism (cf. Blacker 1975) and alternative diagnostic and medical practices (Ohnuki-Tierney 1984) prevalent in Japan today.

Kannushi enjoy no special prestige in following their occupation, nor is it particularly remunerative. Although the advice and comments of *kannushi* about issues relating to ritual are listened to attentively, this authority in ritual matters does not carry over to nonritual matters. *Kannushi* obviously derive a great deal of emotional and ideological satisfaction from their position and from promoting and exercising their religious beliefs. The financial issue does, however, point to some important realities in Yuzawa's festivals.

At the end of every ritual a *kannushi* is handed an envelope with "car fare." The sum enclosed will range from a low of about 3,000 yen (for performing at a small neighborhood shrine) to a high of about 10,000 yen. The more elaborate a ritual, the higher is the sum, but with the exception of performing weddings, where a *kannushi* may be paid even more than 10,000 yen, the higher sum is rare; even at larger rituals the sum rarely exceeds 5,000 yen. Whatever the sum, it is not a fee—the *kannushi* does not charge for his services—but a donation from the group that has requested the ritual. The sum usually correlates with the importance of the ritual and the size and wealth of the group concerned. *Kannushi* perform between one hundred and three hundred rituals a year, earning about 500,000 yen to 1,500,000 yen annually from their activities. One *kannushi* admitted to making about 3,000,000 yen, but he is an exception, devoting most of his time to performing and encouraging the performance of rituals. Only two of Yuzawa's *kannushi* have endowments *(shinden).* For one of them the *shinden* provides for a modest salary and the use of a house. For the other, who is the incumbent of a smaller shrine, the endowment provides only for the use of a house. Of Yuzawa's six *kannushi,* only two support themselves solely through their work as ritual specialists. Three of the other four work at professional (salaried) jobs. The last is a farmer and craftsman.

The full-time *kannushi* and their activities point to major changes that have occurred in the position of shrine officiant in Japan (see also Hagiwara 1963), changes that reflect changes in community and social life.

Increasing specialization of *kannushi* was a product of the increased governmental influence on religious affairs during the Edo period. With the establishment in 1665 of the Yoshida School as the officially sanctioned form of Shinto ritual, the process of professionalization began. It was accelerated with the Shinto law of 1871, which disinherited priestly families, turning shrines into public corporations. This was followed by examinations for priests (1872) and the separation of Shinto and Buddhist priests a year later. By the Showa era, *kannushi* were expected to be full-time professionals. In reality, evidence from rural areas (e.g., Bernier 1975; Embree 1939) indicates that many *kannushi* still supported themselves as farmers and craftsmen, notwithstanding the governmental edicts.

The present *kannushi* of Atago-jinja represents the Meiji Restoration ideal. He is a highly trained individual, supported solely by a grant that maintains him and the shrine. He is engaged fully as a priest and consultant on ritual matters. The other full-time priest in Yuzawa represents a modern adaptation to an older pattern. Not supported by a *shinden*, he has no regular income and supports himself by actively promoting rituals and searching out opportunities for performing them. He approaches to a degree the position of "missionary" that Hagiwara (1963) assigns to Buddhist clergy in contradistinction to Shinto priests. This particular *kannushi* actively promotes the performance of rituals in places or institutions where they have not been performed before or where they have been abandoned. He has also been instrumental in the creation of two new shrines, offering objects to serve as *shintai* and purifying and servicing the shrines. He makes himself available for consultations on matters pertaining to rituals, as do all *kannushi*, but he also solicits consultations about problems such as afflictions, ritual purity, and so on. He has acquired a small car, thereby extending his range far beyond Yuzawa.

As can be seen, a variety of strategies is available to *kannushi* in pursuing their profession. The differences among them can be accounted for by differences in temperament and conviction and by differences in specific economic circumstances. In turn, the differences also affect the relationship of the *kannushi* to the corporations for whom rituals are performed. A less well trained individual or one dependent on a specific group for economic support is likely to be vulnerable to his patrons' specific demands. The incumbent of an endowed position such as Atago-jinja, who is not dependent on any powerful corporation, is much less vulnerable to the whims of his benefactors.

The Network of Experts

As a general rule the fifty-odd neighborhood-association and ritual-association shrines in Yuzawa are each served by a *kannushi* family and have been for generations. However, differences in the circumstances of particular *kannushi* affect this reality. One *kannushi,* who lacks formal training and is, in any case, a full-time salaried employee, performs rituals only at the shrine his family has served for generations. He himself succeeded to the position by default, after the death of a relative. Other *kannushi* operate within a given range, performing as the main officiant at shrines with which they have long-term arrangements, occasionally assisting outside their area at elaborate rituals that require more priests. The *kannushi* officiating at Atago-jinja's main rituals, for instance, include priests from a number of shrines outside Yuzawa.

Festival rituals require greater elaboration than do other rituals for reasons already discussed. Such elaborate rituals—Atago-jinja's main festival is the most prominent example in Yuzawa—require larger numbers of *kannushi* to cooperate in the performance. The greater number of officiants is both a signifier of greater elaboration and a function of it. We have seen how all the actions in a shrine ritual can be performed by a single individual. Dividing the officiant's role among a number of performers demonstrates greater investment of resources. Within Yuzawa and its immediately contiguous areas, therefore, most *kannushi* can expect to perform in concert with their professional colleagues in a number of instances in any given year as each shrine association tries to keep up with (or outperform) its neighbors. In these elaborated rituals, *kannushi* may perform different roles. The *guji* of a shrine will perform as main officiant in the rituals of his own shrine, demonstrating his position by his dress and the part he plays, while in the main ritual of another's shrine he may play a more modest position and dress in regular *kariginu.*

Kannushi also may substitute for others either temporarily or permanently. The current officiant of Mitake-jinja has accepted the position in lieu of the original incumbent, who finds the climb difficult because of his age. A *kannushi* who is ill or away on business or otherwise unable to attend a ritual will find a substitute, usually from among those *kannushi* he knows and has performed with in Yuzawa.

Outside Yuzawa, Yuzawa *kannushi* have fewer long-term relationships to shrines. Villages close to Yuzawa are likely to have a Yuzawa *kannushi* as one of their officiants in a major ritual, but the further away, particularly in the major ritual of some major shrine, the fewer the opportunities for a Yuzawa *kannushi* to participate. The borderline where a Yuzawa *kannushi* will be found as a sole officiant seems to be about three to five kilometers around Yuzawa, although some do carry their activities farther afield. The range of participation in joint elaborate rituals is about twice that and includes most of the small towns around Yuzawa and in neighboring administrative units. The difference is presumably due to the scarcity of large shrines with elaborate rituals that need several *kannushi* and the small number of *kannushi* who can perform in them.

The overlapping of ranges creates a network of ties among *kannushi*. This social and professional network is a major determinant of the form rituals take. Governmental attempts to fix the liturgical order of shrine rituals are a relatively recent phenomenon. In the seventeenth century, the Yoshida priestly family, encouraged by the *bakufu* (the premodern military government), attempted to standardize shrine rituals. Nonetheless, a great deal of variation in ritual forms in shrines persisted. Conformity was imposed in earnest beginning about 1902 (Fridell 1973, 13–14), notwithstanding a stream of government directives that started in 1871. Local ritual variations survived, however, and still exist, protected today by other government directives, the Occupation authorities' Shinto directive of 1945 and later, the Japanese constitution. Although the minutiae of rituals observed at places distant from Yuzawa vary in many details, there is a general similarity. The differences among rituals in different areas are explained by local preferences and history: Japanese communities have traditionally guarded and maintained their own local traditions, both religious and otherwise. The similarities among rituals derive partly from shared cultural history throughout Japan. More important for the general uniformity of ritual practice, however, is the web of relationships between *kannushi,* which extends beyond their immediate areas of operation.

Yuzawa *kannushi* have trained and participated in seminars elsewhere and have even, in exceptional cases, taken part in rituals in such places as Tokyo or Akita City. They are therefore aware of and to some degree conform to the expectations of their peers elsewhere. This tendency toward such conformity is reinforced by Jinja Honchō, which makes conscious efforts to promote uniformity in shrine rituals. Not surprisingly, however, there is a greater degree of uniformity within a "local network" area, such as Yuzawa, where the *kannushi* interact with one another frequently and where individuals participate in the rituals of more than one *kannushi* in the network. Furthermore, within Yuzawa the performance of individual *kannushi* is judged against the performance of other officiants.

At this point, local preferences generally prevail over some abstract "national norm." A *kannushi* who has performed for a given corporate group for a number of years is therefore likely to conform to that group's particular expectations, even though he may conform to the demands of his professional peers when performing with them. When acting as a replacement for one of his peers, a *kannushi*, unaware that there are special performative preferences in the shrine at which he is officiating, may decide to satisfy himself. The generation of a particular ritual form is not uniform, and the variation is dynamic, albeit within certain generally accepted limits. On the whole, the more powerful the social or economic position of the group commissioning a ritual, and the less determined a *kannushi* is to adhere to some other standard, the more the commissioning group can insist on certain standards in the performance. Wealthy individual contributors or sponsors of ritual events can be observed insisting on some specific ritual act in preference to another, with the *kannushi* conforming, sometimes against his own preference. *Kannushi* continuing a relationship going back years or even generations with a particular group of participants are in a different position. In those groups such as neighborhoods, where the participants at a ritual change from one year to another, the participants are often unsure of themselves. Having participated in few rituals throughout their lifetimes, they are in a poor position to criticize the officiant's performance. At most, the members have some general and vague expectations about the *kannushi*'s performance. Members of ritual associations, such as *kōjū*, who may participate in a given ritual year after year, have a position closer to that of individual wealthy sponsors. They are familiar with ritual performance and consequently often have precise expectations of their officiant. In some cases observed, *kōjū* members even overruled a *kannushi* who attempted to alter the order of ritual, the form or quantity of the offering, or some other detail.

The more experience and training an officiant has, the more he is able to fulfill performative expectations and adhere to the complex behavioral rules governing elaborate rituals. This situation has two implications. First, we are likely to find only formally qualified individuals participating in elaborate rituals that require a number of officiants. That is, *kannushi* who have little training or experience are not likely to be found running major rituals on their own, nor are they likely to be members of a team of officiants in a major ritual such as Atago-jinja's main festival.

The other implication brings us back to the other types of officiant described at the beginning of this chapter: carpenters and household heads. In terms of Shinto ideology, any sufficiently pure individual may perform a ritual. In practice, however, the issue of performative competence, or lack of it, is a prime determinant. Carpenters and household heads, or other untrained individuals, lack the performative skills to perform in public rituals. The average individual does not see many roof-raising rituals and is therefore unable to pass learned judgment on the competence of the performance. Individuals who are having a building constructed (and are therefore in a position to commission a *mune age*) rarely do so more than once or twice in their lifetimes. They therefore cannot criticize the officiant's performance from the same position as a member of a *kōjū*, who has seen a given ritual many times. The other participants at a *mune age* are usually carpenters who work with or under the authority of the officiant, who is usually the head carpenter. They often work with him for many years and have become accustomed to his style of performing the ritual. Even if they were inclined to suggest changes or offer criticisms, they would be unlikely to do so, given their subordinate and junior position; instead, they are likely to accept the performance as is, whether it adheres to or departs from some familiar norm. The same is true for a household head: his authority in domestic matters is probably accepted without question in this area as in others. Family or household members are also unlikely to participate in the household rituals of others (the exception being brides, who are expected to quickly adjust to their new household's way of doing things). We can therefore expect to see, and indeed do see, great variation among the rituals of individual households.

In sum, we find that the role of the *kannushi* in shrine rituals and in festivals is tied to a number of factors. It depends to a degree on the *kannushi*'s training, which also affects his relationship with the network of his peers. The network reinforces certain tendencies in performance and keeps some degree of uniformity within a given geographical area where *kannushi* share their activities. From another point of view, *kannushi* are performers, subject to the criticism and observation of their audiences. The structure of the relationship among shrines, their support groups, and their officiants is such that a dynamic balance exists, exerting different pressures in each particular case. Finally, the *kannushi* themselves have much invested emotionally and ideologically in their own performances and beliefs. They act as individuals and make ritual decisions based on their experience, their training, their social position in the community, and other personal factors.

8

The Festival System

I HAVE CONCENTRATED up to this point on analyzing the separate components that go toward creating a *matsuri*. Throughout I have made reference to the idea that *matsuri* are part of a complex, interactive web of events and relationships. I want now to present this relationship in context and to focus on the articulation and mutual effects of *matsuri* and not just their internal components.

All of Yuzawa's *matsuri* are interconnected by common elements. The same individuals—as officiants, as managers, as participants, or as audiences—act in many *matsuri*. The people managing one *matsuri* may well be involved, perhaps in another role, in another one. The audiences, those that participate in rituals as well as those that come to enjoy a *matsuri*'s festivities, are drawn from the same population pool, in this case, the residents of Yuzawa.

Directly related to, and partly as a consequence of, these commonalities, Yuzawa rituals, parades, and festivities bear a great similarity to one another. I have also noted in passing how they differ from similar events outside Yuzawa. This complex of *matsuri* and associated behavior within a given area constitutes a *festival system,* that is, a set of interrelated festival practices in a given territory, sharing a population base, that influence one another to a greater degree than they are influenced by practices outside the system.

The idea that festivals in a local area are related in a systematic way helps explain two apparently contradictory factors. First, it helps explain change in (some or all of) the festivals of the system. It is not only that similar factors are assumed to be operating on festivals within the festival system. More significantly, the systematic relationship among the festivals in the system means that actual relationships among festivals serve as channels along which changes and information propagate. Second, we have seen in the case of Yuzawa that a large set of behaviors and festival

124

elements have been retained (in the eyes of their performers, retained unchanged). Other behaviors have been revived or revitalized once pressures that caused their suspension were removed. This too has happened within the boundaries of a particular system. Paradoxically, the same factors and systemic relationships that transmit change can also ensure continuity.

It must be clear from the outset that the boundaries of a festival system are permeable. They allow change, though often in a determined and controlled fashion. These boundaries may be the consequence of factors embedded in the particular culture the system is part of. They may also be maintained consciously by the participants in the system, who are surprised, and often pleased, at what they perceive as their own uniqueness. The boundaries of this "consciousness of uniqueness" coincide with those of the festival system and are just as elusive. We turn therefore to an attempt to identify the operation and characteristics of Yuzawa's festival system and to the effects—the change and continuity—that it engenders. In order to discuss the festival system in a useful manner, it is necessary to examine first the perceived similarities between Yuzawa's *matsuri* and those outside it and then their differences. It will also prove useful to see how the population involved acts in these events. Finally, we will see how change and continuity are propagated and maintained through the channels created by people participating in the events.

The Systematic Relationship of Yuzawa's *Matsuri*

A festival system generates a feeling of uniqueness among participants. The differences in style between one festival system and another reinforce this feeling. The system's unity is maintained by a set of social forms and practices and a set of commonly used cultural idioms. Performances within a festival system share in those cultural idioms. Items and acts of display, the use of particular symbols and meaningful events, and officiants' performances have local referents.

The three major festivals make up a central pillar in the concept Yuzawa has of itself as a unit. These three festivals affect a large segment of Yuzawa's population, and they also influence the performance of other festivals in Yuzawa. Of the series of annual *matsuri* that comprise Yuzawa's festival system, these three involve the whole town or significant portions of it. The Daimyō Gyōretsu parade with its elaborate festivities and the Inukko and Tanabata festivals differ from others in scale. More p

ple, including tourists, participate in them, and more money is expended on them. They are advertised outside Yuzawa and mentioned in several national guidebooks.

Several *jinja* in Yuzawa in addition to Atago-jinja—including Yuno-hara Hitachi Inari-jinja (Maemori-chō), Mitake-jinja (Yanagi-machi), Yuzawa Shoichi Inari-jinja (Ura-machi), Shimizu-jinja (Minamishin-machi), Okachimachi Inari-jinja (Okachi-machi), and Oji Inari-jinja (Uchidate-chō)—have more than one festival during the year. Not incidentally, all of them are currently neighborhood *jinja*.

Other *jinja* in Yuzawa have a single *matsuri* during the year. Most of these *matsuri* consist of little more than a ritual performed in or before the shrine. These include neighborhood *jinja*, *ujiko jinja*, *kōjū jinja*, and single-family *ujigami*. Many of these small shrines, particularly the family *ujigami*, are in private yards and therefore not easily accessible to the outside observer. There are at least a hundred such small shrines in Yuzawa, most of them no larger than one meter to a side. It proved impossible to attend all their rituals or even, in many cases, discover the identity of the owners. The *matsuri* of neighborhood shrines are generally accompanied by festivities of some sort though generally on a very small scale. These small-scale festivities usually include the distribution of sparklers or gifts to the owning group's children.

Anyone who attends a variety of rituals in Yuzawa can expect to see the same officiant running a number of them. The quirks and idiosyncrasies of Yuzawa's small group of *kannushi*—five men in all—become associated with the "proper" way to run rituals. In Yuzawa, for example, *sakaki* is always used for *tamagushi*. In areas near Yuzawa other evergreens are sometimes substituted. In areas near Yuzawa *kannushi* sometimes wear white robes, which Yuzawa *kannushi* wear only in mortuary rituals. Small continuing differences reinforce the perceived uniqueness of Yuzawa. Since possible participants in a Yuzawa *matsuri* ritual are almost exclusively limited to Yuzawans and since participation in festival rituals corresponds largely to the management of festivals, certain forms of rituals and festivities become recognized by the participants themselves as being significantly and specially Yuzawan. This perception adds to the felt but not always expressed distinction Yuzawa residents make between "our Yuzawa *matsuri*" and other *matsuri*. Those other *matsuri* are often very similar to Yuzawa's, but few Yuzawans attend them (unless they are particularly famous *matsuri*) and no one in Yuzawa is part of their management.

Shared Cultural Idioms in the Festival System

The presence of a shared set of recognizable cultural idioms in the system's festivals additionally characterizes a festival system. Yuzawa residents explicitly recognize such common idioms as "Yuzawa no doku-toku-na mono"—Yuzawa's local specialties—which include festival activities and artifacts as well as items of daily use. One distinctive local specialty is the Tanabata *edoro* lanterns: rectangular frames fitted with a light source, covered with painted pictures. The themes of the pictures are not particularly "Yuzawan" but are copies of *bijin-ga*[1] and other classical Japanese painting. In recent years *edoro* have appeared at other Yuzawa festivals. Children are encouraged to make and paint *edoro* lanterns at the festivals of Kumano-jinja, Okachimachi-jinja, Shinmeisha (in Daiku-machi), and Kanaike-jinja. These lanterns are not used in areas adjacent to Yuzawa.

Festival-goers in Yuzawa share a set of cultural idioms sufficient to create a feeling of difference from other areas without creating a feeling of separation. In Yuzawa, *hairei* performers often offer a handful of rice and a coin in a twist of white paper. *Hairei* is also performed in Tokyo, but without the rice and coins in paper. Even though particular idioms do occur elsewhere (e.g., the paper twists are also used in Kyoto), they are sufficiently distinctive so that Yuzawa residents can ignore other examples throughout Japan and claim the custom as indicative of their own uniqueness. Idioms spread within a festival system more easily than they do outside it because those in a system already share many idioms and social ties. Festivity and ritual forms unique to a single festival within the system may be dropped in favor of more common ones. Exposure to possibilities and pressures from two systems, national and local, lead specific idioms to be adopted. The pressures from each system are not equal. The national system has more power, is more persuasive and pervasive, and has more means, such as the educational system, to serve it. Aided by the national communications media and the ease of travel, the use of *mikoshi* spreads from the metropolis. A local festival system, however, such as that of Yuzawa, has the advantage of immediacy. People who know one another can influence the choice of festival idioms by personal pressure, by example, and by approval or disapproval of others' choices. Neighborhoods therefore adopt particular festival elements, retain them, or change them according to a complex interplay of factors that differ from one neighborhood to another. Individual and organizational factors such as who is interested, who has influence, who has seen a particularly fine *mikoshi* or Ebisu *dawara*, as well as money and the media affect the process.

The Festival System and Social Ties

An identifiable population is the basis of any festival system. Individuals in the system have ties to various festivals in which they may have different roles. Individuals and groups within the system interact more with one another in the context of festivals than they do with those outside that system and are therefore more familiar with that system's idioms and usages than with another's. This is true of participants whether they are laypersons or festival experts.

Included in a given system's population is a set of interrelated social units—corporations—that organize and manage the festivals. These management corporate groups are related because many individuals belong to more than one group. Festival management and organizing groups often have similar internal structures. Even where internal structures differ in detail, they are based on common cultural practices and shared cultural idioms that are at least familiar and comprehensible to the relevant population. At the same time, there is group autonomy to the extent that similar groups may know little about one another's internal workings. Maemori-chō *wakamono-kai* members, for example, were surprised to hear that Fuppari-chō *wakamono-kai* members did not retire at forty-two.

Festivals are commonplace in Yuzawa, especially during late summer. Individuals often participate in more than one during the year, often in different capacities. The town is small enough so that festival markers such as festival music, sound bombs, Ebisu *dawara* parades, flag-bedecked shrines, and colored lanterns can be seen or heard even by those not directly involved in the proceedings. An example of multiple participation in festivals is furnished by Sakai Ichiro, a member of one of the *wakamono-kai* that run the Daimyō Gyōretsu. During the Daimyō Gyōretsu in 1981, he was present at the ritual at Atago-jinja and later accompanied the *mikoshi* in the parade as one of the *mikoshi* guardians. He offered *tamagushi* at his neighborhood shrine twice during the year in his capacity as representative of his neighborhood's *wakamono-kai*. He and some friends visited the midsummer Yunohara *jinja* festivities, where they drank beer "and just had a good time."

Sakai works in a large shop on Yuzawa's main street. During Inukko *matsuri* he was one of the team that constructed the shop's entry in the Inukko concourse. China was in style that year, because of political and diplomatic events, and the team had created a large five-storied Chinese-style pagoda. For Tanabata he helped make paper decorations and later set up a Tanabata lantern and decorated bamboo stem before his shop. He also went to perform *hairei* during the festivals of the shrines of two adjacent neighborhoods.

Sakai's festival-related behavior is not unusual; many people do something similar during the year. His reasons for attending any particular *matsuri* differ. For example, he went to visit the beer garden that was part of the Yunohara-chō *matsuri* festivities with a group of friends on a warm summer night. He professes no particular interest in festivals and said that he went to the Yunohara-chō festival simply to have a good time. He performed *hairei* at one *jinja* because it was required of him as a member of the Daimyō Gyōretsu team. The *wakamono-kai* of the *jinja* in question was to run the Daimyō Gyōretsu the following year. He performed *hairei* at the *jinja* of a neighborhood that borders his own when they had their festival "to maintain smooth relations" and "show that one cares."

Similar personal associations with a large number of *matsuri* underlie a festival system. A majority of the people who participate in a system's festivals are from the same limited population because they have the greatest opportunities and motives for participating in them.

The actual management of a festival is confined to members of the system's population. Management of a major festival such as the Daimyō Gyōretsu connects whole webs of relationships among *matsuri* in the Yuzawa festival system. Moreover, the Daimyō Gyōretsu serves as a focus for the activities of even those groups not involved in its management. Managing the Daimyō Gyōretsu involves a long series of interactions and exchanges, and so the Daimyō Gyōretsu touches the majority of Yuzawans in some way, even if only peripherally. For those individuals involved in managing and preparing it, the Daimyō Gyōretsu becomes a major preoccupation for at least a year. The postfestival assessment meetings and rituals that accompany the year's management of the Daimyō Gyōretsu reinforce the social ties that bind the festival system. The same individuals who run the Daimyō Gyōretsu also attend and run other festivals during the year. As residents of Yuzawa they can be expected to attend still more such events during their lifetimes.

Kannushi are an important element in the web of personal relations that define the system. The relationship among these ritual experts was explored in an earlier chapter. Here we take up another aspect of the *kannushi*'s social world. Through social relationships to a few individuals in the community, a single *kannushi* influences a great many others. The relationships and influence of Hirano Saburo illustrate this point. Hirano inherited the position of *kannushi* from his father and was trained before the war at a *kannushi* institute in Sendai. Sons do not always agree to succeed to their father's office, and Hirano, less fortunate than his father, has not been able to interest his own son in succeeding him. If he insists on passing on his occupation to an heir, he will have to adopt a bridegroom *(muko yōshi)* for his daughter. Hirano is the sole officiant at eight shrines and assists with other *kannushi* at Atago-jinja's rituals. He also performs at weddings, house raisings, ritual cleansings, and house purifications. Because Hirano has a full-time job—he heads a quasi-governmental office in town—he performs as an officiant only in Yuzawa.

Among other places, Hirano performs at Kumano-jinja, the *chōnai-jinja* of a smallish neighborhood, which has only one festival per year. The *jinja* is maintained by the *chōnai-kaichō* who lives just in front of it. Since there are few children in the neighborhood and many elderly couples, the *chōnai-kaichō* says there is not much interest in a boisterous festival, and therefore the festivities are subdued. The *tōban* distribute fireworks to the children, and Tanabata-style lanterns the children have made are hung near the shrine. As at all festivals, a hired fireworks-maker sets off several sound bombs before and after the two rituals. Hirano arrives several minutes before the ritual on the first day of the festival. He puts on his vestments and prepares the *tamagushi*. After the ritual he quickly changes his clothes and says goodbye, since he has another ritual to perform the same day.

In Mitake-jinja, where Hirano also serves, the situation is different. The ritual takes place on a late summer afternoon after work, atop Mount Mitake. Hirano arrives after finishing work at his office. He joins the talk in the small shack where the *wakamono* put up for the night. After he performs the ritual he joins the participants and shares the feast they have brought. After several hours of *naorai* he descends the mountain.

Hirano's ritual-based "network" consists of relationships he has formed at the shrines where he officiates and at the nonshrine rituals he performs. An average of five participants are present at each ritual he performs, some of whom are present every year. They, in turn, see the performances of other *kannushi* or are at least aware of them as they themselves participate in various events throughout the system.

The officiant's position is authoritative in the narrow sphere of ritual. Hirano and other *kannushi* are main sources of reference within the festival system for one important component of festivals, their rituals. *Kannushi* maintain long relationships with a shrine and generally know who are interested in preserving the ritual. *Kannushi* interact in their duties within the system more than outside it, and they influence both participants and one another, since they perform together at some rituals. While all of them have experience in performing rituals outside Yuzawa, most of their experience is within it and is colored by the Yuzawa way of doing things. They therefore perform more like one another than like officiants outside the system. Officiants directly or indirectly communicate to a significant segment of the festival system's population the behaviors that are fit or unfit for ritual. Similar performances by different *kannushi* within the system affect both changes in and the retention of older forms and ritual usage. Old forms are maintained because participants are used to them and because officiants reinforce one another's ritual behaviors. New forms may be accepted when the ritual experts reach some consensus about them and when they start performing them as regular features in the system's rituals.

Change within the Festival System

Changes in a festival may involve changes in the performance of its rituals, in its organization or management, or in the type and scope of its festivities. Changes in a festival system involve aggregate changes in the festivals that make up the system or additions and deletions of those festivals. A fundamental characteristic of festival systems is that, changes in the individual festivals notwithstanding, the festival system itself has great durability. This is true even when individual festivals in the system disappear completely, as has happened a number of times in Yuzawa. In Shin-machi, for instance, nothing is left of the festival except a poorly attended ritual. This attrition is partly balanced by the creation of new festivals. The Shinmeisha *matsuri* of Uramon-machi, a new neighborhood, is an example. Major changes can therefore take place within the system without affecting the system's continuity or boundaries.

Changes in festivities often result from the introduction of a new possibility or opportunity. The presence of the same individuals in several festivals induces and reinforces these changes. Individuals might feel it desirable to introduce successful innovations experienced elsewhere to their own festivals. Festivity events that appeal to contemporary taste obviously have a greater chance of continuing than those that do not. For example, as the once-popular puppet shows lost their charm, the two festivals in Yuzawa that featured the shows lost much of their festivity as well. Other factors also affect the retention of a festival. Of the two festivals that had puppet shows, one revived when alternate festivity events were introduced because the neighborhood that ran the festival remained a social unit. The other festival's festivities disappeared almost completely because, as the head of the *kōjū* said, "People who used to come from all around to enjoy the show and the fireworks lost interest [in the traditional puppet plays] and therefore we could not support anything elaborate [because of the reduced donations], and even fewer people came." The gradual decline of the neighborhood's population is not mentioned but is definitely also a factor.

Demographic changes—in the age of the population, economic base, number of residents—affect the forms of festivity as well. Uwa-machi was settled by the personal samurai[2] of the local *daimyō*. During the festival of Atago-jinja the residents of the neighborhood would construct large papier maché goblins and demons that were animated in some fashion, presumably by strings. The puppets were used to "teach the samurai children the virtues of courage and fearlessness." The custom was abandoned in the beginning of the present century when many *bushi* families, who had lost their prestige and incomes, left the neighborhood. There is no great interest in renewing the custom in Uwa-machi partly because the rationale for it has disappeared and partly because there is no real record describing the details of the custom.

Individual tastes, too, can affect festivity forms. The area in front of Kumano-jinja in Aramachi used to be a sumo wrestling ring. A yearly competition was held on the festival day, supported by a local sumo fan who offered small prizes. Since that individual has moved away from the neighborhood, however, the tournament has been canceled and the ring has made way for a playground.

Festivities are particularly vulnerable to changes in taste and fashion because they are spectator and participant oriented. What is attractive to one group in one locality often becomes attractive to others of the same bent elsewhere. Change spreads from one festival to another within the system. Yunohara-chō adopted a *mikoshi* for the neighborhood's children, for example, because the children had seen *mikoshi* on television and had demanded the same. Other neighborhoods adopted Ebisu *dawara* after seeing how successful they were elsewhere in Yuzawa. The festival system roughly defines the limit of such transfers because the audience of the neighborhood *matsuri* is by and large limited to the population of the system.

Neighborhoods fulfill few major functions in modern Japan, especially compared to work, and sometimes have no major interest in preserving specific neighborhood customs as markers. In the Edo period matters of wealth, occupation, and law separated neighborhoods. Merchants, craftsmen, and soldier-administrators of various crafts and occupations were restricted to separate neighborhoods. Only traces of these differences remain today. Most public services originate from a higher administrative level than the *chō* and most duties—to school, to work, to the authorities —are to higher administrative levels too. Neighborhoods have much less importance today than they did when residents had only their neighbors to rely on. Since the traditional social differences no longer obtain, it is only if there is an individual (such as the sumo enthusiast in Aramachi) or a group (such as the PTA/*wakamono-kai* in Okachi-machi who revived Ebisu *dawara*) interested in some traditional festivity form or in strengthening neighborhood localism that specific local festivities are initiated or reestablished.

At the city level, local merchants and the municipality have an interest in preserving local practices. The Yuzawa festival system's unity is encouraged by local firms, who use local festivals in their attempts to ward off metropolitan economic pressure. While this is not the sole factor in the system's maintenance, the financial backing of such firms enables festivals to be as elaborate as they are.

The grip of Tokyo on the political and cultural life of the nation has been progressively tightened since mid-Meiji by the emergence of modern factors, most notably compulsory state-controlled primary education, mass communications, and the cartelization of the modern economy. All these trends have encouraged the centralization of cultural life (H. D. W. Smith 1973, 369). Festival systems might be said to play a part in the local counterattack against this "tyranny" because they emphasize the unique aspects of the local system. *Matsuri* themselves are one of the last culturally legitimate bastions of localism left. Language, food, dress, housing are gradually becoming homogenized, differing little from Tokyo to Yuzawa. By contrast, in the festival system, change can be controlled to some degree. True, festivals are penetrated by influences from metropolitan culture, but these influences are allowed in those areas considered less important. That many of the old customs of Yuzawa, such as the Daimyō Gyōretsu itself, are actually historical imports is conveniently ignored by most. Children request *mikoshi* and receive them in Kanaike since, at the neighborhood level, it is unimportant whether the focus of community activity, a parade, has the added garnish of being a specifically local item such as an Ebisu *dawara*. At the city level, metropolitan idioms are adopted but not in crucial parts of the festival. The body of the lord's parade is kept as fixed as possible, for example, but the tail can import an Edo *mikoshi* or a foreign anthropologist.

The boundaries of a festival system are not impermeable. They are at best a barrier that must be supported by other effects. For some, the differences in festival practice between Yuzawa and other areas are not important; for others they are. Change occurs as interested parties decide, on an ongoing, changing basis, what can or cannot be adopted. To see how this principle works, we can examine changes in the three critical areas of festival performance: ritual, festivities, and organization.

Changes in Rituals

Japanese governments have historically tried to regulate rituals and other aspects of religion. From the beginning of the Meiji era (1868–1912) to the end of World War II, the government issued rules on the order and elaboration of rituals. It is specious to search for the "pure" and original Shinto or other type of ritual, as many Japanese ethnologists such as Yanagida (1946, 1962, 1970) have. "There is the mistake of claiming to understand Shinto by discovering the 'original form' of Shinto in the hereditary worship of an isolated hamlet in the mountains or along the sea shore" (Ishida 1968, 110). Ishida's reference to Yanagida and Origuchi seems clear.[3] In reality, as R. J. Smith (1974, 213) has noted, "all the faiths blended into popular Japanese religion today have at one time or another been promoted, downgraded, or suppressed by the state." In the case of Shinto, this has meant that great efforts were made to standardize rituals and to force people to comply with government-generated rules. As result of this government intervention, which lasted until 1945, there is a basic similarity among all Shinto rituals.

Changes in rituals tend to be minimal within a festival system for yet another reason, the conservativism of those responsible for and most interested in ritual, both lay people and experts. The *kannushi*, as a ritual expert, has the most invested in the form of the ritual, since that is his stock-in-trade. He is therefore most insistent on doing things his own way. It must also be recalled that most Yuzawa *kannushi* were trained before 1945 and therefore have similar positions on many issues of ritual. *Kannushi* occasionally do introduce innovations, but these are generally in peripheral matters and in conformance with their feelings about the proper form of rituals they perform.

Specific changes within rituals stem from the interaction between the two major ritual roles of officiant and participants. The *kannushi* has a particular training, a specific world view derived from that training, and a distinct commitment to presenting this world view. Because of this training and its effects, officiants tend to maintain rituals in the form they have been taught. The reaction of participants is mixed. Some, used to a certain ritual style, insist that only this style is acceptable. Others—particularly those who change from year to year—are more open to change. For example, one Yuzawa *kannushi* insisted on rearranging an altar and performing music before a ritual he performed as a substitute for another *kannushi*. The *tōban* of that shrine had organized a ritual only once before, and they were in no position to argue when he stated, "I realize your regular officiant does things in another way but I do them my way; please forgive me." The same man also attempted to introduce multicolored (red-green-white) *gohei* instead of the regular white ones. Red and green are used in combination with white in many places, but not in Yuzawa. "These colors are pleasing to the *kami*," the *kannushi* said, and they are also related to the three national treasures: mirror (white), sword (red), and jewels (green). Moreover, said the *kannushi*, the multicolored *gohei* were *"kirei"* (pretty). Some of these innovations were accepted. In other shrines, where the *tōban* were more confident and where opposition developed, they were refused.

Participants who are present year after year are more likely to have fixed notions about ritual behavior. Thus, the powerful head of one *jinja*'s *ujiko sōdai* prompted the *kannushi* during rituals, telling him where to sit and when to start sections of the ritual. In another, where the *ujiko sōdai* is less powerful but still intact, the *ujiko sōdai* head insisted on delaying a festival ritual until new candles were provided. The regular officiant, who obviously did not consider this an important point, waited patiently for new candles to be brought.

In contrast, individuals who attend a ritual for the first or only time in their lives (and this is common for most participants) rarely have any say in the performance. Since a ritual must be a proper performance, the expert in propriety, the officiant, must be relied on. A couple who had bought a house rebuilt the old *ujigami* shrine on the premises. They were not related to the previous owners, but, as they explained, they had been urged to rebuild the shrine because it was the proper thing to do. Once the small structure had been erected, the *kannushi* arranged all the details of the ritual. He told the owners what to do in preparation, what materials to obtain, where to stand and when to bow during the ritual; and, of course, he performed the purification and installation rituals for the new shrine according to his standards. The couple did not know the correct forms of behavior, though they knew there *were* correct forms. The officiant in this instance had free rein to run the ritual as he saw fit, so long as the ritual fit the couple's idiomatic understanding of proper politeness and deference behavior.

Changes within rituals are therefore the sum of influences brought by officiant and participants. The duration of their relationship, how far it extends outside the ritual, the different personalities involved, and the specific ritual point at issue all affect the outcome. Generally, the longer and stronger the relationship, the more the participants are able to influence the officiant, whether toward change or toward retention of forms. The more central the issue is for the officiant, the more he tries to control changes.

The ability of participants to dictate changes in a part of the ritual is particularly strong in the order of offering *tamagushi*. *Tamagushi hoten* reflects the social arrangements of the shrine's support system. The order of offering is a public declaration of relationships with a shrine and its festival. A lesser or greater ability to financially support a shrine or to run its festival is reflected in the order of offering. Large contributors are pressed to offer *tamagushi* first. Such was the case in an *ujiko jinja* in the center of Yuzawa where a wealthy *ujiko* member paid for the reconstruction of the shrine building. During that year's ritual, the steward of the shrine and hereditary *ujiko* head insisted that the wealthy contributor offer *tamagushi* first. In another shrine, the representatives of the corporate units running the shrine deferred to one another for a while before they finally settled on offering one *tamagushi* for both groups. In Atago-jinja, the *jigannushi* who are the shrine's *ujiko* do not make a major managerial or financial contribution to the festival. Their right to offer is residual, and therefore they offer last.

The relationship with a shrine as well as with a festival is transferable. The most prominent case is the transfer of the Daimyō Gyōretsu from its erstwhile performer, the *daimyō*, to the town's *chōnin*. Aramachi illustrates another case. The land on which Aramachi's Kumano-jinja stands is owned by a wealthy resident of another neighborhood. The *shintai* of the *jinja* was transferred to the neighborhood association by the previous owners when they could no longer maintain the shrine. The *jinja* is small and the festival not elaborate. Four *tamagushi* are made available for offering. Only two are actually offered, by the *tōban-chō* and the priest. The ones prepared for the *ujiko* family and the landowner are not used because they do not care to exercise their right, although nominally they are part of the *jinja*'s support group. As we saw in the case of Mitake-jinja, shrines and their rituals may also be transferred as part of an economic transaction.

All of these changes take place within the framework of a single festival system. Innovations and changes may be introduced from outside sources, as in the case of the colored *gohei,* but the channels of introduction are part of the system, and thus the changes reflect local, that is, system, factors and not just impositions from metropolitan culture or some other festival system.

Changes in Festivities

The festivities of several Yuzawa shrines have been reduced to practically nothing, although their rituals are still performed. *Jinja* require an organization and a set of organized management procedures to operate. If such an organization exists, other uses can be made of it, and it can operate and manage festive events as well. Where rituals have been maintained, therefore, festivities can be renewed. Such is the case in Yunohara-chō and Daiku-machi, which started beer gardens and parades; in Okachi-machi, which revived a parade and started a children's party; and in several of Atago-chō's *kumi*, which started new parades. By providing a stable core element in festivals and a basis for organizing and expanding a festival's other events, rituals contribute to the maintenance of festivals. An example can be seen in the Daiku-machi festival.

The Daiku-machi festival is composed of (1) a ritual performed by a *kannushi;* (2) an Ebisu *dawara* parade managed by members of the *waka-mono-kai* but performed by the neighborhood's children; (3) Japanese folk dances organized by the neighborhood's *fujin-kai* (women's association) folk dance club; (4) a beer garden operated by the *wakamono-kai* offering cold beer and grilled snacks; (5) a keg of cold sake offered all comers, supervised and paid for by the *chōnai-kai* officers (who also partake liberally themselves); and (6) individual activities of participants in the *matsuri* including drinking, eating, dancing, lighting fireworks, and the like.

The Daiku-machi shrine, Shinmeisha, was erected during the heyday of Japan's nationalism by a *kōjū* of the richest men in town. This group still supports the shrine, but as the shrine is within the area of Daiku-machi, it has become the neighborhood shrine, and its festival is attended and supported largely by the neighborhood residents.

The *wakamono-kai* in Daiku-machi had made Ebisu *dawara* before the war, though the custom was stopped during or soon after the war. In 1978 the *kannushi* encouraged the *wakamono-kai* to renew the custom as a means of involving the neighborhood's children in the festival. The Ebisu *dawara* made by the *wakamono-kai* is carried through the neighborhood by the children, then brought up the steep steps of the Shinmeisha shrine; at the shrine the *kannushi* waves his *harai gushi* over the bale and the children and enjoins them to "be good, study hard, and obey your parents." The children are rewarded with snacks and soft drinks.

A group of neighborhood women taught by an accredited teacher initiated the dancing. They demonstrated their skills at the Daiku-machi festival for the first time in 1978 and have been doing so ever since. After they perform, they invite spectators to join in, and they demonstrate the steps for those unfamiliar with them.

In 1980, Daiku-machi's *wakamono-kai* introduced a beer garden after a group from Daiku-machi had seen neighboring Yunohara-chō's successful venture. The year before, the Yunohara-chō *wakamono-kai* needed to raise funds for decorating the neighborhood, a trip for the neighborhood's children, a party for themselves, and straw to make large *shimenawa* for the neighborhood shrine's *shintai,* a large tree. Until 1979 they had received part of the monies they needed from household festival donations. In the late 1970s, residents' grumbling about financing the *wakamono-kai*'s drinking parties increased until the *wakamono-kai* finally gave up claims to the donation money, which was thenceforth used for altar offerings for the festival and to finance the neighborhood's mothers' and children's day trip. With the donation money no longer available to them, the *wakamono-kai* decided to open a beer garden in an empty lot near the shrine during the festival to raise money. They rented equipment for dispensing draft beer and for making grilled snacks. Not only was this form of festivity a success, judging by the number of participants and their favorable reactions, but the *wakamono-kai* were also able to finance their activities in a socially respectable and enjoyable manner.

The Daiku-machi *wakamono-kai,* who had attended the first year of the beer garden, adopted the beer garden idea when the time for their own festival came around. It too was successful both financially and socially.

The beer gardens show that there are no exact prescriptions for festivities. Festivities are what people enjoy, and to retain their public they need to change along with participants' tastes. They must constantly adapt or they might disappear. The beer gardens also illustrate that changes occur within a pattern: the Yunohara *wakamono-kai* (a traditional institution) changed its behavior to meet new circumstances. Once started, the idea was quickly copied by other places such as Daiku-machi. The agents of transfer were individuals from the population base of Yuzawa's festival system.

A new festival may be initiated for social reasons as a focus for community feeling. However, it is preceded by the building of a shrine and the performance of yearly rituals in that shrine, as was the case in Uramon-machi. In other cases, such as in Hirashimizu-machi number 2, festivities that included a song contest were started after the neighborhood association took over an *ujigami* shrine and built a neighborhood association hall around it, thus preserving both the shrine and its ritual.

Where there is no ritual, no festival can be initiated in a neighborhood. Where festive events have disappeared, as they did in many festivals following the war, festivities cannot be renewed unless a ritual has been preserved as seed. Several abandoned shrines in the precincts of Yuzawa's central park, which I have been told "used to have quite exciting festivals," may attest to the difficulty of reviving festivals in the absence of a retained ritual. This supports the contention by other studies of festival behavior (Yanagawa 1974; Blacker 1975, 315–316) that festivals in Japan survive partly because they are sources of entertainment. *Matsuri* entertainment possibilities have been overtaken by television, radio, cinema, discos, and the like. "As elsewhere in the world, the former role of Japanese religions in providing recreation and entertainment . . . has been largely taken over by secular agencies" (Norbeck 1970, 105). While these other forms of entertainment have been gradually supplanting *matsuri* in the present century, Japan's prosperity has lately led to a search for the "authentic" and the "traditional." One aspect of this search is the *mingei* (folk art) movement, founded and expressed by the writer Yanagi Soetsu (Yanagi 1926) and others. Another is the conscious search for the cultural roots of modern Japan's very urban culture. In what might be called "the *furusato* movement," urban residents are

driven to find country provenance. While this interest was sparked by
intellectuals such as folklorist Yanagida (1962, 1970), it has now become
a feature of Japanese cultural life. Part of this movement is the revival
of interest (sometimes commercial) in, and consequently the revival of,
traditional festivals. Abetting the *mingei* movement is the easy access
to the countryside provided by automobile ownership and public trans-
port. Individuals who do seek out festival events, however, do so
not as folklorists, but as seekers of diversion (Economic Planning Agency
1972).

Festivals all over Japan have changed to meet this new demand for leisure-time entertainment. According to Yanagawa, "there have been
remarkable changes in the manner of celebration. After 1955, for example, the Chichibu Tourist Association became a co-sponsor along with the
traditional sponsors, the *machi* of Chichibu," of the Chichibu festival
(1968, 157). And as Graburn (1983) notes, tourism and religion have
become inextricably fused in modern Japan.

On a smaller scale, the same thing is happening in Yuzawa's neighborhood *matsuri*. Keeping the public interested means providing rewarding
and entertaining activity, giving the public what it wants, even at the
expense of traditional activities. Preserving festival elements for their own
merits is of interest only to a few elderly purists and ethnographers. "The
old festival puppet plays were really not very amusing, and even in my
childhood I did not recall much about them. The kids today are much
happier with the cartoon films," one middle-aged man responded when I
lamented the absence of the traditional puppet-play.

Festivals are no longer the sole entertainment available to the public
but only one alternative among many. Participating in a festival, with its
old-fashioned, traditional, nonmodern connotations, often bores many
young Japanese (or so they say). Sitting in company with one's friends,
family, or date and drinking cold beer on a hot summer night is pleasant,
whether the beer and the occasion mark a festival or not. Festival-goers
these days do not necessarily have any social or emotional ties to a festival
beyond its "entertainment value." This lack of ties does not indicate that
the "festival religion" (Davis 1977b) is maladaptive, as Norbeck (1970,
160) and Morioka (1975, 160) both claim. Change is a necessary aspect of
festival continuity. If festivals don't change, the public loses interest, and
a festival disappears. Changes in festivals are the inevitable reaction of a
healthy festival system to changes in conditions outside the festivals
themselves.

Organizational and Social Changes

In Shinto, state intervention has affected not only the rituals but also the organizations that maintain them. Changes in shrine support organizations came about by fiat of the American Occupation authorities after World War II. Neighborhood associations are no longer able to force contributions for the neighborhood shrine but must rely on voluntary contributions. In small cities like Yuzawa the difference is not great; neighborhood opinion can enforce compliance with neighborhood rules. In the large cities, in contrst, neighborhood sanctions often do not carry much weight (Steiner 1965, 222). Even in Yuzawa, people who strenuously object to paying the contribution to a shrine are exempt. Such is the case with Christian families and with members of Sōka Gakkai. Nonetheless, support for shrines and for their rituals and festivals is high. Over the years, people have found ways around government edicts. They continued supporting their shrines in the traditional manner (Akaike 1976) during the American Occupation, just as they fought, sometimes passively and sometimes actively, to maintain those same shrines during the shrine consolidation efforts of the Meiji government in the early part of the twentieth century (Fridell 1973).

Historically, most of Yuzawa's shrines had been the property of small groups, usually *ujiko* or *kōjū*. Membership in these groups was limited by social categories, residence, or descent. Yunohara Hitachi Inari-jinja, Kanaike-jinja, Senkoin Inari-jinja, and Onsawa-jinja were owned by the *daimyō* and granted as favors to groups of his followers. Kumano-jinja, Yunohara-jinja, Shoichi Yuzawa Inari-jinja, and Atago-jinja were all the *ujigami* of a family or group of families. With the exception of Senkoin Inari-jinja, all have been converted to neighborhood shrines in which *tōban* membership is open to all resident households in the neighborhood and in which all households are expected to participate. Responsibility for shrines and for festival management has changed from *ujiko* to *chōnai-kai*—in other words, from a restrictive group based on descent to a more open group based on residence. In Ura-machi, for example, ten families comprised the *ujiko* that owned the Shoichi Yuzawa Inari-jinja. In 1970 the original shrine building burned down. The *ujiko*, financially unable to rebuild the shrine and keep up its festivals, approached the *chōnai-kai* to take over the shrine. The *chōnai-kai* met several times to debate the issue and finally agreed to take over the shrine provided the building also serve as the neighborhood association hall.

Changes need not come from such dramatic causes. The Yanagi-machi *wakamono-kai*, who are drawn from neighborhood residents, agreed to take over a *kōjū* shrine on Mount Mitake as agents of the *chōnai-kai*. They had been requested to do so by the owners, whose age made climbing the mountain difficult. Kumano-jinja in Aramachi was maintained by a *bushi* family. That family had received the responsibility for the shrine from another family, now extinct, who had received it from the Satake *daimyō*. The shrine is now Aramachi's *chōnai-jinja* and was transferred to the *chōnai-kai* at the request of the *bushi* family.

As these examples show, the groups responsible for shrine support are often replaced. Groups that want to acquire shrines for religious or social motives and can support them and their festivals are able to do so. The general trend is from narrow ascriptive to broad residential support. And at least in Yuzawa, the picture is not a simple one of formerly wealthy elements in a community losing their ritual privileges to formerly excluded elements, as is the case in villages studied by Davis (1977a) and Bernier (1975). *Shintai* and a *kannushi* to perform the rituals are readily available for the asking, as the new neighborhood shrines in Uramon-machi and Okada-machi illustrate. In Yuzawa the replacement of one group by another is often instigated by those who own shrines and are no longer able to care for them because of advancing age (Kumano-jinja) or for economic reasons (Shoichi Yuzawa Inari-jinja). Changes do not come about as result of a struggle, but they reflect, as do changes in shrines elsewhere, changes in the social fabric in Japan.

The changes within management groups are less easily noticeable. These groups differ internally from one another. Their internal arrangements fit their circumstances, and when the groups adapt, they do so over a long time. The Fuppari-chō *wakamono-kai*, which presumably started out as an association of men under the age of forty-two, now accepts men of all ages. The start of this change is not easily traced. Similar changes probably occur in other groups over time.

Festival Continuity

A number of factors support the continuity of festivals within a given system by providing different degrees of flexibility to the entire system. That is, the variation and adaptability of these factors allows the adaptation, and thus the persistence, of the institution as a whole.

Corporate autonomy. The internal autonomy of the corporations that support festivals in Yuzawa ensures a variety of approaches to festival management. Each group has its own reasons for deciding what to incorporate into its festival and what to leave out. This idiosyncrasy ensures flexibility in the face of changing external conditions. The different internal arrangements of each of the groups that run the Daimyō Gyōretsu are a case in point. A festival run by few corporations, such as that of Daikumachi, is relatively easy to change in terms of arrangements and operations.

Economic interests. The dominance of Yuzawa's small local manufacturing and distributing firms is gradually being eroded by large out-of-town companies. Of Yuzawa's ten largest factories (exclusive of sake breweries), six are branches of companies headquartered elsewhere. Two of Yuzawa's four department stores and all the banks are branches of regional chains. The problem is particularly acute for shops and factories dealing in local products—pickles, wood products, dyed goods, and sake —that must compete against the combined inroads of the greater market power of the large companies and the shift of Japanese taste from traditional to new. Beer is replacing sake and synthetic fabrics replacing homespun. Cheese is becoming a regular item in the diet. The head of the Sake Cooperative summed it up: "We are gradually selling less sake because people's taste has changed. Now local firms can either cooperate as we have done in the Sake Coop, or change their line of business as some breweries have, or go under, as others have." Three of Yuzawa's sake breweries have "gone over to the enemy," as it were: they are now distributors for national beer and soft-drink companies. Substitute any local product for sake and the picture is similar. The financial support that commercial concerns give to many local *matsuri* is partly an expression of this need to defend a commercial market. Such support includes financing, use of premises, and allowing employees time off for festival activities. The local firms' interest in fostering the festival system is only part of their efforts to protect their market, but it is a highly visible one. Every festival carries a commercial display of some sort, and all of them are of local firms. Lanterns bearing the name of Ryozeki (a brewery) illuminate Maemori-chō's festivals. Sake for Yanagi-machi festivals is provided by Ononosato, the Yanagi-machi brewery. On the whole, the larger Yuzawa companies respond with displayable contributions when solicited for funds to help festival projects in their neighborhood and the town.

Ritual interests. Rituals are relatively invariant. *Kannushi* confer among themselves on matters relating to ritual and, when necessary, replace one another. Their major concern is that the prescribed "proper" form of addressing the *kami* be followed. *Kannushi* can impose their own generally conservative outlook on rituals because they are usually more knowledgeable about ritual requirements than are the participants. *Kannushi* are therefore capable of making changes in rituals or stopping such changes—or both. The same *kannushi* who pioneered the taxicab *harai*, for instance, considers himself very conservative and insists on punctilious altar arrangements. All the *kannushi* take great pains to ensure that shrine support groups perform the rituals by informing those responsible for them by mail several weeks in advance. Because there is such a committed individual, because a ritual is a relatively small part of the festival's outlay, and because some participants feel the need for, or the desirability of, rituals for other reasons, *matsuri* rituals tend to continue even when other events in a festival disappear. On the other hand, once a ritual is started, festivities can be added if there is an interest. The same kind of organization needed to maintain and perform rituals—if only to collect donations and arrange the shrine building and altar—is a potential tool that can be used to manage festive events as well.

The qualities of place. Urban Japanese still attempt to maintain ties with their *furusato* (place of origin). In practical terms this might mean little more than an occasional visit, although the idea of maintaining relations with the country is highly valued (Prime Minister's Office 1988). The idea of *furusato* is reinforced by television and other media that use the concept for advertisements wherein the countryside's bucolic charms are used to promote various products. Local communities fearful of losing their work force and anxious to attract firms providing jobs are also interested in promoting the virtues of the countryside. The normal problems of crowded life in big cities combined with the ease of transportation and the intellectual *mingei* (Moeran 1981) and folklorist movements give the idea of *furusato* added force. Local communities are making efforts to emphasize their local qualities. Their motives derive from a desire to attract tourists, from efforts to stem the drain of young and trained people and attract back those who have left, and from a very real sense of local pride. Local officials and other individuals in Yuzawa express great pride in the town. This natural pride finds its expression in various ways, not the least of which is the support of the local festival system. The concept of Yuzawa includes the idea that the community has something worthy of care and preservation. The three major festivals of the Yuzawa festival system are preserved for their own sakes as acknowledged cultural treasures and for the town's sake as a place with its own cultural traditions and values.

9

The Broader Perspective

*M*ATSURI in Yuzawa and the Yuzawa festival system are components of a much broader festival system that encompasses the whole of Japan. Despite some differences, generalizations can be made about Japanese festivals. Furthermore, the data from Japan are a subset of a cluster of phenomena—festivals—that can be seen worldwide. In this final chapter I will also attempt to make some broader generalizations than I have so far. Emphasis will be on the Japanese case, but I will draw on studies of other cultures as well.

Matsuri in Japan

From the data and analysis I have presented in the previous chapters, several factors appear to contribute to the continuation of *matsuri* in modern Japan. The conclusions are bolstered by Yanagawa's (1974), Sonoda's (1975), and Bernier's (1975) studies of *matsuri*. Ooms (1967) touches on the subject peripherally. Yamamoto (1978), Akaike (1976), and Davis (1977a) deal with the effects of social, economic, and political changes on *matsuri*. Of these studies, Akaike, Sonoda, Yamamoto, and Yanagawa concentrate on the persistence of *matsuri* in modern settings without coming to conclusions valid for other areas. The others treat *matsuri* continuation peripherally.

Matsuri as an Inculcation of Community Feeling

That *matsuri* can become foci for community unity was recognized and used by the Meiji authorities in their attempt to establish new, broader community loyalties in the countryside (Fridell 1973, 18, 93). Guthrie (1976, 177), Johnson (1976, 122–123), and Norbeck (1970, 105) suggest that *matsuri* continue to be popular because they reinforce the feeling of community solidarity.

In the Chichibu-jinja *matsuri,* farmers and residents from Chichibu's outlying districts join the *matsuri* of the urban area (Akaike 1976, 159). In Chichibu, three community festivals emphasize different communal attitudes: one centers on the neighborhood of Kamimachi (Akaike's 1976 subject community), another on the town of Chichibu of which Kamimachi is part. In Yuzawa's Daimyō Gyōretsu, the nonformal tail of the parade includes participating marchers from outlying settlements of Yuzawa-shi. These *matsuri* serve as opportunities for creation and display of a community spirit that transcends the immediate neighborhood. The mobilization of people throughout a community aids in establishing feelings of trust and cooperation. Not incidentally, most of these community-forming activities are marked by, or end, with a communal feast. The feast, as Embree (1939, 266; 1944, 1–2) has noted and as was seen from the Yuzawa examples, is an integral and important part of festival rituals. So important is it and the feeling of communal solidarity it engenders, that for many Yuzawa respondents the feast was the major and most important part of a *matsuri,* just as for many respondents "the creation of communal solidarity" was in itself the prime reason for having a *matsuri* in the first place.

Matsuri also help socialize newcomers into established communities. Yamamoto (1978) points out in her study of the Namahage festival that the Namahage custom survives partly because it is a useful device in socializing newcomers to the community's ways.[1] Brides, adopted bridegrooms, and children are all subject to the Namahage's harassment. The demonlike figures threaten only those not yet accustomed to the community's ways, those whose lack of socialization is likely to disturb the community or its households. There is nothing comparable to the Namahage in Yuzawa. Nonetheless, certain public festival activities, such as carrying a *mikoshi* or other ported object are viewed by many as socialization mechanisms.

The data and analyses cited suggest that *matsuri* persist, in part, because they help communities maintain themselves. The danger of such a viewpoint is that it makes it easy to fall into a functionalist interpretation, one in which *matsuri* are seen to exist merely as devices in the survival strategies of Japanese communities. However, as we have seen, other factors are just as important. *Matsuri* may well help in maintaining a community. What is more important, and much less controversial, is that they are believed by their participants to help the community function. This native interpretation is valid because, within the desired values of

Japanese society, maintaining group feeling is widely considered to be a desirable and important trait of any social form. That the sole or even the main reason for *matsuri* persistence is that they help maintain communities is not and cannot be argued. Other reasons factor as strongly.

Matsuri as an Expression of Shared Cultural Idioms

Matsuri also persist because, as Sonoda (1975, 32–33) notes, they serve as expressions of and vehicles for common cultural idioms. Tokyo's Edokko culture, once a prime factor in the shared festivities of the Kanda *matsuri*, has been losing ground in the face of a more general metropolitan culture (which derives from it to a certain extent). Cultural idioms such as speech patterns, certain occupations, and specific festival customs are no longer maintained or have been intentionally suppressed. Intraneighborhood cohesion is splitting the Kanda *matsuri*, whose unifier was a consciousness of cultural uniqueness shared by a multineighborhood urban culture.

In Yuzawa, shared cultural idioms of the town as a whole play a major part in the three central *matsuri*. The social bonds within a neighborhood are not much stronger than are the bonds with the rest of the town. The boundaries of the shared cultural idioms (effectively the boundaries of the festival system) coincide closely with the social boundaries of the town. The size of the community probably has much to do with this factor. Tokyo neighborhoods are much larger than Yuzawa's, and the spatial boundary of Edokko *shitamachi* neighborhoods is less clearly defined than the spatial boundary between Yuzawa and its neighboring villages and towns.

Matsuri as a Display

The idea that *matsuri* engender community solidarity must not obscure the fact that few Japanese communities are internally egalitarian. Festivals are often used to express a real or claimed communal superiority as well as a real or claimed solidarity. I have discussed the opportunities festivals give for the demonstration and display of individual or group power and prestige. In Akaike's study of a Chichibu neighborhood, status displays are a major motive for one of the three festivals performed in the neighborhood. Displays of power and wealth during the *matsuri* were a necessary step for those intent on entering Chichibu, and later national, politics. Another festival served as a vehicle for expressing communal solidarity and for socializing children into the neighborhood community. A third festival functioned as a display of communal solidarity (Akaike

1976, 154–155). Davis (1977a) and Bernier (1975) both describe cases in which once-powerful family coalitions strove to maintain claims to ritual priority long after their economic and political prominence had disappeared. In Yuzawa, too, displays such as those that accompany the riders in the Daimyō Gyōretsu, as well as the altars erected during the *matsuri,* are claims to economic power in the town. The presence of a father's or of a grandfather's name, *mon* (family crest), or place of business printed on the decorations accompanying the rider sensitizes and accustoms residents to the who-is-who of the town's wealthy and powerful. Competition is supposed to be muted in town, but at least some suppressed emotion is evident during *matsuri.*[2]

Matsuri as a Form of Recreation

R. J. Smith (1978, 6) notes that recreation is a largely ignored aspect of festivals. It must not be forgotten that people prepare and perform *matsuri* partly because they enjoy doing so. Recreation deserves more serious attention as a motive for performing *matsuri* than it has received heretofore (in, e.g., Guthrie 1976, 177; Norbeck 1970, 105). *Matsuri* persist in many places (certainly in Yuzawa) partly because they are a source of entertainment. As long as they continue to be entertaining, they will be performed and attended in Yuzawa as elsewhere (Bernier 1975, 167; Yamamoto 1978, 134). At the same time—and this point is not acknowledged by either Yamamoto or Bernier—such continued interest must be accompanied by adjustments in the entertainment. Since *matsuri* are no longer the only or the major source of entertainment for the Japanese populace, they must be able to compete with other recreational forms; therefore they must offer what will be likely to attract their participants.

Matsuri and Change

All the *matsuri* discussed here are undergoing or have undergone change. Change—in the idioms used, in the choice of *matsuri* events, or in the forms of social organization that support the *matsuri*—is a factor in *matsuri's* vitality. Although sometimes abrupt, the change may be the cumulative and continued effect of internal social change, economic factors, and taste.

Demographic changes are also important to the development of *matsuri*. This is as true of neighborhoods in downtown Tokyo as it is of rural villages. *Shitamachi* neighborhoods in downtown Tokyo have become depopulated as homes have made way for businesses (Sonoda 1975); villages become depopulated as young men leave permanently (Bernier 1975) or seasonally, as they do in villages in the Tohoku in winter, to search for employment. Morioka's hypothesis (1975) that population migration from rural areas affects shrine support because fewer people are there to manage and arrange festivals in areas of emigration appears to be correct, if imprecise. Transitory residents in the cities may not care enough to join shrine management or to support the shrine since they do not expect to remain long in the community. Small towns like Yuzawa, however, do not have such drastic population changes because economic and working conditions have improved over the past decade until such towns have nearly as many amenities as the crowded cities and in some ways, such as the low price and larger size of residences, may even surpass them. As Yanagawa (1968, 156) notes, the urban context does not work against *matsuri*. Rather, the massive demographic shift from agricultural areas to urban areas to cities and within cities during the better part of a century does not allow the growth of stable managerial organizations for festivals in areas of high emigration and immigration.

In Yuzawa, where the population has been relatively stable and where strain from emigration and immigration does not appear to be high, *matsuri* continue, and new ones are even started. The emigration of junior sons to the large cities appears to have been offset by the immigration of some of the outlying farming populace and by the return of some who had left. Thus the managerial frameworks do not appear to be too unduly disturbed.

Festivals outside Japan

Since festivals are not unique to Japan, it is possible to make some cross-cultural generalizations about festivals from data gathered elsewhere. Obviously only a sample of the studies of festivals can be presented here, but certain features seem to repeat themselves sufficiently to assume that they are generally common. Such generalizations must be approached with caution because of great differences in the social and cultural environments of the festivals involved. There are also great differences in the theoretical approaches adopted by various students of festivals.

Two major themes emerge from analysis of festivals in other cultures: entertainment and community. Entertainment is clearly a major motivation for creating a festival. Grimes (1976, 193) notes that entertainment is easily the most elaborate part of the festival of Santa Fe in New Mexico. Individuals and groups devote most of their resources to it. Grimes' informants saw entertainment as a major motivation for attending the festival.

It has been noted before that festivals can produce contradictory effects. This is particularly true when dealing with the effects of festivals that emphasize local pride or sense of community. Riegelhaupt (1973) reports that the festivals of Portuguese peasants are foci for communal solidarity, while at the same time they intensify animus to the interests of the (Catholic) church. The same effect was observed in Malta (Boissevain 1969), where festivals are used as displays by one community against another. Hanchette (1982) indicates that both cooperation and competition between castes in a village in India are expressed in festival tasks.

In Malta as in Yuzawa, festivals are generally related to religious events. However, religion in Malta is the province of an organized and powerful church that has influence and power beyond any festival body in Yuzawa. Moreover, as Boissevain notes, Maltese *festas* are colored by the tension between political parties and the Catholic church. Notwithstanding these basic differences, it is possible to distinguish two types of events in Maltese *festas* that approximate the distinctions I have pointed out in Yuzawa *matsuri*. The formal part of a *festa* is managed by a priest and is related to the church ritual. The less formal part of the *festa*—the fireworks, band parades, and other entertainment—is run by associations. Moreover, and this characteristic is basic to all festivals, "the organization of the annual *festa* requires a long period of planning and preparation. This work calls for a certain degree of centralization" (Boissevain 1969, 62). Like *matsuri, festas* too require some organized management.

Santa Fe, New Mexico, a town that has merged Spanish, Indian, and Anglo cultures, differs markedly from Japanese towns in history and social background. The fiesta in Santa Fe is both a civic celebration of the town's unity and an ethnic and religious event in which the citizens do not all share alike (Grimes 1976, 94). The local fiesta emphasizes the unity of the town, but it also extols the virtues of its different ethnic groups. The "spirit," as Grimes calls it (I have called it "image"), of festival is maintained partly by the presentation of organized events, partly by offering entertainment, wearing special dress, playing special music, and eating special foods. Entertainment "is the prime source of continuity. It forms the background for the other events, thus giving people

something to do between events" (Grimes 1976, 194). As in Yuzawa's
Daimyō Gyōretsu, various groups acquire proprietary rights to events in
the Santa Fe fiesta. These rights are preserved and exercised in each festival and are also transferable, like festival rights in Yuzawa.

Class differences affect European festivals to a greater degree than they
do Japanese *matsuri,* and class conflict appears to be an overt or hidden
theme in parades (Brandes 1980, 18–25) and other festival events (Press
1979, 1–29) in Europe. Class tension is not evident in Yuzawa's festivals,
perhaps because it is not a major theme in Japanese society as a whole.
Nonetheless, the presence and dominance of economically powerful individuals is acknowledged and often welcomed, since they financially
underwrite Yuzawa's festivals.

R. J. Smith (1978, 4–6) and Davis (1977a, 28–29) have suggested that
part of the problem in dealing with ritual in Japan is that religious belief
is not a particularly salient aspect of life in Japan. In other words, religious belief is not a major motive for action for most actors. Festivals do
not create cosmologically meaningful explanatory systems because interest in such problems is low. This lack of interest obviously affects the
"religious" nature of Japanese festivals. In other religious complexes,
however, the cosmological explanatory functions of religion are important
driving forces for rituals and festivals. Ostor's study of the festivals of a
Bengali town (1980) is such a case. In Vishnapur, the town studied, the
relationship between god and humankind and the general cosmological
issues incidental to that relationship were of primary importance. Ostor's
informants appear to have been eager to comment on and elucidate their
cosmologies whereas Yuzawa informants were uninterested in doing so.
Ostor's point—that festivals are part of the mechanisms for generating
meaning (1980, 10)—is not applicable to Yuzawa.

Notwithstanding this major difference, Vishnapur *pujas* (festivals)
resemble Yuzawan *matsuri* in two ways. First, like the Daimyō Gyōretsu,
the raja's *puja,* which is the central ritual in Vishnapur, unifies the town
and serves as a model for the community (equivalent to Yuzawa neighborhood) *pujas.* "The raja's *puja* unifies and defines the town as a single
unit, and the town is encompassed by the king's goddess. . . . The raja's
puja tells us most about the whole system because it is a model for other
Durgapujas in the town; it is the most encompassing of all *pujas*" (Ostor
1980, 25). Festivals thus both unify the town as a single festival system
and divide it into separate residential communities and ritual groups,
each of which displays its own festival in contrast to others.

Second, some festival elements change over time. "The public community worship of the goddess is a recent phenomenon, about one hundred and fifty years old. Its development has been parallel to the emergence of community involvement in temple worship and *puja* organization" (Ostor 1980, 33). Likewise, community involvement in Yuzawa festivals is also a relatively new phenomenon resulting from changes in social patterns within the community and from changes in Japanese social and political life.

The Nature of Festivals

It is clear from the examples given in the preceding section that festivals are similar in as many ways as they are different. This section addresses the question of whether it is possible to analyze festivals across cultures within a single theoretical framework. Such attempts have, of course, been made. Here I intend to point out some of the major points, and drawbacks, of a few theoretical approaches, seen against the background of comparative data. To expand some of the conclusions from the cross-cultural material, it is necessary to briefly restate some of the cross-cultural findings about festivals.

On the whole, there is agreement about a number of features associated with festivals: (1) Festivals are dramatic performances (Farber 1983; Manning 1983; Grimes 1976). (2) Festivals are a forum for presenting social myths and ideology (Farber 1983; Grimes 1976). (3) Festivals constitute a form of entertainment (Manning 1983) and thus are related to leisure. (4) Festivals are public and probably an urban-related phenomenon. Even in rural areas, it is apparent that the governing limit is population: the greater the pool of participants, the more prominent the festival. (5) Festivals are participatory and nonforced. It is difficult, perhaps impossible, to force people into a festival. This characteristic hints that spontaneity (generated intentionally or not) is an important element.

Any discussion of festivals must assess the relationship between ritual and festivity. Festivity has been associated with two other phenomena— play and "communitas"—and both must also be addressed in order to understand festivals. "Festival," what Manning (1983, 7) calls "celebration," embraces both play and ritual. Festivities are the realm of play, whereas in contrast, ritual is the domain of more "serious" belief (Handelman 1977). Ritualization or ceremonialization of activities in a festival maintains an orderly framework around the disorder and lack of control implicit in festivities. Like all play, festivities must have rules in order to allow the freedom in them to exist without the threatening possibility of the disorder implicit in that freedom spilling over into daily life. A realm of activity entirely without rules becomes anarchy. At the very least, play rules exist to determine the limits—starting and ending time, borders, and behavior limits—within which festivity takes place. Among other things, ceremonialization of certain activities within and at the beginning and end of festivity lends weight to the ability of the organizers to control festivity and to limit its excesses and define its boundaries. Whether a festival is controlled by those who dominate the social order or by those who are subordinate in it, boundaries must be established lest licensed playfulness become, through excess, a serious concern. The seriousness with which this potential for disorder is treated in Yuzawa is seen in the care with which all phases of the major *matsuri* are coordinated with the Yuzawa police station, which also defines the *matsuri*'s physical and temporal limits.

One major problem in discussing festivals is the consequence of Turner's idea of "communitas." After formulating the concept in *The Ritual Process* (1969), Turner continually tried to fine tune a concept that on the face of it should be irreducible. The problem is, if there are different types of communitas, then it stands to reason that communitas has identifiable structure and can thus be classified as to type and kind. A concept dealing *ab initio* with formless social interchange is of little worth. When combined with attempts to modify the initial position, the concept becomes untenable. That Turner has difficulties identifying what is going on in festive events does not mean that what is happening is unamenable to structured analysis. To the contrary, the fact that Turner has had to struggle mightily with the concept itself (compare the use of the concept in Turner 1969, 1972, and changes by 1983b, 1986), modifying it and creating subsets of what appears to be, or should be, an irreducible concept, should have indicated something wrong with it. In Turner's later writings (1983a) it seems that he was coming closer to recognizing that formal structure, ordering, management are necessary prerequisites for any kind of free social flow: "just as a river needs a bed and banks to flow, so do people need framing and structural rules to do their kind of flowing" (Turner 1983a, 122).

In practice one can hardly fault Turner. The idea of festivity is difficult to deal with analytically. But other evidence, as for example Abrahams' (1982) identification of categories of festive action in relation to objects, indicates that it is possible. Moreover, "joy," "happiness," "excitement" can be analyzed and verified, if only at a physiological or psychological level.

Turner seemed to be returning to a better formulation of the problem of both form and lack of it in festivals when he noted that social drama is a set of loosely integrated processes with some patterned aspects, some persistence of form, controlled by discrepant principles that are often situationally incompatible with one another (Turner 1986, 74). Highly structured events such as rituals serve as anchors around which swirl generally formless events, created by the manipulation, observance, violation, play with, and breaking of rules, norms, precepts, and relations. Festivals are successful, generally, as a human set of behaviors because they are areas in which rules (or certain sets of them) are optional. This "fuzziness" of rule application generates a host of complex and varied situations and does away with the need for a variety of communitas types. Recognition that this is the case allows for a different strategy in dealing with festivals.

An alternative to Turner's interpretation of festivals as a release, perhaps fleeting, from the determinate order of daily life is suggested by Buechler (1980). Buechler's point that festivals can be used as a means for communicating social data is well taken. In this Buechler takes up an idea initially proposed by Leach (1972). The use of the Daimyō Gyōretsu as a means for communicating social realities had been pointed out earlier. What Buechler does not say, however, is even more interesting. First, it is clear that while festivals can be used as media for communicating social relations and changes in them, they can also be used for a variety of other things. The Yuzawa festivals clearly illustrate this latter point. Festivals are manipulable (Buechler 1980, 318), and at least outside the Andes, they are also manipulated for other ends than communicating social position.

The residents of the Andean community of Compi participate in *fiestas*, which I (and other non-Spanish speakers) take to mean festivals. These *fiestas,* however, differ from "festivals" as discussed here: Compi residents' festivals are more similar to the rituals in Yuzawa *matsuri* than to festivals. Small face-to-face groups such as Andean villagers in Compi are too enmeshed in sets of social obligations to "flow" into the playfulness of festivity. That kind of playfulness requires a certain degree of anonymity provided by a crowd in which some, at least, are strangers. In comparison, Andean townsmen (see Robert Jerome Smith's [1975] description of *fiesta* in a small Andean town) are as playful and immoderately festive as are festival-goers elsewhere. This observation leads to the suggestion that demographic, not cultural, differences are important: festivities are part of the context of urbanization. Festivals require the presence of some minimum critical mass before they can emerge as the phenomenon we can identify as a festival. They are thus prominently urban or periurban phenomena. The idea that festivals are urban phenomena must be refined. At the least, festivals require some critical mass of people: the presence solely of kin and neighbors probably inhibits and limits the loosening of social roles obligatory in festival. This is not to say that villagers or residents of a neighborhood do not, or cannot, have ritually regulated play or enjoy themselves by creating an atmosphere of celebration. What it means, rather, is that mass festivities are qualitatively different from smaller affairs because they are quantitatively different in terms of personnel.

A second factor is also relevant. Small face-to-face groups do not require the organizational sinews that form the structure of festivals. These of course may well exist because they are required for the prosecution of rituals. Vogt's description of the minute personnel requirements of the Central American *cargo* systems are examples of that sort (Vogt 1969). But the involvement of a large number of people from within a small population in the organizational side of things excludes them to a large degree from the abandonment or seeming abandonment of participating freely in the festivities. Finally, though actions in smaller communities and groups may be ritualized, it is doubtful that major rituals can be sustained in small family groupings such as those described by Buechler, and such major rituals have a direct bearing on the emergence of differentiated managerial structures and thus on the essential sinew of festivals.

It seems from the evidence provided above that the limiting factor on festivals is the density and availability of population. Where population is low, play, games, presentation, ritual, and other amusement are possible and almost inevitable. Festivals, with their concomitant flow and structured looseness, are not. Once population passes some critical point, festivals become possible, perhaps even necessary. Indeed, as Robert Jerome Smith points out, festivals cast their net over the surrounding population, who are as necessary for the festival as the townspeople themselves. What the critical population point is, that is, the minimum size that allows the generation of a festival of any sort, is difficult to assess. I would hazard that it may well be a function of specific cultural factors in the population concerned.

Festivals and Modernity

That festivals are urban (or at least, associated with population concentrations) does not help in understanding them. It merely provides for a basic requirement from which festivals can start. Rising population densities are, however, associated with another phenomenon—modernity—which is important for understanding festivals in Japan. It must be kept in mind that Yuzawa is a modern town. It is separated by time from the community from which the Daimyō Gyōretsu, Tanabata, and other festivals originated. Because festivals change in response to changes in their cultural and social environment, we must search for some explanation for festivals in the pervasive, complex, cultural matrix we call "modernity." The creation of more and more festivals, in or outside Japan, is a consequence of modernity and its increased separation of leisure from work, increased regimentation of time, increased formalization of social relations. MacCannell's (1976) theory of modernity is relevant here since he suggests a comprehensible framework for understanding festivals. One consequence of modernity is "cultural productions" in which a number of elements play their parts: (1) a model "for"; (2) norms and themes derived from the model; (3) a medium (radio, ritual, festival); (4) an audience (fans, participants); and (5) producers (those who create, control, manage the cultural production). Cultural productions emerge as a means for modern societies to redefine and explicate their existence, perhaps to bring weaknesses or problems to the fore, certainly to celebrate and reaffirm their own successes, because visible success—material, cultural, ethical—is the ruler by which modernity is measured. All five of MacCannell's criteria are to be found in *matsuri*. The idea that *matsuri* are an expression of modernity effectively turns the idea that they are cultural remnants on its head. True, a social and performative model—traditional festivals—exists. But modern *matsuri,* as shown, have evolved well beyond that. They are active expressions of modern living, symbols in a very subtle sense of modern, not traditional, Japan. The clothes worn in the Daimyō Gyōretsu, the physical symbols used are conspicuous examples of historical events and situations. But at a deeper level, it is the participation of townspeople and tourists in modern clothes, the wealth that the festival implies, the control of the aristocratic parade by commoners, that are the symbols. The control of a public event by the community exemplifies Japanese society, and unlike the search for symbolic meaning in every item of ritual or ceremonial event (see, for example, Turner 1982, 16), it does what symbols are intended to do—unconsciously to make people aware that they are modern Japanese in a modern world, one they have made and made their own. In previous chapters I have deliberately not gone deeply into the "symbolic" meaning of the parade items. In a sense (although I do not make this the center of my argument), the items in the Daimyō Gyōretsu are symbols of what is not. They are nice to look at, but none of the people looking at the parade wants to return to the situations the symbols espouse. Bushidō (the samurai code of conduct), as Mishima Yukio had occasion to notice, is dead. So are the motivations and social structures that supported Bushidō—the *bakufu,* the four classes system, and all they imply and were dependent upon. It is nice to be reminded that they once existed, that they are a foundation of what is real, but they no more represent Japan for the average Japanese than does the *Chanson de Roland* for the average Westerner.

Conclusions

Four basic generalizations can be made about festivals. First, "festival is (and can be used as) a prime device for promoting social cohesion, for integrating individuals into a society or group, and maintaining them as members through shared, recurrent, positively reinforcing performance" (Robert Jerome Smith 1975, 9). Second, "changes occur constantly in everything from festival organization to songs" (ibid.). Third, a festival is based on some form of sharing a common cultural idiom. Such an idiom may be newly cultivated, as in Santa Fe, or very traditional, as in Vishnapur or Yuzawa, but it encourages a sense of common identity and common participation. Fourth, whatever their structure or intent and no matter how seemingly wild and unstructured, festivals need some organizing sinews to hold them together. "[The *fiesta*] spirit must be generated, it does not occur on its own initiative" (Grimes 1976, 193). These general insights can be applied to the Yuzawa case as a sort of summary of what festivals mean. The degree to which these insights are directly applicable to any particular festival in any particular festival system depends of course on specifically local variables.

Yuzawa Festivals in Perspective

Matsuri in Yuzawa continue, but they are undergoing changes. For analytic purposes the study of *matsuri* in Yuzawa was divided into three main

areas: ritual, festivity, and the organizations that support and manage
matsuri. It must be emphasized that these are interrelated. Ritual, festivity, and the managerial organizations are changing in different ways and
for different though related reasons. Cumulatively, these changes constitute changes in *matsuri* and in festival systems of which they are part. Paradoxically, these changes in detail and in the elements of *matsuri* allow
matsuri as social and cultural phenomena to be flexible. To be flexible
means to be able to adjust to new circumstances, a prerequisite for continued existence in a changing world.

The form of *matsuri* rituals is dependent upon a core of religious belief
and practice, on modes of polite interaction commonly used in Yuzawa,
and on the social and economic arrangements that support the ritual.
While I have treated *kami* analytically as social beings, it is not clear how
much the belief in *kami* has to do with preserving the form of rituals.
Belief is extremely subjective and methodologically difficult to verify.
Informants in Yuzawa do not assign belief in *kami* a major part in their
motivations for ritual participation or in their ideas about rituals. Moreover, anthropologists disagree about the weight to be assigned the factor
of belief in Japan (compare Bernier 1975, 165–169 with R. J. Smith
1978, 6). Whether we accept the natives' denial at face value or not, the
realm of belief and its attendants—"world view" and cognitive maps—
are too ambiguous to serve as reliable signposts for understanding why
and how festivals, only partly dependent on rituals and religious factors,
operate.

In purely social terms, individuals with an interest in their "proper"
performance of rituals, for whatever motive, are those who affect rituals
the most. These individuals, both officiants and participants, tend to be
conservative about the introduction of changes into "their" rituals.
Change in ritual forms appears to be relatively slow for that reason, and
rituals tend to maintain the same form all over the system. Such changes
as do occur are minor: differences in nuance, coloring, personal quirks
that do not affect the core behaviors found in all local rituals. Polite
usages in Yuzawa do change, albeit slowly. Older people often refer to
the lack of propriety among the young. Notwithstanding the lower standards of formality in daily life, special occasions such as rituals still call for
extremely formal behavior and for extremely polite interaction for the
reasons that have been enumerated earlier. Generally speaking, the more
money and manpower involved in a festival, the more elaborate its ritual
will be in terms of the number and variety of roles, the altar offerings,
and the shrine paraphernalia.

Festivities, in contrast to rituals, change considerably. In some cases in Yuzawa they have been abandoned altogether. In other *matsuri* in Yuzawa new types of festivities have been introduced instead of or in addition to older types. One basic factor underlies these changes. The attraction of a festival for a population is dependent on its ability to offer recreation. This in turn depends on taste and fashion, which change with time and without regard to what occurs in the festival. Even "preservation" movements such as the *mingei* folk craft movement are, to some extent, a matter of taste and fashion. To attract a population, therefore, festivities must be able to change to cater to current taste. In Yuzawa's three major *matsuri,* which are the focus of interest and pride for the entire town, new types of festivity are being introduced. Partly as a result of these changes, partly as a result of other local factors discussed in Chapter 4, the number of festival participants is growing.

The idioms, the particular cultural forms that are used for festivity, come from two main sources. There are idioms deriving from local culture that strengthen and reinforce feelings of the unity of Yuzawa and its uniqueness vis-à-vis the rest of Japan. Local groups such as the town administration and local firms interested in "protecting" the town from metropolitan economic and social intrusion make use of these. Their choice of which elements to use is of course selective. They must, for instance, encourage Yuzawa-shi as a unit, rather than just the traditional unit of the town (i.e., the urban part). Thus, while conserving the festivities, they must also introduce and encourage certain changes.

Other idioms that color festivities derive from national culture. These, which include ritual-cum-festive implements such as *mikoshi,* enter Yuzawa festivals through the media and other contacts Yuzawans have with the rest of the nation. As Yuzawans become aware of them, these idioms are incorporated into Yuzawa's festivities.

The support of festivals is undergoing a steady change too, one that is to be seen elsewhere in Japan. On the one hand, many of the organizations that support festivals are changing their basis of recruitment. They are becoming less exclusive and are accepting people that have historically been excluded. Residence and sometimes mere maintenance of a business in a neighborhood are becoming acceptable criteria for membership. On the other hand, there is an exchange of responsibilities. Groups based on historical and consanguinal ties that are no longer able to maintain their shrine's festivals are giving up the privilege of running a shrine and their duty to support it. Groups based on residence are taking their place and accepting the responsibility for those shrines. In other words, *ujigami jinja* are turning into *chōnai-jinja*. Exclusive ritual organizations are no longer so important, perhaps because the economic and status differences that were their bases no longer exist. Certainly such organizations can no longer support the burden of providing personnel and economic support implicit in maintaining a shrine and its festival. They become less exclusive by necessity.

Exceptions to the general rule that managing bodies of shrine support organizations are becoming less exclusive include the Maemori-chō and Ōmachi *wakamono-kai*. These exceptions depend on efficient organization, a large number of supporters, and committed support by those able to bear the financial burden.

Festivals add to the self-identity of a community in two ways. The nature of Yuzawa as a unit different from other such units in Japan is reinforced by those elements of festivity that are specifically Yuzawan, such as the Daimyō Gyōretsu parade, the Inukko, and the lanterns at Tanabata. The elaboration in festival display, which is most noticeable in festivity, demonstrates Yuzawa's abilities as a cohesive and internally cooperating community. To a lesser degree, the same applies in the festivals of Yuzawa's neighborhoods, whose displays contrast with others in the town. This affirmation of self-identity, therefore, is a major motive for such groups to support their festivals, and much of their support is committed to the idea of the *matsuri* as a display.

Change, Religion, and Festival Continuity

I introduced the discussion of Yuzawa's festivals through a discussion of religion. Religion is interwoven through the performance of festivals as a social fact. It is therefore apt to return to the subject of religion at the close.

Rituals make sense through reference to moot entities—the *kami*—who are addressed as social beings, thus making the ritual comprehensible to participants. Rituals serve as a relatively unchanging core for festivals, and the manpower that manages rituals is also able to manage festivities. Rituals supply an organizational focus and sometimes a motif for festivals, but the religious aspect is not too important to most festivalgoers. The continuation of religious belief depends on religious behavior being seen as part of ongoing daily life, either as an extension of recognized social arrangements and interactions or as a part of a different institution, festival, which in turn is seen consciously as part of the expression of a community's identity and unity.

Some of Yuzawa's festivals have disappeared completely. Others remain only as a ritual. Yet this is not an indication that festivals are doomed to disappear. The three major festivals remain. They are supported by well-organized groups that include the municipality, and they involve a large population. They are continually attracting larger audiences as outlying communities of Yuzawa-shi join in them. They are made attractive because while they preserve and represent the uniqueness of Yuzawa, they also allow the infiltration of national culture, something these outlying communities can share in.

Neighborhood festivals are changing as their managers seek new means of attracting participants. New festivals are created in neighborhoods that did not have them as the success of other festivals within the system becomes apparent. The residents of neighborhoods that do not have festivals see them consciously as means of creating and enforcing community solidarity.

In general terms, those festivals in Yuzawa that survive, and even thrive, do so because they have a broad population base from which to draw managers and an organized corporate unit that is willing and able to assume the responsibility for a festival. To a great degree festival success also depends on the ability of the festival to attract a participating population because it is interesting and entertaining, or because it is felt to contribute something to the group concerned.

These principles also apply outside Yuzawa and outside Japan. Where there is a committed and self-conscious population unit, where such a unit has within itself some managerial structure that can maintain a sustained organizational effort, where such a population has or can create shared displays and cultural idioms, and where the population feels that what passes in the festival is entertaining and fun, festivals can be maintained or created. A corollary to these qualifications is that the continuation of festivals is predicated on change, since all of these bases of festivals change independently with time.

Notes

1. Some of the arguments and distinctions made in the debate can be found in Foster (1965), Kushner et al. (1962), W. E. Moore (1963), and Steward (1963). Studies with specific reference to Japan include Bellah (1958) on religious change; Brameld (1968) and R. E. Ward (1965) on social and political change; Norbeck (1961) on cultural change; and two collections, one edited by Dore (1967) and the other by Jansen (1965) on modernization in a number of fields.

Chapter 2

1. Numbers given within the publication reflect this unreliability. The numbers cited do not agree with those in Table 3 of the same publication (see Agency for Cultural Affairs 1981, 298).

2. For example, the registry of shrines counts only two shrines in Yuzawa, whereas, by my own count, Yuzawa has thirty-three shrines excluding household and ancestor worship shrines in private yards. Yuzawa is not exceptionally religious; a similar count could be made elsewhere in Japan with the same results.

3. There is also a new year according to the old lunar calendar, but because of formal recognition of the Gregorian calendar by the government the lunar new year is poorly observed.

4. A *shi* is a local government unit usually titled "city" in English publications. *Shi* differ in size and in rural-urban mix.

5. The two words are different readings of the same character.

6. Similar systems are used all over Japan. For example, in Okayama prefecture, "announcements, requests or instructions, usually in mimeographed form, are sent to the house of the elective official of the *buraku* [hamlet], the *buraku kaichō*. . . . He circulates a board carrying the notice by passing it on to his immediate neighbor, who reads the notice, then passes it on to his next neighbor. The board goes from house to house . . . until it has made the full round and returns to the leader's house" (Beardsley, Hall, and Ward 1959, 249). See also Hendry (1981) for a detailed description of the system's operation.

7. Maemori-chō is divided into six *kairanban* circuits, but all the *kairanban*

messages originate from the headman of the whole neighborhood. There are heads for each circuit, but Maemori-chō generally acts as a single unit.

8. This is a commonly held view of Japanese local-central government relations in social science literature. It has been challenged by Reed (1982). However, Reed deals largely with relationships between prefectural governments and the central government. In neighborhood-city relationships, the lower echelon's scope of affairs includes some sanitation activities and beautification campaigns, communicating municipal pronouncements, and collecting a small service fee. Other activities, such as entertainment or trips, may be undertaken at the discretion of the neighborhood association, but they are strictly self-initiated. The municipality does not, in Yuzawa at least, see the neighborhood associations as much more than convenient channels for contacting resident households. In many cases, the Yuzawa municipality did not even know the identity of the neighborhood headman.

9. Because there are few flush toilets in Yuzawa, disinfectants are regularly distributed by the *chōnai-kai*.

10. Tohoku (the Northeast) encompasses the northernmost prefectures on Japan's main island of Honshu, including Akita. Traditionally the area has been one of the poorest in Japan, both because of climatic conditions and because of communication difficulties with the national social and economic centers in the Kantō (Tokyo area) and Kansai (Kyoto-Osaka area).

11. In a somewhat disapproving tone, Fukutake (1974, 103) wrote of this trend in the early 1970s:

> Today, the home television set provides everyday amusement for almost everyone. But people have a great deal of free time, and even though they may spend three hours a day watching television, they do not rely on this for all their amusement. Sightseeing trips (whose popularity has resulted in a rapid growth in the tourist industry) and Sunday drives are a wholesome kind of amusement but they cannot be indulged in every day. A great many divert themselves from frustrations by drinking in bars or at street stands, or by amusing themselves at professional wrestling or boxing matches.
>
> Recently, even in rural towns, newly built bowling alleys have attracted the young. . . .
>
> In any case recreation and leisure have come to be regarded as one of the goals of human life. . . .

12. There is a certain ambivalence among the Japanese toward the countryside, and the two different terms used evoke these attitudes. *Inaka* (the countryside) implies "not sophisticated, quiet, and far from the exciting life of the metropolis," as one group of young Japanese summed it up for me. *Furusato* arouses slightly different sentiments: "a place where my relatives live"; "the place where I feel at home, even though I was not born there"; and "where I go to feel at home" were some descriptions offered by the same group. The evocation of *furu-*

sato can often produce lachrymose recollections of natal (or family) homes in the country, particularly from bar acquaintances. *Inaka* and its customs, on the other hand, are the frequent subject of witticisms by metropolitan comics.

13. One *koku* equals 180 liters, or roughly 5.2 bushels of grain. Traditionally, one *koku* is the standard measure of rice sufficient to feed one man for a year.

CHAPTER 3

1. Salt is a major purifying agent in Japanese tradition, exemplified by the handfuls of salt thrown by sumo wrestlers before they enter the ring. Every ritual altar includes a small plate of salt.

2. One reason I elaborate on this point is the persistent argument in anthropology over definitions of religion in which the concept of the "supernatural" features prominently. Some, like Spiro (1966), have argued that the "supernatural" is a major element in all religions. Others, such as B. Ward (1979) and Saliba (1976), have argued that the concept reflects Western ethnocentrism. While my sentiments lie with the second party, I think the argument lies outside the competence of anthropology (see Turner 1969 for a discussion of the limits of psychological analysis in anthropology). Guthrie (1980), noting that the salient characteristic for anthropology of "supernatural beings" is their social character, effectively leaves the "supernatural" argument to theologians and frees anthropologists to concentrate on the effects of godheads on society. Not to prejudice the issue, which is outside the scope of this work, I refer to gods and spirits as "moot entities." Shinto moot entities are labeled *kami*.

3. The importance of correct dress to ritual can be assumed from the fact that even in the worst weather a *kannushi* wears his robes without an overcoat. The *kannushi* at the *dondo-yaki* later commented that it was so cold his fingers froze to the sake cup he offered for *naorai*.

4. The number three is ritually significant in several contexts. A wedding's main ceremony is referred to as *san san kudo* (three times three cups), referring to the ritual consumption of three cups of sake. The lacquered sake cups used for the New Year come in nesting sets of threes. Trays of offerings at shrines are added to altars in multiples of three.

5. Acquiescence is not necessarily the same as acceptance. In a different context Howe (1981, 296) says of those who take part in fox hunting in England that "willing, induced, or coerced, their participation is taken as a conventional sign of acquiescence to a class structure represented and dramatized in the hunt."

6. When asked why they engaged in a practice that involved long hours of effort, some fencers replied that they wanted to engage in physical activity, others that they felt it was a civic duty, and still others that they felt they owed a social debt to the senior fencer. With one exception, no one stated that he practiced fencing for spiritual improvement, although the sport's spiritual dimension was always emphasized nominally during practice. Among tea ceremony practition-

ers, reasons given privately for joining were largely social, for the lessons brought housewives together.

Although Kondo (1985) is arguing a different point, her data also indicate that acquiescence to the practice is a primary component in getting adherents to accept the "messages" imparted by the tea ceremony.

7. Prideaux (1970) and Martin (1964) discuss Japanese honorifics and formal levels of speech. Briefly stated, for the speaker, verb suffixes indicate higher or lower levels of "respect language" toward the listener. Usually prefixed to nouns, honorifics indicate the level of "respect" accorded the subject. Stock greetings are usually extremely respectful, though there are regional variations. *Dōmo* in the Yuzawa dialect is equivalent to the whole set of daily greetings for acquaintances in standard Japanese.

Words used in Yuzawa are often a mixture of standard Japanese and Akita dialect; thus these greetings, and the words transcribed here may differ somewhat from the standard Japanese familiar to the reader.

8. See, for example, Befu (1974), Moeran (1986), and Ben-Ari (1986) for detailed descriptions of the forms and etiquette of drinking parties.

9. The use of this vocal effect is characteristic of formal theatrical productions, such as Noh theatre (Bethe and Brazell 1978; Hoff 1978, 141–164). Percussive signals are also used to punctuate sections of a performance in other performing arts in Japan, such as *rakugo* storytelling (Hrdlickova 1969, 188). Particularly in dance, performance segments can also be punctuated and emphasized by "freezing" the action in a tableau (Valentine 1986, 119).

10. During one ritual, an elderly lady entered the shrine, walked in front of the participants, stationed herself between them and the officiant at the altar, performed *hairei*, and left. She was not part of what was going on, and her actions did not disturb the concentration on the single focus of the event. Not only are rituals concerned with a single focus of action, but that focus is geared to a limited group of participants. The single *hairei* performer was not one of the recognized participants and did not affect the focus of the event.

11. The *kannushi's* detachment from the interaction is intentional. Even when children had difficulty making the offering properly during the *shichi-go-san* ritual, the *kannushi,* seated two meters away, did not rise to help, but offered advice from the sidelines.

CHAPTER 4

1. Ebisu, the *kami* of luck, is part of the folk pantheon of seven lucky gods (plenty, luck, the arts, longevity, wisdom, protection, good fortune) who sail the *takarabune* (treasure ship). Equivalent, perhaps, to the representation of Santa Claus, their images are displayed in many shops and particularly restaurants. Ebisu has more serious (and terrible) aspects as the *kami* Koto-shiro-nushi-no-kami (Shinto Committee 1958), as the dwarf *kami* Sukunabikona, and as Hiruko

(Ouwehand 1964, 82–83). *Tawara* (or *dawara*), woven rice straw mats that are rolled into a cylinder shape and bound with straw rope, were the traditional means of storing and transporting rice.

2. Some large *machi*—Atago, Maemori, Hirashimizu—are divided into sub-units called *kumi*. In Atago-chō each *kumi* brings its own Ebisu *dawara* to the shrine. See chap. 2, n. 6.

3. "The youth association supplies the initiative and most of the labor force for many tasks connected with the community's ceremonial life" (Beardsley, Hall, and Ward 1959, 253).

4. The *wakamono-kai* of one Atago-chō *kumi* regularly volunteers its services to help at the retired citizens' home. The Ebisu *dawara* was made by the *wakamono-kai* and is carried by the residents.

5. From 1903 to 1945 the national and prefectural governments ranked all the shrines in the country. The great majority of small neighborhood shrines were "unranked." One shrine in each *mura* (administrative village) was granted the rank of *gōsha*. Several large shrines in each prefecture were granted the rank of *kensha*. Above those were ranked a number of special categories: shrines listed in the Engi-shiki, shrines related to the imperial family, etc. Above these was the highest-ranking national shrine, Ise-jingu. Ranks were conferred based on the number and financial ability of a shrine's registered supporters. A shrine that aspired to the title of *gōsha*, for instance, had to present a list of subscribers to the shrine, their contributions, and guarantees that they would support a resident *kannushi*, together with the formal application to the prefectural governor.

6. The first change took place because the Go Chō, who were responsible for the finances of both events, felt they could no longer support the double financial burden. The second change was to accommodate the schoolchildren who are the parade's mainstay. The *guji* (chief priest) agreed at the time that the lord's parade would precede the *mikoshi* parade.

7. The Tokugawa authorities tried to enforce an orderly (by their criteria) usage of rank indicators. Fringed standards indicated wealth in one thousand *koku* of rice (thus, the Yuzawa *daimyō*, who has ten standards in his train, indicating an income of ten thousand *koku*, or 1,800,000 liters of rice, holds the lowest rank of *daimyō*), and other badges were used according to a complicated system of privilege and title. The sumptuary regulations were often ignored by nobles with greater claims or pretensions than the Tokugawa were prepared to accord them. As the power of the Tokugawa government declined toward the end of its rule, outlying nobles like the Satake arrogated to themselves unauthorized rank markers. As this process took time and changed from one period to another, it is difficult to tell now what, precisely, the Yuzawa *daimyō* was claiming.

8. The four *jigannushi* families are descendants of families who had fields in present-day Atago-chō. One family found in its field a statue which, after consulting with the other three families, all agreed to worship. These families form

the *ujiko* of the shrine, although the evolution of Atago-jinja affairs has reduced their importance, as has happened in other *ujigami* shrines (see Ashkenazi 1981 for the process of transferring shrine responsibilities).

9. The importance of proper dress in traditional Japan is of course indicated by the Chūshingura tale, in which false advice on proper dress by the tale's villain leads to the quarrel that is later avenged by the forty-seven masterless samurai, or *ronin*.

CHAPTER 5

1. Most restaurants in Japan accept delivery orders, and specialty restaurants will supply *bentō* (box lunches), some of which are elaborate.

2. One question a foreigner is almost always asked in Japan is, "What is the *shushoku* in your country?" *Shushoku* is generally defined as "staple," but its implications are greater. The question really implies, "What is the staff of life, that without which, even when one is full, one feels that one hasn't truly eaten?" In Japan, as in most of East Asia, the answer is rice. For someone from a European culture (including Americans), where bread has long since ceased to be the staff of life, the answer is not so simple. I generally found myself having to give an exposition on eating habits, rather than just saying "bread." (The latter reply had, in some instances, meant that I was presented with a two-inch-thick slice of bread instead of a bowl of rice.) Dore (1978, 86) was faced with the same problem, and his solution was as inelegant as mine.

3. The New Year is less a festival in the sense used here than an individual and family holiday.

4. The Inukko concourse is the local name of the area allocated by the municipality for the construction of *inukko* (snow sculptures of dogs) and *odokko* (snow shrines), between Yuzawa's municipal buildings and central park. In the summer the area serves as the town's softball and sports grounds.

5. *Mochi* is a traditional festival delicacy. It is popularly associated with strength, health, and well-being. In Akita, cakes of *mochi* are eaten rolled in sweetened bean paste or toasted soybean flour and sugar.

6. Lanterns are generally ordered from one of the two lantern makers in Yuzawa. They cost 15,000 yen and up, depending on size, shape, and coloring.

7. The National Rice Council promotes rice in pamphlets, in television commercials, and on billboards. In one subway ad in Tokyo, a perplexed and very obviously foreign businessman is holding a bowl of rice and saying to himself, "I wonder what makes Japanese business so successful. It must be the rice they eat."

8. An example not as conspicuous in Yuzawa because of the weather is the *shichi-go-san* festival. The ritual was originally a family and private rite of passage. In postwar Japan "there are certain 'rites of passage' in which Shinto priests came to participate in and after the Meiji period, although they were primarily folk customs within families in most cases. The festivals for children of seven,

five, and three years of age . . . [are one] example of this" (Hirai 1968, 148). In Tokyo, mothers and children usually visit a *jinja* for the ritual dressed in fine kimono. The price of such an outfit starts at about 250,000 yen for an adult and about 150,000 yen for a child—a significant outlay. The kimono are ostentatious displays of the ability and desire to sustain conspicuous consumption.

9. Families in Yuzawa of both *chōnin* and *bushi* descent possess genealogical records to demonstrate the antiquity of their lineage. The competition between *chōnin* and *bushi* lineages is a muted issue in Yuzawa today.

10. Many neighborhoods and hamlets join in the tail of the parade, which, unlike the beginning of the parade, is informal, with no fixed roles. Nevertheless, I was told it is "only polite" to ask the *tōban*'s permission. Moreover, the parade organizers are legally responsible for the parade's conduct. The trucks children ride in are draped with indigo bunting stenciled with the badge or trademark of a sponsor. Shops and merchants outside the Go Chō must apply several times before the managing group gives them permission to sponsor a truck or float.

11. There are few salaried workers among active *wakamono-kai* members, partly, I was told, because their employers are loath to give them time off to participate in the *wakamono-kai matsuri* affairs.

CHAPTER 6

1. "New Religions" include a group of syncretic relgions that began emerging in Japan in the early nineteenth century. There are several hundred in Japan today, and membership varies from hundreds to millions. Their doctrine generally borrows from Shinto, Buddhism, and even Christianity impartially. They are proselytizers and usually exclusivist. They tend to limit their members' participation in neighborhood life. Chinnery's findings illustrate how important neighborhood *matsuri* can be: in the village she studied, Tenrikyō (one of the largest New Religions) was accepted fully as legitimate once its members started participating in the village *matsuri*.

2. Not necessarily ancestor worship. In Yuzawa, members of an *ujiko* support a *jinja* that was established by an ancestor or ancestors. The rights in the *jinja* descend to the *ujiko* members through that relationship. *Ujiko* members maintain a *jinja* that was worshiped by their *ie* because it was worshiped by ancestors in their *ie* without regard to whether or not they actually also worship those same ancestors. On ancestor worship (which is usually associated more with Buddhist than with *jinja* practices), see R. J. Smith (1974) and Ooms (1967).

3. See, for example, a survey of the arguments in Mouer and Sugimoto (1980).

4. In many Yuzawa firms it is the custom for a son to assume his father's name upon the latter's retirement. This is true of inns, shops, and small traditional factories (e.g., for wood utensils). The change of name, along with the transfer of the shop's or inn's official seal, is registered at the municipality. Those without

male progeny often adopt a son-in-law as heir, a custom known as *muko yōshi*, whereupon the son-in-law takes on his father-in-law's surname and assumes the obligations of a son. The specific purpose of *muko yōshi* is to preserve the *ie*.

5. The situation is different in some of the New Religions, although even they count their adherents by household rather than by individual. Also, in some shrines, such as many *kōjū* shrines and traveling *kō*, membership is by individual. "Membership by household" is, however, a sufficiently valid generalization for most *jinja* and *otera*.

6. The canal, fed from the Omono River, is used for snow disposal in winter and as a source of water for the fire department's water pumps. It was originally constructed during the Edo period to provide water for the Go Chō and also served as part of the *daimyō*'s defense works.

7. Japanese refer to their place of employment as *uchi* (my/our house), and the emotional connotations are of a shared in-group.

8. Traditionally, shrine grounds have been used as arenas for sporting events. Three of Yuzawa's neighborhood shrines have sumo wrestling rings (all now defunct) on their grounds. One has an archery range and served as the seat of the local traditional archery club.

9. Shrines that have been placed on another shrine's grounds for safekeeping or because there is no longer anyone to worship at them. This is becoming more common in Japan as families and individuals migrate to the big cities. See Ashkenazi (1981).

10. The paths leading to the entrance of most shrines are bent, and the entrance to shrines is inevitably blocked by an offertory box. Only *kami* walk directly into a shrine.

11. The reverse is also probably true. An elaborate ritual in a simple festival would be incongruous, even risible, and no such case was observed in Yuzawa.

12. Officials at Jinja Honchō and at Kokugakuin University, where *kannushi* are trained, were emphatic that *kannushi* should always offer *tamagushi* first, the position of honor.

13. A discussion of the law, its effects on Shinto, and other legal and social issues concerning Shinto can be found in Creemers (1968).

14. While equivalents of "elect" and "appoint" are used in Japanese, I refrain from using the English words here. The choice of representatives in rural Japan is not an election per se, but a winnowing out of candidates, none of whom pushes himself forward aggressively. I was told that Maemori-chō rarely holds full elections for *gojikai* posts: "People know whom they would like to have and they consult among themselves and he is chosen." Even in local government bodies actual balloting is often more a confirmation of an already accepted consensus. Dore (1978) has described the process in rural areas in greater detail.

15. Judging by the festival dates (spring and autumn), the mother mountain

(Mitake is a holy Shugendō mountain near Tokyo), and the custom of staying overnight near a tended fire, which is similar to mountain ascetic practices elsewhere (Earhart 1970; Blacker 1975), the shrine may have originally been a Shugendō shrine until the suppression of the sect in the 1870s. Only traces of that mountain ascetic practice remain.

16. Most members are over forty (forty-two has traditionally been the age of accession to full male adult responsibilities in Japan). Some Go Chō *wakamono-kai*—Maemori-chō, Yanagi-machi, and Ōmachi—rigidly adhere to this age limit. Fuppari-chō and Tamachi do not adhere to an age limit.

17. See also Ashkenazi (1988b) for some management implications of *hansei-kai.*

CHAPTER 7

1. Since this book is concerned specifically with *matsuri,* I do not discuss issues relating to Buddhist priests (bonzes) and their rituals. Because of their complexity, the issues of the Buddhist aspect of Japanese religion must necessarily be dealt with elsewhere. This is true of bonzes' competence as well, which is dependent upon and directed by their membership in a sect organization. Christian missionaries and ministers are not discussed here either, since their influence is negligible and they have no formal role or influence in *matsuri.* See Ashkenazi (1991).

2. It should be added that *kannushi,* on the whole, emphasize the almost down-to-earth nature of their trade. I never heard a *kannushi* give a mystical explanation for the rituals he performed, and none of the *kannushi* in Yuzawa saw anything mystical about their activities. There were no trances or uses of shamanistic effects. Indeed, such effects were frowned upon.

CHAPTER 8

1. Literally, "paintings of beauties," a fashion in portrait painting, usually of courtesans, that developed in the Edo period.

2. During the Edo period, two groups of samurai were quartered in Yuzawa: vassals of the southern branch of the Satake lords and vassals of the Satake main house in Akita City. The Yuzawa fief was responsible for the upkeep of the main house's vassals but had no control over them. The local *daimyō*'s vassals were settled on the approaches to the *daimyō*'s mansion and at other strategic points.

3. An interesting example of "legitimizing" a reconstructed practice as authentic is that of Shugendō, or ascetic mountain worship. The current Shugendō of the Haguro-san sect, to which some Yuzawa shrines are related, has evolved an elaborate hagiography and provenance to demonstrate the authenticity of its rituals. The Haguro sect had been proscribed from 1873 to 1946, and its practices today are a "revivification" of dimly remembered secret practices that the current membership nonetheless claims are authentic (Earhart 1970).

CHAPTER 9

1. The Namahage festival takes place on the Oga peninsula in northern Akita prefecture. In the festival, the young men of the villages dress in traditional demon masks and straw raincoats called *namahage*. They visit the village households, particularly those with new brides or unruly children. The Namahage sing songs, threaten their victims, caper, and generally harass the household until bought off by promises of future proper behavior, sake, and food.

2. One interesting question concerns internal conflict. During the period of fieldwork, and even later, there was no evidence of real conflict. There were several minor disagreements about issues in the Daimyō Gyōretsu, but these caused no evident strains in town. Nonetheless, there were traces of past disagreements that had been carefully smoothed over. One segment of Atago-chō had withdrawn from the neighborhood about 1960. There was competition between Maemori-chō and Atago-chō over primacy in town. The sole case of real disagreement during the period of fieldwork was the increasing demand by the *yakkofuri* for some form of payment for their services. See Ashkenazi (1990).

Glossary

amazake	甘酒	sweet, lightly fermented rice gruel
ashigaru	足軽	footsoldier; the lowest *bushi* rank in the Edo period
bakufu	幕府	shogun's military government during the Edo period
bettō	別当	steward of a shrine
[O]bon	盆	Festival of the Dead
bōzu	坊主	Buddhist priest
bunke	分家	branch house
bushi	武士	warrior; the military/administrative stratum in the Edo period
chō	町	neighborhood (*machi* is an alternative reading)
chōchin	提灯	small, round paper lantern
chōnai-kai	町内会	neighborhood association
chōnai-kaichō	町内会長	neighborhood headman
chōnai-kaikan	町内会館	neighborhood association hall
chōnin	町人	townsmen (merchants and craftsmen in the Edo period)
daimyō	大名	autonomous lord of Edo period with an income of 10,000 koku or more
dawara		*See* Ebisu dawara
dondo-yaki	どんど焼き	a rite in which old New Year's ornaments and ritual paraphernalia are burned
Ebisu dawara	恵比寿俵	a decorated straw bale paraded through a neighborhood during a festival
ebōshi	烏帽子	tall, brimless, black gauze hat worn by *kannushi* during rituals

enka	演歌	popular ballads
fuda	札	a slip of paper printed with the name of a shrine's *kami* usually placed in one's *kamidana*
furusato	故里	one's place of birth or original residence
Go Chō	五町	the five Yuzawa neighborhoods that run the Daimyō Gyōretsu in yearly rotation: Maemori-chō, Yanagi-machi, Omachi, Tamachi, and Fuppari-chō
gohei	御幣	an altar ornament of zigzag-shaped strips of folded paper suspended atop an upright wand
gu	宮	shrine, a suffix attached to Hachiman shrines, as in Hachiman-gu
guji	宮司	chief priest of a shrine
guji aisatsu	宮司挨拶	segment of a ritual in which the officiant thanks the participants
hairei	拝礼	individual act of worship at a shrine
hakama	袴	long, loose culottes worn as part of formal Japanese costume
hansei-kai	反省会	assessment meetings held after the Daimyō Gyōretsu
happi	法被	a short surcoat worn during festivals
harai	祓	segment of *jinja* ritual in which the officiant waves a *harai gushi* over participants to purify them
harai gushi	祓串	a wand or branch to which paper streamers are attached by flax; used in a ritual to purify precincts and participants
hare	晴れ	pure; purity
hatsu matsuri	初祭り	the first festival of the year at a shrine
honke	本家	main house
ie	家	household, house (the house of . . .)
inaka	田舎	countryside; rural as contrasted to urban
inukko	犬っこ	snow statues of dogs made during Inukko *matsuri*
jichin-sai	地鎮祭	ground-breaking ritual

jigannushi	地願主	the four families who originally worshiped the *kami* of Atago-jinja
jinja	神社	a Shinto shrine
Jinja Honchō	神社本庁	Association of Shinto Shrines
kabuza	株座	a religious monopoly in which stock (*kabu*) owners maintain a monopoly on major shrine functions and benefits
kagura	神楽	a dance performed for the entertainment of *kami* during a ritual or festival
kairanban	回覧板	a communal message board passed from house to house in a neighborhood
kami	神	Shinto deity; object of veneration
kamidana	神棚	shelves within a house fitted with a small shrine for ancestral and household *kami*
kanmuri	冠	hat worn by *guji* during rituals
kannushi	神主	a priest trained to officiate at *jinja* rituals
karaoke	カラオケ	singing to recorded music
kariginu	狩衣	loose surplice of brocade silk worn by *kannushi*
kegare	汚れ	impure, polluted; impurity, pollution
kifu	寄付	donations from a household for a shrine or festival
kōjin	降神	segment of shrine ritual; the request to a *kami* to attend a ritual
kōjū	講中	a ritual association whose membership is individual
koku	石	amount of rice sufficient to feed one man for one year; in practice 180 liters
koreisai	古例際	main festival of a shrine
koseki	戸籍	household registry maintained for each family in Japan
kumi	組	section of a neighborhood
machi	町	neighborhood (*chō* is another reading)
matsuri	祭り	festival
miki	神酒	consecrated wine

miko	巫女	shrine maiden
mikoshi	神輿	a palanquin paraded through a shrine parish during a festival
mikoshi-shuku	神輿宿	the midday resting place of the Atago-jinja *mikoshi* during Daimyō Gyōretsu parade
miyaza	宮座	shrine support group
mochi	餅	pounded glutinous rice
montsuki	紋付き	formal Japanese robe with the owner's crest on sleeves and back
muko yōshi	婿養子	adopted son-in-law
naorai	直会	feast at the end of a ritual; also, sharing of wine and food from altar
New Religions	新宗教	religious sects that arose in Japan roughly since the nineteenth century
ninjō	人情	human feelings (as opposed to duty)
norito	祝詞	segment of a *jinja* ritual in which the *kannushi* addresses the *kami*
O-bon	お盆	see *bon*
odokko	お堂っこ	a shrine made of snow constructed during the Inukko *matsuri*
otera	お寺	Buddhist temple
sai-chō	祭長	the (lay) sponsor of the Atago-jinja *koreisai*
sakaki	榊	an evergreen used in *jinja* rituals (*Cleyera ochnacea* or *Cleyera japonica*)
sanbō	三方	a raised tray used for offerings (*sonaemono*)
sankin kōtai	参勤交代	the system by which daimyō were required to reside in Edo for a fixed period each year during the Edo period
Satake	佐竹	clan that ruled Yuzawa during the Edo period
seiza	正座	formal sitting on one's knees
sekihan	赤飯	rice cooked with red beans eaten as a festive dish
shi	市	administrative municipality
shichi-go-san	七五三	festival for three- and seven-year-old girls and five-year-old boys
shimenawa	締縄	a rope or hawser of rice straw marking a consecrated area

shinkō shiki	神幸式	a ritual parade; the review of a parish by its *kami*
shintai	神体	a material object representing the kami in which the *kami*'s spirit is believed to reside
shitamachi	下町	working-class neighborhood
Shugendo	修験道	a syncretic and ascetic mountain worship sect proscribed by the Meiji government and revived after 1946
sode ginu	袖衣	formal clothes consisting of *hakama*, robe, and a stiff-shouldered upper garment
[O]sonaemono	供え物	food offerings on a shrine altar
tamagushi	玉串	an offering consisting of a sprig of evergreen, usually *sakaki*, with paper streamers attached by flax
tamagushi hōten	玉串捧典	segment of ritual in which *tamagushi* are offered
tawara		*See* Ebisu dawara
tatsu-mai	竜舞	a dance performed by two to four dancers in tall dragon masks
tekiya	的屋	itinerant fair-booth operator
tōban	当番	group that rotates responsibility for a shrine among its members, who may be individuals or subgroups
tōban-chō	当番長	head of a tōban
torii	鳥居	gatelike arch marking the approach to a *jinja*
ujigami	氏神	clan/family *kami* and *kami* worshiped by an *ujiko*
ujiko	氏子	shrine support group based on ancestral practice
ujiko jinja	氏子神社	*jinja* run by an *ujiko*
ujiko sōdai	氏子総代	management committee of an *ujiko*
wakamono-kai	若者会	young men's association of a neighborhood
yakkofuri	奴振り	a group of men in Yuzawa who carry the *daimyō*'s badges of rank in the Daimyō Gyōretsu parade
yoi matsuri	宵祭り	the eve of a festival
yukata	欲衣	light summer robe

References

Abrahams, Roger D. 1982. The language of festivals: Celebrating the economy. In *Celebration*, ed. V. Turner, 161–177. Washington, DC: Smithsonian Institute Publications.

———. 1988. An American vocabulary of celebrations. In *Time out of time: Essays on the festival*, ed. A. Falassi, 175–183. Albuquerque: University of New Mexico Press.

Agency for Cultural Affairs. 1981. *Japanese religion*. Tokyo: Kodansha.

Akaike, Noriaki. 1976. Festivals and neighborhood associations. *Japanese Journal of Religious Studies* 3 (2–3): 127–174.

———. 1981. The Ontake cult association and local society: The case of the Owari-Mikawa region in Central Japan. *Japanese Journal of Religious Studies* 8 (1–2): 51–82.

Akita-ken Jinja Shinto-shi Committee. 1979. *Akita-ken Jinja Shinto-shi* (The history of Jinja Shinto in Akita prefecture). Akita: Shinto-shi kai.

Ando Seiichi. 1960. *Kinsei Miyaza no Shiteki kenkyu* (A historical study of early modern *miyaza*). Tokyo: Yoshikawa.

Anesaki, Masaharu. 1963. *History of Japanese religion*. Tokyo: Charles E. Tuttle Co.

———. 1970. *Religious life of the Japanese people*, rev. ed., ed. Kishimoto Hideo. Tokyo: Kokusai Bunka Shinkokai.

Ashkenazi, Michael. 1981. Guest shrines and folk Shinto. *Journal of Intercultural Studies* 8:29–36.

———. 1988a. The varieties of paraded objects in Japanese festivals. *Ethnology* 27 (1): 45–56.

———. 1988b. A native model for Japanese quality circles. In *Japanese management at home and abroad*, ed. T. Blumenthal, 15–28. Beersheva: Ben Gurion University Press.

———. 1990. Religious conflict in a Japanese town: Or is it? In *Japanese models of conflict resolution*, ed. S. N. Eisenstadt and E. Ben-Ari, 192–212. London: Routledge & Kegan Paul.

————. 1991. Japanese responses to missionary activity. *Social Compass* 38 (2): 141–154.

Bachnik, Jane. 1983. Recruitment strategies for household succession: Rethinking Japanese household succession. *Man* 18:160–182.

Barth, Frederik. 1973. *Ritual and knowledge among the Baktaman.* New Haven: Yale University Press.

Basabe, Fernando. 1968. *Religious attitudes of Japanese men.* Tokyo and Rutland, VT: Sophia University and Charles E. Tuttle Co.

Bauman, Richard. 1975. Verbal art as performance. *American Anthropologist* 77 (2): 290–311.

Beardsley, Richard, John Hall, and Robert Ward. 1959. *Village Japan.* Chicago: University of Chicago Press, Phoenix Books.

Beattie, John H. M. 1966. Ritual and social change. *Man* n.s. 1:60–74.

Befu, Harumi. 1962. Corporative emphasis and patterns of descent in the Japanese family. In *Japanese culture,* ed. R. J. Smith and R. K. Beardsley, 42–46. Chicago: Aldine Publishing Co.

————. 1974. An ethnography of dinner entertainment in Japan. *Arctic Anthropology* 11-suppl.: 196–203.

Bellah, Robert N. 1958. Religious aspects of modernization in Japan and Turkey. *American Journal of Sociology* 64:1–5.

Ben-Ari, Eyal. 1986. A sports day in suburban Japan: Leisure, artificial communities and the creation of local sentiments. In *Interpreting Japanese society,* ed. J. Hendry and J. Webber, 211–225. Oxford: JASO.

Benedict, Ruth. 1937. Ritual. In *Encyclopedia of the social sciences,* 396–397. New York: Uloe William.

Bernier, Bernard. 1975. *Breaking the cosmic circle: Religion in a Japanese village.* Ithaca: Cornell University East Asia Papers.

Bestor, Theodore. 1985. Tradition and Japanese organization: Institutional development in a Tokyo neighborhood. *Ethnology* 24 (2): 121–136.

Bethe, Monica, and Karen Brazell. 1978. *Noh as performance: An analysis of the kuse scene from YAMAMBA.* Ithaca: Cornell University East Asian Papers.

Blacker, Carmen. 1975. *The catalpa bow.* London: George Allen & Unwin.

Bocock, Robert. 1974. *Ritual in industrial society.* London: George Allen & Unwin.

Boissevain, Jeremy. 1969. *Saints and fireworks: Religion and politics in rural Malta.* London School of Economics Monographs in Social Anthropology. London: Athlone Press.

Booth, Alan. 1982. *Devils, gods and cameramen.* Tokyo: Kinseido.

Brameld, Theodore. 1968. *Japan: Culture, education and change in two communities.* New York: Holt, Rinehart & Winston.

Brandes, Stanley. 1980. *Metaphors of masculinity: Sex and status in Andalusian folklore.* Philadelphia: University of Pennsylvania Press.

Buechler, Hans C. 1980. *The masked media: Aymara fiestas and social interaction in the Bolivian highlands.* The Hague: Mouton.

Caillois, Roger. 1950. *L'homme et le sacre.* Paris: Gallimard.

———. 1979. *Man, play, and games.* New York: Schocken Books.

Casal, U. A. 1967. *The five sacred festivals of ancient Japan: Their symbolism and historical development.* Tokyo: Sophia University and Charles E. Tuttle Co.

Chiba, Masaji. 1970. *Matsuri no hoshakaigaku.* Tokyo: Kobundo.

Chinnery, Thora. 1971. *Religious conflict and compromise in a Japanese village.* Vancouver: University of British Columbia Publications in Anthropology.

Christian, William, Jr. 1972. *Person and god in a Spanish valley.* New York: Seminar Press.

Cohen, Abner. 1980. Drama and politics in the development of a London festival. *Man* 15 (1): 65–87.

Cohn, Werner. 1962. Is religion universal? *Journal for the Scientific Study of Religion* 2:25–33.

Cox, Harvey. 1969. *The feast of fools.* Cambridge: Harvard University Press.

Creemers, Wilhelmus H. M. 1968. *Shrine Shinto after World War II.* Leiden: E. J. Brill.

Davis, Winston. 1976. Parish guilds and political culture in village Japan. *Journal of Asian Studies* 35 (1): 25–36.

———. 1977a. The Miyaza and the fishermen: Ritual status in coastal villages of Wakayama prefecture. *Asian Folklore Studies* 36 (2): 1–29.

———. 1977b. *Toward modernity: A developmental typology of popular religious affiliations in Japan.* Ithaca: Cornell University East Asia Papers.

———. 1980. *Dojo: Magic and exorcism in modern Japan.* Stanford: Stanford University Press.

DeGlopper, Donald. 1974. Religion and ritual in Lukang. In *Religion and ritual in Chinese society*, ed. A. Wolf, 43–70. Palo Alto: Stanford University Press.

Dore, Ronald P. 1978. *Shinohata.* New York: Pantheon Books.

Dore, Ronald, ed. 1967. *Aspects of social change in modern Japan.* Princeton: Princeton University Press.

Douglas, Mary. 1982. *In the active voice.* London: Routledge & Kegan Paul.

Douglas, Mary, and Jonathan Gross. 1981. Food and culture: Measuring the intricacy of rule systems. *Social Science Information* 20 (1): 1–35.

Dundes, Alan, and Alessandro Falassi. 1975. *La terra in piazza: An interpretation of the Palio of Siena.* Berkeley: University of California Press.

Durkheim, Emile. 1947. *The elementary forms of the religious life*. Trans. J. W. Swain. London: George Allen & Unwin.

Earhart, H. Byron. 1969. *Japanese religion: Unity and diversity*. Belmont, CA: Dickenson.

———. 1970. *A religious study of the Mount Haguro sect of Shugendo*. Tokyo: Monumenta Nipponica, Sophia University.

Economic Planning Agency. 1972. *The Japanese and their society*: Part II of the report on national life, 1972. Tokyo: Economic Planning Association.

Eisenstadt, S. N. 1990. Patterns of conflict and conflict resolution in Japan: Some comparative indications. In *Japanese models of conflict resolution*, ed. S. N. Eisenstadt and E. Ben-Ari, 12–38. London: Routledge & Kegan Paul.

Embree, John F. 1939. *Suye Mura*. Chicago: University of Chicago Press.

———. [1944] 1969. *Japanese peasant songs*. Philadelphia: American Folklore Society; New York: Kraus Reprints Co.

Evans-Pritchard, E. E. 1969. Witchcraft explains unfortunate events. In *Reader in comparative religion: An anthropological view*, 4th ed., ed. W. Lessa and E. Z. Vogt, 362–366. New York: Harper & Row.

Farber, Carole. 1983. High, healthy and happy: Ontario mythology on parade. In *The celebration of society*, ed. F. Manning, 33–50. Bowling Green, OH: Bowling Green University Popular Press.

Firth, Raymond. 1963. *Elements of social organization*. Boston: Beacon Press.

Foster, George M. 1965. *Traditional culture and the impact of technological change*. Evanston, London, Tokyo: Harper & Row and John Weatherhill.

Frake, Charles. 1960. A structural description of Subanun religious behavior. In *Cognitive anthropology*, ed. Stephan Tyler, 470–486. New York: Holt, Rinehart & Winston.

Fridell, Wilbur. 1973. *Japanese shrine mergers 1906–12*. Tokyo: Sophia University Press.

Fukutake, Tadashi. 1974. *Japanese society today*. Tokyo: University of Tokyo Press.

Garbett, C. K. 1970. The analysis of social situations. *Man* 5 (2): 214–227.

Geertz, Clifford. 1966. Religion as a cultural system. In *Anthropological approaches to religion*, ed. Michael Banton, 1–44. New York: Praeger.

Gluckman, Max. 1962. Les rites de passage. In *Essays on the ritual of social relations*, ed. M. Gluckman, 1–52. Manchester: Manchester University Press.

Goffman, Erving. 1956. The nature of deference and demeanor. *American Anthropologist* 58:473–503.

———. 1963. *Behavior in public places*. New York: Free Press.

———. 1967. *Interaction ritual*. New York: Doubleday, Anchor.

Goody, Jack. 1977. Against "ritual": Loosely structured thoughts on loosely defined topics. In *Secular ritual*, ed. S. F. Moore and B. Myerhoff, 25–35. Essen: Van Gorcum & Co.

Graburn, Nelson. 1983. *To pray, pay and play: The cultural structure of Japanese domestic tourism*. Aix-en-Provence: Centre des Hautes Etudes Touristiques.

Grimes, Ronald L. 1976. *Symbol and conquest: Public ritual and drama in Santa Fe, New Mexico*. Ithaca: Cornell University Press.

Guthrie, Steward. 1976. *A Japanese new religion: Rissho kosei kai in a Japanese farming village*. Ph.D. dissertation, Yale University.

———. 1980. A cognitive theory of religion. *Current Anthropology* 21 (2): 181–204.

Hagiwara, Tatsuo. [1963] 1980. The position of the Shinto priesthood: historical changes and developement. In *Studies in Japanese folklore*, ed. R. Dorson, 221–236. New York: Arno Press.

Hall, John. 1971. *Japan from prehistory to modern times*. Tokyo: Charles E. Tuttle Co.

Hanchette, Suzanne. 1982. The festival interlude: Some anthropological observations. In *Religious festivals in South India and Sri Lanka*, ed. G. Welbon and G. Yocum, 219–241. New Delhi: Manohar.

Handelman, Don. 1977. Play and ritual: Complementary frames of metacommunication. In *It's a funny thing, humour*, ed. N. J. Chapman and H. Foot, 185–192. London: Pergamon Press.

Harada, Toshiaki. 1973. The village tutelary deity and the use of holy rods. In *Studies in Japanese folklore*, ed. R. Dorson, 215–220. Port Washington, NY: Kennikat Press.

Hardacre, Helen. 1988. The Shinto priesthood in early Meiji Japan: Preliminary inquiries. *History of Religions* 27 (3): 294–320.

Hendry, Joy. 1981. *Marriage in changing Japan: Community and society*. London: Croom Helm.

Herbert, Jean. 1967. *Shinto—At the fountain head of Japan*. London: George Allen & Unwin.

Higo Kazuo. 1942. *Miyaza no kenkyū* (A study of *miyaza*). Tokyo: Kobundo.

Hirai, Naofusa. 1968. Industrialization and Shinto—A historical study. In *Proceedings [of] the second international conference for Shinto studies*, 146–150. Tokyo: Kokugakuin Daigaku Nihon Bunka Kenkyusho.

Hoff, Frank. 1978. *Song, dance, storytelling: Aspects of the performing arts in Japan*. Ithaca: Cornell University East Asia Papers.

Hori, Ichiro. 1968. Folk religion in Japan. Chicago: University of Chicago Press.

Horton, Robin. 1960. A definition of religion and its uses. *Journal of the Royal Anthropological Institute* 90 (1–2): 201–226.

Howe, James. 1981. Fox hunting as ritual. *American Ethnologist* 8 (2): 278–300.

184   References

Hrdlickova, V. 1969. Japanese professional storytellers. *Genre* 2:179–210.
Hsu, Francis L. K. 1975. Iemoto: *The heart of Japan.* New York: John Wiley & Sons.
Huizinga, Johann. 1955. *Homo Ludens.* Boston: Beacon Press.
Hymes, Dell. 1975. Breakthrough into performance. In *Folklore: Communication and Performance,* ed. D. Ben Amos and K. Goldstein, 11–71. The Hague: Mouton.
Inoue, Nobutaka, Mitsugu Komoto, Hirochika Nakamaki, Masanori Shioya, and Masato Uno. 1979. A festival with anonymous kami. *Japanese Journal of Religious Studies* 6 (1–2): 163–186.
Irvine, Judith T. 1979. Formality and informality in communicative events. *American Anthropologist* 81 (4): 773–791.
Ishida, Ichiro. 1968. Shinto and the history of Japanese culture. In *Proceedings* [of] *the second international conference for Shinto studies,* 108–111. Tokyo: Kokugakuin Daigaku Nihon Bunka Kenkyusho.
Iwai, Hiroaki. 1974. Delinquent groups and organized crime. In *Japanese culture and behavior,* ed. T. S. Lebra and W. Lebra, 383–395. Honolulu: University of Hawaii Press.
Jansen, Marius, ed. 1965. *Changing Japanese attitudes toward modernization.* Princeton: Princeton University Press.
Jensen, Adolf. 1963. *Myth and cult among primitive peoples.* Chicago: University of Chicago Press.
Jinja Honcho. 1964. *Shinto shrines and festivals.* Tokyo: Jinja Honcho.
Johnson, Erwin. 1976. *Nagura Mura: An ethnohistorical analysis.* Ithaca: Cornell University Press.
Jordan, David. 1972. *Gods, ghosts and ancestors.* Berkeley: University of California Press.
Kato, Shuichi. 1971. *Form, style, tradition: Reflections on Japanese art and society.* Trans. J. Bester. Berkeley: University of California Press.
Kelly, William. 1990. Japanese no-Noh: The crosstalk of public culture in a rural festival. *Public Culture* 2 (2): 65–81.
Khare, R. S. 1980. Food as nutrition and culture: Notes towards an anthropological methodology. *Social Science Information* 19 (3): 519–542.
Kitagawa, Joseph. 1966. *Religion in Japanese history.* New York: Columbia University Press.
———. 1987. *On understanding Japanese religion.* Princeton: Princeton University Press.
Konchanomai, Pensri. 1977. Shinto and the Japanese way of life. Ph.D. diss. Kasetsrat University, Bangkok.
Kondo, Dorinne. 1985. The way of tea: A symbolic analysis. *Man* 20 (2): 287–306.

Kuroda, Toshio. 1981. Shinto in the history of Japanese religion. *Journal of Japanese Studies* 7 (1): 1–22.

Kushner, Gilbert, Mickey Gibson, John Gulick, John J. Honigman, and Richard Nonas. 1962. *What accounts for sociocultural change?: A propositional inventory.* Chapel Hill: University of North Carolina, Institute for Research in Social Science.

Lane, Christel. 1981. *The rites of rulers: Ritual in industrial society—The Soviet case.* Cambridge: Cambridge University Press.

Leach, Edmund. 1966. "Ritualization in man." *Philosophical Transactions of the Royal Society* series B, no. 251:403–408.

————. 1968. Ritual. *International encyclopedia of the social sciences.* Vol. 13:520–526.

————. 1972. Two essays concerning the symbolic representation of time. In *Reader in comparative religion,* ed. W. Lessa and E. Z. Vogt, 114–135. New York: Harper & Row.

————. 1976. *Culture and Communication.* Cambridge: Cambridge University Press.

Lebra, Takie Sugiyama. 1976. *Japanese patterns of behavior.* Honolulu: University of Hawaii Press.

————. 1984. Nonconfrontational strategies for management of interpersonal conflict. In *Conflict in Japan,* ed. E. S. Krauss et al., 41–60. Honolulu: University of Hawaii Press.

Linhart, Sepp. 1986. Sakariba: Zone of "evaporation" between work and home? In *Interpreting Japanese society,* ed. J. Hendry and J. Webber, 198–210. Oxford: JASO.

Lokowandt, Ernst. 1978. *Die rechtliche entwicklung die staats-Shinto in der ersten hälfte der Meiji-zeit (1868-1890).* Wiesbaden: Otto Harrossowitz.

MacCannell, Dean. 1976. *The tourist: A new theory of the leisure class.* New York: Schocken Books.

Maemori-chō jinja gojikai. N.d. Pamphlet. Maemori, Yuzawa.

Manning, Frank E., ed. 1983. Cosmos and chaos: Celebration in the modern world. In *The celebration of society,* ed. F. Manning, 3–32. Bowling Green, OH: Bowling Green University Popular Press.

Martin, Samuel. 1964. Speech levels in Japan and Korea. In *Language in culture and society,* ed. Dell Hymes, 407–415. New York: Harper & Row.

Middleton, John. 1970. The religious system. In *A handbook of method in cultural anthropology,* ed. Raoul Naroll and Ronald Cohen, 500–508. New York: Natural History Press.

Moeran, Brian. 1981. Yanagi Muneyoshi and the Japanese folkcraft movement. *Asian Folklore Studies* 40 (1): 87–99.

────. 1986. One over the seven: Sake drinking in a Japanese pottery community. In *Interpreting Japanese society,* ed. J. Hendry and J. Webber, 226–242. Oxford: JASO.

Moore, Roy Avril. 1968. Samurai social mobility in Tokugawa Japan. Ph.D. diss., University of Michigan, Ann Arbor.

Moore, Sally F., and Barbara Myerhoff. 1977. Introduction. In *Secular ritual,* ed. S. F. Moore and B. Myerhoff, 3–24. Essen: Van Gorcum & Co.

Moore, Wilbert Ellis. 1963. *Social change.* Englewood Cliffs, NJ: Prentice-Hall.

Moriarty, Elizabeth. 1972. The communitarian aspects of Shinto Matsuri. *Asian Folklore Studies* 31 (2): 91–140.

Morioka, Kiyomi. 1975. *Religion in changing Japanese society.* Tokyo: University of Tokyo Press.

Mouer, Ross, and Yoshio Sugimoto. 1980. Competing models for understanding Japanese society: Some reflections on new directions. *Social Analysis* 5 / 6: 194–204.

Müller, Fredrich Max. [1882] 1976. *Lectures on the origin and growth of religion.* London: Longmans Green & Co. Reprint. New York: AMS Press.

Murakami, Shigeyoshi. 1980. *Japanese religion in the modern century.* Trans. H. Byron Earhart. Tokyo: University of Tokyo Press.

Murcott, Anne. 1982. On the social significance of the "cooked dinner" in S. Wales. *Social Science Information* 21 (4 / 5): 677–696.

Myerhoff, Barbara. 1977. We don't wrap herring in a printed page: Fusion, fiction and continuity in secular ritual. In *Secular ritual,* ed. S. F. Moore and B. Myerhoff, 199–224. Essen: Van Gorcum & Co.

Nakane, Chie. 1967. *Kinship and economic organization in rural Japan.* London School of Economics Monographs in Social Anthropology. London: Athlone Press.

────. 1970. *Japanese society.* Berkeley: University of California Press.

Namahira, Emiko. 1977. An analysis of "Hare" and "Kegare" in Japanese rites of passage. *Minzokugaku Kenkyu* 40:350–368.

Norbeck, Edward. 1961. Postwar cultural change and continuity in northeastern Japan. *American Anthropologist* 63:297–321.

────. 1967a. Associations and democracy in Japan. In *Aspects of social change in modern Japan,* ed. R. P. Dore, 185–200. Princeton: Princeton University Press.

────. 1967b. Anthropological views of religion. In *Religion in philosophical and cultural perspective,* ed. J. Clayton Feaver and William Horosz, 414–435. Princeton: D. Van Nostrand Co.

────. 1970. *Religion and society in modern Japan.* Houston: Tourmaline Press.

Ohnuki-Tierney, Emiko. 1984. *Illness and culture in contemporary Japan.* London: Cambridge University Press.

Okano, Haruko. 1976. *Die stellung der frau in Shinto.* Wiesbaden: Otto Harrossowitz.

Ooms, Herman. 1967. The religion of the household. *Contemporary Religion in Japan* 8 (3–4).

Ostor, Akos. 1980. *The play of the gods: Locality, ideology, structure and time in the festivals of a Bengali town.* Chicago: University of Chicago Press.

Ouwehand, Cornelius. 1964. *Namazu-E and their theories.* Leiden: E. J. Brill.

Plath, David W. 1964. Where the family of God is the family: The role of the dead in Japanese household. *American Anthropologist* 66 (2): 300–317.

———. 1969. *The after hours.* Berkeley: University of California Press.

Ponsonby-Fane, R. A. B. (Richard). 1964a. *Studies in Shinto and shrines.* Kyoto: The Ponsonby Memorial Society.

———. 1964b. *Visiting famous shrines in Japan.* Kyoto: The Ponsonby Memorial Society.

Press, Irwin. 1979. *The city as context: Urbanism and behavioral constraints in Seville.* Urbana: University of Illinois Press.

Prideaux, Gary D. 1970. *The syntax of Japanese honorifics.* The Hague and Paris: Mouton.

Prime Minister's Office. 1988. *Opinion survey on eating habits and roles of farm villages.* Tokyo: Foreign Press Center.

Rappaport, Roy. 1967. Ritual regulation of environmental relations among a New Guinea people. *Ethnology* 6 (1): 17–30.

———. 1979. *Ecology, meaning and religion.* New Haven: Yale University Press.

Raz, Yaakov. 1987. Personal interview, June 1987.

Reed, Steven. 1982. Is Japanese government really centralized? *Journal of Japanese Studies* 8 (1): 133–164.

Richardson, Miles. 1982. Being-in-the-market versus being-in-the-plaza: Material culture and the construction of social reality in Spanish America. *American Ethnologist* 9 (2): 421–436.

Riegelhaupt, Joyce F. 1973. Festas and padres: The organization of religious action in a Portuguese parish. *American Anthropologist* 75 (1): 835–839.

Roberts, John M., Saburo Morita, and L. Keith Brown. 1986. Personal categories for Japanese sacred places and gods: Views elicited from a conjugal pair. *American Anthropologist* 88 (4): 807–824.

Robertson, Joy A. 1987. A dialectic of native and newcomer: The Kodaira citizens' festival in suburban Tokyo. *Anthropological Quarterly* 60 (3): 124–136.

Roof, W. Clark. 1974. Explaining traditional religion in contemporary society. In

Changing perspectives in the scientific study of religion, ed. J. Eister, 295–314. New York: John Wiley & Sons.

Ross, Floyd Hiatt. 1965. *Shinto: The way of Japan.* Boston: Beacon Press.

Sadler, A. W. 1972. Carrying the Mikoshi: Further field notes on the shrine festival in modern Tokyo. *Asian Folklore Studies* 31 (1): 89–114.

———. 1974. At the sanctuary: Further field notes on the shrine festival in modern Tokyo. *Asian Folklore Studies* 33 (1): 17–34.

———. 1975a. Folkdance and fairgrounds: More notes on neighborhood festivals in Tokyo. *Asian Folklore Studies* 34 (1): 1–20.

———. 1975b. The shrine: Notes towards a study of neighborhood festivals in modern Tokyo. *Asian Folklore Studies* 34 (2): 1–38.

Saler, Benson. 1977. Supernatural as a Western category. *Ethos* 5 (1): 31–54.

Saliba, John A. 1976. Religion and the anthropologist 1960–1976. *Anthropologica* 18 (2): 179–223.

Sasaki Chiyoge. N.d. Mitake jinja, Shin-mei-sha, Atago-jinja, Shokaijinja. Yuzawa.

Saso, Michael. 1978. *The teachings of Taoist Master Chuang.* New Haven: Yale University Press.

Shinto Committee for the Ninth International Congress for the History of Religions. 1958. *Basic terms of Shinto.* Tokyo: Jinja Honchō.

Skorupski, John. 1976. *Symbol and theory: A study of theories of religion in social anthropology.* Cambridge: Cambridge University Press.

Smith, Henry De Witt, II. 1973. The tyranny of Tokyo in modern Japanese culture. In *Studies on Japanese culture,* 367–371. Tokyo: Japan PEN Club.

Smith, Michael Garfield. 1974. *Corporations and society.* Chicago: Aldine Publishing Co.

Smith, Robert J. 1974. *Ancestor worship in contemporary Japan.* Palo Alto: Stanford University Press.

———. 1978. Foreword: The eclipse of communal ritual in Japan. In *The Namahage,* 1–8. By Yamamoto Yoshiko. Philadelphia: Institute of the Study of Human Issues.

Smith, Robert Jerome. 1975. *The art of the festival.* University of Kansas Publications in Anthropology. Lawrence: University of Kansas Press.

Sonoda, Minoru. 1975. The traditional festival in urban society. *Japanese Journal of Religious Studies* 2 (2–3): 103–135.

Sopher, David. 1967. *Geography of religions.* Englewood Cliffs, NJ: Prentice-Hall.

Spae, Joseph J. 1972. *Shinto man.* Tokyo: Oriens Institute for Religious Research.

Spiro, Melford E. 1966. Religion: Problems of definition at explanation. In *Anthropological approaches to the study of religion,* ed. M. Banton, 85–125. New York: Praeger.

Steiner, Kurt. 1965. *Local government in Japan*. Palo Alto: Stanford University Press.

Steward, Julian. 1963. *Theory of culture change*. Urbana: University of Illinois Press.

Tsukahira, Toshio. 1966. *Feudal control in Tokugawa Japan: The Sankin Kōtai system*. Cambridge: Harvard University Press.

Turner, Victor. 1967. *The forest of symbols*. Ithaca, NY: Cornell University Press.

————. 1968. *The drums of affliction*. Oxford: Clarendon Press.

————. 1969. *The ritual process (structure and anti-structure)*. Chicago: Aldine Publishing Co.

————. 1972. Betwixt and between: The limited period on rites de passage. In *Reader in comparative religion*, 3d ed., ed. W. Lessa and E. Z. Vogt, 330–347. New York: Harper & Row.

————. 1974. Metaphors of anti-structure in religious culture. In *Changing perspectives in the scientific study of religion*, ed. J. Eister, 63–84. New York: John Wiley & Sons.

————. 1983a. *Carnaval* in Rio: Dionysian drama in an industrializing society. In *The celebration of society*, ed. F. Manning, 103–124. Bowling Green, OH: Bowling Green University Popular Press.

————. 1983b. Liminal to liminoid, in play, flow, and ritual: An essay in comparative symbology. In *Play, games and sports in cultural contexts*, ed. Janet Harris, 123–164. Champaign, IL: Human Kinetics Publishers.

————. 1986. *The anthropology of performance*. New York: PAJ Publications.

Turner, Victor, ed. 1982. *Celebration: Studies in festivity and ritual*. Washington, DC: Smithsonian Institute Press.

Ushiomi, Toshitaka. 1964. *Forestry and mountain village communities in Japan*. Tokyo: Kokusai Bunka Shinkokai.

Valentine, James. 1986. Dance space, time, and organization: Aspects of Japanese cultural performance. In *Interpreting Japanese society*, ed. J. Hendry and J. Webber, 111–129. Oxford: JASO.

Vogt, Evan Z. 1969. *Zinacantan: A Maya community in the highlands of Chiapas*. Cambridge: Harvard University Press.

Waal Malefijt, Annemarie de. 1968. *Religion and culture: An introduction to the anthropology of religion*. London and New York: Macmillan Co.

Wakamori, Taro. [1963] 1980. Initiation rites and young men's associations. In *Studies in Japanese folklore*. Reprint. Ed. R. Dorson, 291–304. Port Washington, NY: Kennikat Press.

Wallace, Anthony F. C. 1966. *Religion: An anthropological view*. New York: Random House.

Wang, Shih-Ching. 1974. Religious organization in the history of a Taiwanese town. In *Religion and ritual in Chinese society*, ed. A. Wolf, 71–92. Palo Alto: Stanford University Press.

Ward, Barbara. 1979. Not merely players: Drama, art and ritual in traditional China. *Man* 14:18-39.

Ward, Robert E. 1965. Japan: The continuity of modernization. In *Political culture and political development*, ed. L. Pye and S. Verba, 27-82. Princeton: Princeton University Press.

Wolf, Arthur. 1978. Gods, ghosts and ancestors. In *Studies in Chinese society*, ed. A. Wolf, 131-182. Palo Alto: Stanford University Press.

Yamamoto, Yoshiko. 1978. *The Namahage*. Philadelphia: ISHI.

Yamashita Magotsugu and Motegi Hisaei. 1965. *Yuzawa-shi shi* (History of Yuzawa). Yuzawa: Akita-ken, Yuzawa-shi Mukashi Iin-kai.

Yanagawa, Keiichi. 1968. Matsuri and modernization. In *Proceedings* [of] *the second international conference for Shinto studies*, 155-157. Tokyo: Kokugakuin Daigaku Nihon Bunka Kenkyusho.

————. 1974. Theological and scientific thinking about festivals: Reflections on the Gion festival at Aizu Tajima. *Japanese Journal of Religious Studies* 1 (1): 4-49.

Yanagi Soetsu (Muneyoshi). [1926] 1955. *Kogei no Michi*. Tokyo: Nihon Mingeikan.

Yanagida, Kunio. 1946a. *Nihon no Matsuri*. Tokyo: Kobundo.

————. 1946b. *Shinto to Minzokugaku*. Tokyo: Meiseido.

————. 1962-1964. *Yanagita Kunio Shu, Teihon*. 28 vols. Tokyo: Chikuma Shobo.

————. 1970. *About our ancestors*. Trans. F. H. Mayer and Y. Ishiwara. Tokyo: Japan Society for the Promotion of Science.

Yunohara Hitachi Inari-jinja Gojikai. N.d. Yunohara Hitachi Inari-jinja Gojikai bylaws. Maemori-cho, Yuzawa-shi. Mimeo.

Yuzawa-shi Kyōiku Iin-kai. 1981. *Watakushitachi no Yuzawa*. Yuzawa: Kyōiku Iin-kai.

Index

About the Author

Michael Ashkenazi received his doctorate in anthropology from Yale University in 1983. He has spent a total of six years in residence in Japan, doing research on festivals and business management. He has taught in Israel, Canada, and Japan and published on such topics as martial arts, festivals and rituals, food, and Japanese business practices and organizational behavior. He is currently senior lecturer in anthropology at Ben Gurion University, Israel.